Lauren's Ride

Lauren Byrne

I hope you enjoy our ride.

Lauren's Ride

John Byrne

SHOWTIME
BOOKS

SHOWTIME
BOOKS

Published by Showtime Books
140 Sheldon Ave., Staten Island, N.Y. 10312

www.showtimepublications.com
bwshowtime@aol.com

ISBN 978-0-9911860-4-4

Photos used by permission of the author.
Some photos used on Day 36 courtesy of Flint Gennari, FineArtPhotos.
Back cover photo courtesy of the Nicotra Group.
Cover design by Gatekeeper Press.

Text set in Minion Pro and Myriad Pro

To my family,

friends,

fellow firefighters,

supporters

and complete strangers

who made the dream

of "Lauren's Ride"

come true.

Contents

Foreword

This is not just an account of my bicycle ride across the country. Many people have ridden bicycles across our great nation. My ride is different. It's the story of a brother's love for his sister. It's a tale of firefighters everywhere bonded by brotherly love, faithfulness, a desire to serve and a willingness to work together. It's a young man's search for his roots ending at his grandfather's firehouse on the other side of the continent. It's a demonstration of everyday Americans willing to help and give — in any way they can.

My purpose in telling this story is to describe and share the unusual acts of kindness, love, strength, challenges and determination I experienced during my 36-day cross country jaunt.

The idea of a bike ride from California to New York at first seemed impossible. The idea of writing a book seemed even more challenging. You should understand that I struggled academically with a learning disability most of my school life. Writing this book was difficult. I was rewarded, however, by the passionate sensation of reliving each and every wonderful experience that thrilled me during the 36 days.

I gained respect and admiration for the many generous people I met in each and every state through which I pedaled. With this sense of gratitude, I invite you to ride along with me to share these wonderful experiences.

John Byrne
September, 2020

Here's to the crazy ones. The misfits. The rebels. The troublemakers. The round pegs in the square holes. The ones who see things differently. They're not fond of rules. And they have no respect for the status quo. You can quote them, disagree with them, glorify or vilify them.
About the only thing you can't do is ignore them. Because they change things. They push the human race forward. And while some may see them as the crazy ones, we see genius. Because the people who are crazy enough to think they can change the world, are the ones who do.

— *Steve Jobs*

I'm Ready to Ride

IT'S SEPT. 9, 2012. I'm seated on my bicycle here at the Golden Gate Bridge in California surrounded by a throng of family and friends. The sun is just about rising, the air a bit cool. The reason I'm here: I intend to pedal 3,600 miles to the Brooklyn Bridge in New York in 36 continuous days.

I chose this unusual bicycle trip as a way to raise money to buy a specially-equipped car for my paralyzed sister, Lauren.

I'm pretty sure I can do it. After all, I'm a bicyclist. I'm a firefighter. I'm determined,

But who knows? People tell me I'm insane. A cross country journey like this is a grueling physical effort, they say. The human body simply can't endure this abuse. I understand. But I'm 26 years old. I'm in top physical condition. And I've carefully planned this venture with others for the past six months. What could possibly go wrong?

Before I shove off, let me give you a glimpse into my background. I think you'll understand why I've chosen this special journey.

Catch you later.

PART I

Growing Up in California

I AM FOUR YEARS OLDER than my sister Lauren. As we grew up, our early years were filled with vivid memories and exciting adventures. Some of my earlier memories were at day care. Sharon McCown owned and operated what I believed to be the best day care center in our community. Our summers were full of all kinds of local trips — from waterslide parks to zoos.

I began playing Little League baseball when I was about five years old. It was the best part of my childhood. My first team was the Red Sox. This is where I met my childhood best friend, Chris Chambers. Chris and I went to the same school, too. His dad was team coach and my dad, Dan, was assistant coach. I was just an average baseball player, but I really loved to play. I remember my dad would always leave work early to get to every one of my practices and games. One time when I was playing third base, I remember a line drive was hit right into my glove. This play proved my dad wrong, because he always told me that I had to *try to catch* the ball. On this play the ball came to me! My mom, Judy, never missed a game either, and Lauren was always behind the backstop to cheer me on. My mom was team mom and official scorekeeper. This was my childhood.

My dad became team coach the following season. I became a pitcher and second baseman. I was an average fielder, and I could actually hit the ball, too. I always looked forward to team practice and game days. My mom was still the official team mom. Lauren made friends with sisters of other players. A highlight of Little League would be to come home after every game, go through the scorebook and rehash every pitch and play. It was during this time in my childhood that I felt the most loved. My dad had high expectations of all his players. He even taught us about things other than baseball. One afternoon, for example, he brought a dead fish to practice just to demonstrate how important a good handshake was, and how poor a bad one felt. He had each player shake the dead fish. Ugh! It made the point. He expected us to always be on time for the games and to always exercise good sportsmanship. He'd always tell us he would rather have a team of average players who played well together rather than have one phenomenal player. My dad was a good role model. He was a union roofer, working 37 years as a member of Local 40, Roofers and Waterproofers of San Francisco. Many days the temperature reached 120 degrees. It was normal for him to work under a blazing sun. But he was never late for a practice or game. I made a lot of friends playing Little League baseball.

I was never an all-star player, but when our team needed a hit, I guess I was a good clutch hitter.

When I think of my dad, I think of a hard-working American who always provided for his family. My dad was born in Neptune, N.J., the youngest of 9 brothers and sisters. He was raised in nearby Belmar, on the Jersey Shore, by a strict, yet honest and loving, Irish father and a loving German mother. Times were tough in those days, with 11 in the family, so the value of a dollar was always appreciated. Dad spent his childhood with his family — and 47 cousins.

When he was 18, dad moved to California to pursue his dream of having a family of his own. He hitchhiked his way out with only $200 in his pocket. Over the years, he turned that $200 into so much more. He moved to the West Coast to work in a better environment and to become a Bay Area roofer. After a few years in California, he returned to New Jersey for a visit home. That's when he met my mom, Judy Quigg. They were introduced to each other by his friend, Andy Meuerle. Andy, by the way, is the person who, many years later, gifted me the bicycle I'm sitting on now. When dad's visit home was over, he convinced my mom to return to California with him. Years later she did. They married in 1983.

Here I am with mom, dad and Lauren in a
backyard photograph taken in 1995. I'm 9
and Lauren's 5. Ah, those were the days!

My dad was fully involved in my childhood. He taught me the importance of hard work and honesty. As an example, he explained how karma worked: if a man stole money and then invested that stolen money in the stock market, the value of that stock would eventually fall. Growing up, we visited so many places, including Disneyland, Universal Studios, the top of the World Trade Center, the Empire State Building, Rockefeller Center at Christmas and the Statue of Liberty. My dad took me camping and he taught me to fish.

But my most enjoyable years with dad were spent when he was my baseball coach.

When I think of my mom, I think of a person who would do anything for her children. She was always there for Lauren and me — no matter the day or time. My mom was there for every event in which Lauren and I participated. She showed up at every soccer game that Lauren played and at every community theatre production in which Lauren acted. When we cried, mom cried; when we smiled, mom smiled. Like dad, mom was born in Neptune, N. J. She was the youngest of two girls. She

Lauren and mom at Stanford University fountain.
Lauren's about 7 years old.

grew up in nearby Freehold, N.J. Her father, John Quigg — my grandfather, and the man after whom I was named — was a volunteer firefighter with the Freehold Fire Department. He was born and raised in Freehold. During World War II he served with the U.S. Coast Guard. After the war, when he returned to civilian life, my grandfather worked for the federal government at Fort Monmouth, a short car commute from his Freehold home. He eventually met and married Elsie Williams, my grandmother, who lived in nearby Staten Island, N.Y. Mom and her sister, my aunt Susan, grew up one block from singer Bruce Springsteen. Mom had an enjoyable childhood. As a child, she would visit the firehouse to hang out with her dad. Whenever there was a big fire in Freehold, mom was there to watch my grandfather help put it out.

Mom went to school to become a computer programmer. When she traveled to California that first time, she wanted to see what Silicon

I loved playing baseball, especially
since dad was team coach. Here's me
and the coach before a game.

Valley was about. It didn't take her long to decide she'd stay and work in California. Mom was always our biggest fan. I remember she would stay up many nights dealing with my homework issues. She suffered with me through my childhood school learning pains. We even went to counseling together so she could help me work through the hard times. My mother worked and worked around the clock — all this while we were growing up. She is a great mom! Whether I was right or wrong, mom was there for me. I give her credit for her patience, because I truly believe I might not be alive today if it weren't for her. Mom balanced discipline and fun perfectly for Lauren and me.

When I was still a child, my parents began to realize that I was a bit more active than other children. Hyperactive was the word. I think they first realized it the nights mom would put me in the car and drive around town, sometimes for hours, until I eventually fell asleep. Later, during my early school years, teachers gave me backrubs to help me fall asleep at nap time. As early as second grade I was having trouble keeping up with other students. And I was having trouble staying focused. School officials diagnosed the problem. I had attention-deficit disorder, or what is commonly referred to as ADD. I was so hyper, for instance, that I would drive my dad crazy after his long work days. He would ask me to just sit still for two minutes when I kept running in front of the television set. I remember mom would spend hours with me every night trying to help me with basic homework assignments.

I had a second grade reading ability — in the fifth grade. I struggled. Through my mom's support, with the interest of great teachers, and with constant extra reading help in the learning center, I was able to graduate elementary school on time. But I'll tell you, it wasn't easy.

I was a hard worker when I *wasn't* in school. I helped my dad on weekends by mowing the lawn and sweeping the sidewalk. At eight years old, I would go to a neighbor's house and vacuum. I earned a dollar. At 10, I mowed our neighbor's lawn. Then I started a lawn mowing service. By the end of that summer I had 10 customers. Many of them were attracted by the flyers I handed out as I went trick-or-treating on Halloween. I was truly a young entrepreneur. I did this for several years, sometimes earning several hundred dollars a week. Receiving a gas-powered weed-wacker from my grandmother for Christmas even added to the services I could provide!

At 14, the earliest I could officially work, I took a job at McDonald's. I remember that during the Christmas season my friend and I would sing to customers as they approached the drive-through window. I kept the McDonald's job through junior high school.

In junior high I experienced the same problems I had in elementary school. Things began to brighten, however, when I got to high school. I remember my first day of high school. A teacher explained the importance of becoming involved in school activities. A few days later, I happened to visit Stage 1 Theatre, where mom and Lauren were rehearsing for the musical *Little Shop of Horrors*. I remember that I had casually walked into the theater to watch their rehearsal. Lights were bright and sound was clear on this big stage right in front of me. Amazing, I thought! I had never seen a live theatre production before.

At one point the director, Steve Harrington, turned to me. "Hey, I need you to hang a light," he ordered. And so I did.

That was the beginning. The next community theatre production was *Annie*, another musical. Mom thought I was joking when I said I wanted to be cast in the show. But I was serious. So Lauren, mom and I all auditioned. You guessed it. We all got parts. Lauren was an orphan, mom was Mrs. Pugh and I was part of the ensemble, or chorus. Before long the three of us participated in our community theater as a family. And we received awards at the end of each show.

Theatre. This is where I met my high school best friends, Ben and John Reynolds. We hit it off right from the start. The three of us handled all the backstage work from there on. We built sets, set up sound equipment and aimed and focused lights for our high school and for Stage 1 Theatre productions. This led to a job at the Lorraine Hansberry Theater, an African-American theater in nearby San Francisco. My job there during the shows included set construction, operating the lights and working backstage. I worked at the theatre five nights a week.

I soon realized I could use my hyper condition to an advantage by being involved in positive things. I also realized that I had a lot more energy than most people, and if I focused that extra energy in the right areas, things would go well for me.

Despite my extra theatre work, I was still struggling in high school. In sophomore year, I was failing English and I was absent 26 times from my biology class. With English and biology aside, however, I was doing much better overall. It was only those two subjects that I couldn't seem to master. What was happening was that I would usually cut class if I hadn't done the homework. You know what I'm talking about. I'm sure you did it once or twice when you were in high school.

Senior year, I went out for the football team. I made the varsity squad. I played on special teams and I always tried my best, whether it was during practice or on game day. A few times during practice the coach even yelled at me for tackling the quarterback. I couldn't help it, I told him. I had only one speed. I went from the coach telling me during try-outs that I was fat, slow and had no muscle, to being in on most tackles on kickoff and punt return. After football season, I joined the varsity wrestling team and filled in the spot of the 215 pound weight class. I had a winning record by the end of the season, which qualified me for sectional competitions.

During career day near the end of my senior year, a group of fire-fighters visited our school and discussed firefighting. I could tell they loved their work. They described their workday and what they did to help people during crises. I learned about other aspects of their job, too, including salary and benefits — and the brotherhood associated with being a firefighter. I was intrigued when they told us every day was filled with new, different and exciting experiences. Hmmm, I thought. This could be for me. The more they spoke, the more I liked firefighting.

The visit by those firefighters convinced me to take the next step to follow in my grandfather's footsteps. That night, I excitedly told my family about the firefighters' visit. And I told them that's what I wanted to do in my life.

I told them I wanted to become a firefighter.

One of my dad's friends, Greg McCarthy, was a firefighter in nearby Redwood City. So, later that week, dad arranged a ride-along – which was an opportunity for me to actually ride on a fire engine. I remember the ride-along like it was yesterday: On one run, I actually got to hold the intravenous (IV) bag for a heart attack victim. Wow! From that moment, I realized one thing was certain: *I definitely intended to become a firefighter!*

Two days after I graduated high school, in June, 2004, I moved to my Aunt Jean's house on the California central coast. I signed up for fire technology classes and for a class to become an Emergency Medical Technician (EMT) at Allan Hancock Community College. During my EMT class, the instructor, a California Department of Forestry engineer, who later became my good friend, asked if anyone knew what an assessment was. I answered that I knew it. I was the only one in class who knew it. I had spent hours the night before studying. So I started yelling at the "patient," "Ma'am, my name is John Byrne, and I'm here to help." That's the beginning of an assessment.

By the way, I soon learned that the California Department of Forestry became the California Department of Forestry and Fire Protection. Today it's called Cal Fire for short.

By the end of that week I attended a firefighter awards ceremony. The next day, I walked into the Nipomo, Calif., fire station, my local firehouse. I introduced myself to Capt. Felix Camacho and asked if there was any way I could volunteer with the fire company. He explained the position of Paid Call Firefighter. This was a unique program whereby a volunteer could respond from his or her own home, instead of from a fire station. Dejected, I told him I didn't think I had the experience for that. He answered by telling me I didn't need experience — *that the fire company would actually train and pay me.* I was now ecstatic! I'm back in the game, I thought!

I loved knowing I was on my way to becoming a firefighter. This first step, becoming a Paid Call Firefighter, would allow me to learn the job of firefighting while I was paid — all while I attended school. I was proud to enter firefighting at the age of 19. I did as many ride-alongs as I could, and I asked hundreds of questions. One time, I was at the fire station for so many days in a row that firefighters asked me to leave because they said they were about to have a private meeting with the chief. Later I found out they really didn't meet with the chief at all. That was an excuse. They just needed a break from me. The guys compared me to a Golden Retriever coming in with my tail wagging and knocking over things, but always trying to learn and better myself. I volunteered with the Nipomo Fire Company for about a year, and I was voted firefighter of the year. My hard work was beginning to pay off. My next career step would be to attend a fire academy with the goal of obtaining a permanent firefighting position.

Life was on a track that I had never imagined possible. What was next to come, I wondered?

Lauren's Injury

SUMMER WAS JUST BEGINNING, and I was hard at work completing my Allan Hancock College online fire technology and general education classes. I was doing everything I could to increase my chances of being selected for the next class of Allan Hancock College Fire Academy, which was set to begin in the fall. I had now spent a full year living with my Aunt Jean and my cousin Jake in Nipomo. Jake was three years younger than I was.

Things were going well in my life. Jake and I were looking forward to an exciting and eventful summer. We had many projects to work on around the house, some of which helped pay for a portion of my rent. I had now been a Paid Call Firefighter with the San Luis Obispo County Fire Department for about a year. Everything seemed to be going great. I really loved the direction in which my life was moving. I was even doing well in school — for the first time ever. I scored a 3.9 Grade Point Average (GPA) in college, compared to my lousy 2.1 GPA in high school.

Lauren had just completed her freshman year in high school and was set to take on a summer job teaching children at the pre-school center down the street from our house. Dad was winding up his last few years of being a Bay Area roofer, and mom was still working part time.

Everything in our lives was going just as planned. Or so I thought.

June 21, 2005, was the summer solstice. It was a special day for our family because it was our late grandfather, Thomas Byrne's, birthday. He had passed away a few years prior. I remember sitting in my aunt's living room, doing my homework and talking with my aunt and cousin. We were talking about Grandpa Tom and how we had missed him telling stories. I spent a good part of the morning sitting in the living room taking online quizzes for my fire technology classes. Casper, my aunt's cat, was sprawled out next to me on the couch. I remember the sun reflecting off the outdoor swimming pool into the house. It was becoming a warm day.

Lauren, meanwhile, was 230 miles away at our childhood home in Newark. She was enjoying the summer weather, too. Since it was turning out to be such a nice day, she decided to invite some of her friends over for a swim in our backyard pool. Her best friend, Erin Reis, was the only one who could make it. So Lauren and Erin spent the afternoon swimming in our above-ground Doughboy pool. Then they took a break to eat. Years before, dad built a wooden pool deck. After eating, Lauren and Erin decided to go back in the water.

Then it happened.

Lauren was walking on the deck. Somehow she tripped and fell head first into the pool, apparently hitting her head on the pool bottom.

She was floating face down. She remembers that she tried, but couldn't lift her head out of the water. Her lungs quickly filled with water. Everything became darker and darker and darker, she later said. Then Lauren passed out.

Erin didn't notice Lauren fall into the pool. But when she saw Lauren floating face down, she thought Lauren was messing around. When she moved closer, she realized Lauren wasn't joking. Erin yelled at her. Lauren didn't answer. Erin had learned CPR (cardio pulmonary resuscitation) as a Girl Scout. She quickly and carefully lifted Lauren's head out of the water so her friend could breathe. She began mouth-to-mouth resuscitation, moving the lifeless Lauren to the side of the pool as she did.

At the side of the pool, Erin simultaneously grabbed for her cell phone and punched in 911. She was holding Lauren up and still giving CPR as she dialed. Back then, cell phones did not use a GPS signal to automatically find the cell phone location and route the call to the nearest police department. So Erin's call went to a distant office of the California Highway Patrol. With time of the essence, Erin's cell phone call for help was transferred from one California jurisdiction to another. We learned later that Erin's emergency call for help never reached the correct agency. Meanwhile, Lauren was still not breathing. Erin was continuing mouth-to-mouth while trying to call for help and holding Lauren up in the pool at the same time. The minutes were ticking by. Erin realized she was getting nowhere with the call for help. She thought fast, then called her mother to plead for help. Erin's mom quickly dialed 911 to report the incident, then sped to Lauren's house in her car. She took Erin's brother, Jared, with her. They raced into the backyard and pulled the unconscious Lauren from the water, easing her onto the pool deck. Lauren was beginning to breathe on her own.

Meanwhile, the Newark Fire Department — our local fire department — had received the call for help at 3:17 p.m. and dispatched firefighters to the house. Battalion Chief Anthony Connell happened to be riding in his car a few blocks away, and heard the alarm on his fire radio. He sped to the house, and was there in a minute after the original dispatch. Chief Connell found Lauren on the backyard deck. He began the assessment, asking questions about what had happened. There seemed to be a bit of confusion because Lauren was just regaining consciousness — and this was a traumatic event for Erin. The two girls didn't have all the answers right off the bat. Erin didn't remember Lauren falling into the pool. First, Lauren said she passed out. But then she said she remembered hitting her head on the bottom. Now other firefighters arrived at the house. They continued the assessment and took vital signs. An American Medical Response (AMR) ambulance was requested at 3:22 p.m. with a Code 3 — which means using emergency lights and siren. The ambulance reached Lauren six minutes later, at 3:28. The crew noticed Lauren couldn't move her extremities, so they loaded her onto a gurney for the hospital to check for water in her lungs. That was 23 minutes later, at 3:51 p.m. Meanwhile, Chief Connell called our mom and explained what had happened.

But here's something interesting. The ambulance started towards the hospital via Code 2 — driving with no lights and no siren. The seriousness of Lauren's injury was not being noted. En route, the ambulance medic performed several tests to see if Lauren could feel or move her feet. Lauren couldn't move her legs. It was 3:58 p.m. when the medic finally attempted to secure Lauren's head and neck because of a possible spinal injury. Lauren had told the medic several times that she thought she hit her head on the pool bottom. Lauren says she remembers the medic getting upset as she questioned her, and asking if she had maybe taken drugs and then passed out. The medic told Lauren that she hadn't hit her head in the pool, and then accused Lauren of lying. The medic then poked a needle on the end of Lauren's foot to see if Lauren could feel it. Lauren remembers she was scared and intimidated. In the ambulance report, the medic makes it clear that Lauren couldn't move her legs, and that in fact she may have hit her head on the pool bottom. The ambulance eventually arrived at the hospital, leisurely observing all traffic lights along the way. The ambulance crew never upgraded to Code 3 for a major trauma of a broken neck with loss of movement to her legs. The seriousness of Lauren's injury was not being understood.

My phone rang about 4 p.m. that day. I was sitting on my aunt's couch doing school work. It was mom. She sounded panicked. "John, Lauren is on her way to the hospital," she said. "I just got off the phone with the fire department. They told me Lauren passed out in the pool. She should be okay. They said they're checking her lungs for water." I listened, then I asked mom if I should come home. She said no, just stand by. It sounded like Lauren would be okay. Both mom and dad were now on their way to Washington Hospital in Fremont, Calif., where Lauren had been taken.

After I got off the phone, I remember I just sat there and thought for a moment. Something was wrong. I wondered how my sister could have passed out in the pool. I had just completed an EMT class and, from what mom was saying, it didn't really make sense that she passed out in the pool, just like that. Lauren had no medical problems.

I began to worry.

MEANWHILE, BACK HOME, AFTER MOM CALLED ME she called dad. He was working in San Jose, about 30 miles from Washington Hospital. He left work and quickly drove to the hospital, figuring that Lauren was being checked for water in her lungs because of a near drowning. Mom and dad got to the hospital at about the same time. Erin and her mother were now at the hospital, too. Mom wasn't really worried because doctors were treating Lauren as if her condition wasn't anything to worry about. Believe it or not, the hospital staff was more concerned about the number of people with Lauren in the emergency room. The ambulance staff told dad that Lauren was fine, that she was waiting to have her lungs X-rayed. Dad found Lauren still lying in her wet bathing suit.

"Dad, I can't move my legs," Lauren told her father as she wept. Apparently ambulance personnel never passed information to the hospital staff that Lauren couldn't move her legs. Dad very quickly told the hospital staff what Lauren said about her legs. It was only then that the emergency room staff began to treat Lauren for a broken neck. X-rays of her neck now showed that her C-6 and C-7 vertebrates were shattered. Doctors ordered an MRI, but Lauren was now shivering and developing hypothermia.

A few minutes later, my phone rang again. It was mom. This time she was crying. "Your sister has a broken neck," she told me through sobs. "She's going into emergency surgery. They're telling us she…might… not…survive."

Hearing this is something I hope no sibling or parent ever has to hear. I told mom I was leaving my aunt's house right away. I told my aunt what had happened, grabbed my stuff and was on the road in minutes. But as I began the long drive, the severity of what was happening finally hit me.

I began to cry like I had never cried in my life. I was screaming to God, "Why is this happening? Please let her be okay."

The fire station where I volunteered was a few miles from my aunt's house. It was located at the freeway entrance that I would take to head north. I realized I could barely drive three miles without falling apart, so I pulled over to the fire station. The crew was watching television. Somehow I pulled it together to say, "My sister was involved in a bad accident, and she might not make it." There was silence. They turned the television off. The guys helped me call my cousin Jake, who came to the station to drive me up to the hospital that was hours away.

Back at the hospital, Lauren came out of a second MRI while doctors prepared for surgery. First, they had to fasten a halo to her head. A halo brace holds the head in place so that the bones of the spine (vertebrae) can heal from an injury or surgery. The halo is held in place by four screws, or pins, in the skull. We later learned that two more bolts had to be screwed in because the initial bolts went in the wrong places and didn't secure her head correctly. With the halo in place, technicians rushed Lauren into surgery.

When Jake and I finally reached the hospital, it hit me that Lauren might not be alive. I can remember that I pictured our last day together. Her summer job was coming up, and she had to do more paperwork. So I went with her. We had talked about how great she was doing in school, and about her bright future. She had received awards in her sign language classes and had been the perfect student.

Now this.

ON THE DRIVE TO THE HOSPITAL I cried most of the way. I called mom a few times, and the only news she had was that Lauren was in surgery. Jake and I prayed for her to be okay. Looking back, I never would have been able to make that drive myself. Thank God for Jake.

We reached the hospital about 8 p.m. I hugged mom and dad, and we all cried. There was no word from anyone. Just silence as we waited. Lauren's friends began to arrive at the hospital. Everyone was praying for Lauren.

Finally, after hours of surgery, Dr. Moses Taghioff, the surgeon, appeared in the waiting room. He said the surgery had gone well, and that Lauren was in stable condition. He also gave us a sliver of good news: it appeared that Lauren's spinal cord was not completely severed. He suggested we go home to sleep, that he would call us if Lauren's condition changed during the night. We had a lot of questions. But there seemed to be no answers.

Back home, we gathered in the living room, as we had done before so many times as a family. This time, Lauren was missing. An eerie feeling surrounded us. I can't explain it. We were in shock. No one ever plans for something like this. I mean, how can you plan for a freak accident?

The next day, June 22, dad was up at 5:30 in the morning and headed to the hospital right away. Lauren was asleep when he got there. He talked to nurses to learn as much as he could. Lauren was now on a respirator, so a tube went down her throat into her lungs to help her breathe. They explained she would probably not need the respirator permanently. Lauren needed it temporarily because of swelling. Dad remembers Lauren waking up and that he explained what had happened to her and what the doctors knew, which was not much. She was highly medicated. Mom and I got there a little later. I was a mess. I wasn't strong enough to see my sister in that condition. I broke down and cried. Lauren saw me crying, and she began to cry. She was in pain, she was scared, and she had a halo screwed into her skull. And we had no idea the extent of her injury. The surgeon who had operated on Lauren came into the room. He explained the operation: he replaced her C-6 and C-7 vertebrae with cadaver bones by screwing the bones together. He explained the difference between an incomplete injury and a complete injury. Lauren had an incomplete injury — which meant there was hope for recovery. Wow! This was the greatest news we could have heard. So, we all heard it. Recovery was possible! Recovery mode had just begun for Lauren. The surgeon conducted some reflex tests with her feet. A small movement occurred. He gave our family hope.

"I feel she will walk again someday," he told us.

The next few days were more challenging. Lauren was taken off the respirator, and with each day she became more stable. We worked as a family to make sure someone was always with her. We took different shifts. Mom took the late shift, staying as late as she could every night. A few nights she never even left but slept on the hospital floor. It was difficult for her to leave when visiting hours were over. Lauren still had the halo screwed in her head, and her only movement was limited movement in her arms. The halo was attached to a huge vest that was strapped around her upper torso to keep her spine completely still. They had to move Lauren every few hours to prevent bed sores. We prayed and we prayed, and we believed things would change and that this would be only temporary. On Lauren's fourth night in intensive care, a patient with a massive head injury was yelling all night. The yelling frightened Lauren. Nurses told her to push a button if she needed help. But she learned quickly that she couldn't move her fingers to push the button, and still had a tube in her throat which prevented her from speaking. When nurses realized Lauren was panicking, they tried to comfort her by calling dad. Dad rushed back to the hospital at 4:30 a.m. This was one of many scary events for Lauren.

With Lauren's injury, we had to learn different jobs at home. Things that Lauren did. And we didn't always do them correctly. For instance, Lauren had pet turtles, so dad volunteered to care for the turtles. Each day he fed them a few pieces of green food and a few pieces of black food. Days later, when Lauren eventually began to speak, dad matter-of-factly wondered out loud why the turtles loved the green food but hardly ate the black food. Now, for the first time since she had been hospitalized, Lauren laughed. "Dad, that's not food. It's charcoal from the pool filter," she told him with a smile. Lauren's loud laughing reached the nurses. They came rushing in. Here Lauren was bedridden in intensive care, and she was laughing uncontrollably. Lauren always tried to find fun in things.

Lauren also realized something sad that week. Nurses explained that they would now help her to sit up, initially for at least 30 seconds. Lauren thought it would be fairly easy. But as they pulled her up, she got sick and almost passed out. That's when she realized her condition was serious.

Lauren stayed at Washington Hospital for a week. She then transferred to Santa Clara Valley Medical Center. We received support from our family, friends and community in many forms and acts of kindness. The acts came in the form of buying food for us at the hospital, organizing fundraisers, moral support and gifts. This community support got us through the horrible time. We realized we couldn't do it alone. It's amazing that many people offer help during tragic times. An example is Stage 1 Theatre, the theater that mom, Lauren and I volunteered at for many years. Many of our theater friends helped us. They organized fundraisers that raised thousands of dollars — my parents both had to stop working to be there for Lauren, so our household income disappeared. Lauren's favorite dog, Hoppy, visited with a gift — 1,000 Origami Cranes made as a Japanese tradition. Hoppy and Kaz, his owner, played a huge role in keeping up Lauren's spirits. They visited Lauren every night for years.

I WAS NOW ATTENDING Allan Hancock College in Santa Maria, Calif. Dad told me that he and mom could take care of Lauren. He wanted me to keep things going with school and the rest of my life. As difficult as it was, I went back home and attended classes each Monday through Thursday. I would drive up to see Lauren every Thursday night and stay over until Sunday. In the first few weeks, Lauren was limited in what she could do. With this, she kept a positive attitude. As her brother, I wanted to help in any way I could, but there was not much I could do. I bought a DVD player so she could watch our favorite childhood movie "Liar, Liar." One night, Lauren asked me to sing to her. Me? Sing to her? I wasn't sure if she was all there mentally because I was a horrible singer. [They say sometimes you take on traits from the donor of the cadaver bones; my first thought was, he might have been crazy.] But I sang every time I visited Lauren. Through my singing, I think Lauren and I began to form a closer relationship.

Santa Clara Valley Medical Center was thought to be the best medical facility in the state for spinal cord rehabilitation and treatment. Lauren knew she would work hard to eventually walk, but even simple tasks such as lifting a cup to drink was then impossible. For hours every day Lauren would try simple tasks. Over and over. One day, it took everything she could to just move her finger. But she did it. The doctors marveled. Dad said if she could move her finger once, she could move it again. But her finger became so tired from that one movement, she wasn't able to move it again for a week. The injury also affected her vocal chords. Her voice was now weak; it was softer than a whisper. Lauren had so much to overcome and regain. At this point, Lauren was most concerned about getting better so she could get back to school in September, just a few months away. Sadly, she was naive about the seriousness of her injury.

Later, during therapy, Lauren decided to go back into the swimming pool. Because she had nearly drowned, this would be a huge fear to overcome. It was one of many. The first time she went to the pool, just seeing it was enough for her that day. As days went on, she was at therapy every chance she got. While at the medical center, Lauren met other patients with similar injuries. The first few months at the medical center were the most difficult for Lauren and everyone who knew her. It was so hard for me to see my sister in such bad shape. Everything she felt, mom, dad and I felt. Lauren felt that, at times it was harder for those around her to see her in this condition than it was for her. So dad and Lauren decided to have an important talk about her future.

Dad and Lauren understood that the initial ambulance responders may have made mistakes in attempting to treat her. Many people had contacted us about lawsuits against AMR and Washington Hospital. Negligence apparently had occurred because she was sitting in the hospital for more than an hour with a broken neck while the hospital staff was not treating her.

Had she received treatment sooner, and had appropriate precautions been taken, her injury might have been less severe. The ambulance report clearly showed the crew had documented her loss of movement. But the ambulance crew apparently never passed that report along to anyone at the hospital. She and dad discussed it more and agreed that yes, Lauren would indeed walk again. They would not look back at what could have been or should have been, because that would not change her condition. So she and dad agreed that, from that moment on, she'd use all her energy to regain what she had lost. It was an important moment for Lauren's future.

In the third week at Santa Clara, Lauren had her hardest day. Doctors realized that her halo bolts again had been installed incorrectly because they kept shifting across her skull. When they tried to tighten the front bolts, they would tear her skin with the side bolts, and vice versa. So, on a weekend when her regular doctors were off, they decided to screw two more bolts into her head to keep her head and spine stable.

They gave her morphine to combat the pain. But Lauren said it was the worst pain she had ever felt.

They would turn the bolts with a torque wrench so the proper pressure was applied. They had to increase her level of morphine a few times and Lauren just pleaded with dad to ask them to stop.

Later, she told me it was torture as they screwed the bolts into her head while she couldn't move.

There were many up and down days for Lauren, but she never looked back, just forward. There were so many challenges ahead of her, and someone was always there when needed. That night, Aunt Jean stayed with Lauren, and the two of them laughed all night. For one of Lauren's most difficult days in her life, she was pretty strong.

LAUREN SPENT SIX WEEKS at Santa Clara. And she did, in fact, progress. Finally, she was set to be discharged. We made a few changes at home. We installed ramps for the wheelchair she would be using in many areas of the house. We changed door knobs so she would be able to open a door. We brought in a special medical bed and set it up in the dining room. There were so many things to change, but we knew they'd be only temporary.

Whenever we came across something that Lauren could not do, mom would always say — and emphasize — the word yet after. "Lauren can't pick up a cup — yet." This left room for improvement and for hope. If you say you can't do something, you are correct. If you say you can't do it yet, it keeps hope alive. The mind is so powerful, and Lauren and our family knew that.

When Lauren finally came home from the hospital, we had a lot to figure out. Lauren had obstacles to overcome and a lot of things to re-learn, just to function. Three of dad's sisters who lived in New Jersey were nurses: Grace, Patty and Dee. They came to California to begin home care for Lauren. They were a great physical help, and they added a mental confidence only they would be able to give. They gave Lauren the proper care to help bring her back from her grave condition. My parents also needed a break from Lauren's 24-hour care.

I couldn't imagine being so limited and remaining as positive as Lauren. Lauren never complained. She found light in every situation. At the hospital, her positive attitude inspired everyone around her. She had a long road to travel, but Lauren was determined to do anything she put her mind to. She was scheduled to return to the hospital, after her halo was removed, to begin a more regimented therapy. At home she spent every effort learning how to move her arms and regain other muscles.

September was approaching. But with all the hospital visits and therapy ahead, it looked as if Lauren would miss her sophomore year of high school.

The Next Seven Years

LAUREN RETURNED TO THE HOSPITAL after her halo had been removed. With the halo off, a more regimented therapy could now begin. Lauren struggled with simple functions. She couldn't brush her teeth, or even hold a cup of water. She lost movement to most parts of her body. Every doctor we spoke to had little to no insight as to the functions she might regain. She faced the unknown, but many people at the hospital kept Lauren's spirits up. Her therapy began quickly. She spent hours each day as part of a skills group led by Katsura Kobayashi. Here she learned to pick up foam blocks and make basic finger movements. With therapy sessions she regained many motor skills. Lauren soon realized she could become more independent simply by developing a positive attitude.

Renee Coates was Lauren's occupational therapist. Lauren could not have asked for a better occupational therapist to help her get through this unknown and challenging time. Lauren loved Renee's energetic and joyful spirit. Renee would assist Lauren in relearning such basics as how to hold a toothbrush and a hair brush. These were major accomplishments for Lauren. Renee taught Lauren how to dress herself. Every function that she gained back was a milestone for Lauren and our family. Lauren would also practice how to transfer from her wheelchair to a car. This was a trying time for Lauren because many easy tasks now seemed impossible.

Lauren had a physical therapist, too. Shonna Moran pushed Lauren physically in areas with movements to which Lauren was limited. Shonna helped Lauren learn various stretches and would work on balancing and transferring from a chair. She also showed Lauren how to roll over and sit up from a flat position. Lauren was learning that because she had lost movement and strength. It would now take patience, a positive attitude and hours of practice to learn to do a simple thing such as just sitting up.

It was not only Lauren's therapists and nurses who gave her support and guidance. Other patients, such as her roommate Cambry Kaylor, were inspirational. Cambry and her family were facing the same challenges that we were. Cambry had broken her back in a horse riding accident the same day Lauren broke her neck. Lauren and Cambry bonded quickly with their positive attitudes. They inspired each other and learned from each other day after day. They saw each other struggle and overcome each challenge.

The people Lauren met and worked with all played a large part in her progress. These people not only offered guidance in her recovery, they gave her love and strength through friendships. It was such a relief to have these special people providing so much support in so many areas. We were blessed to have met them.

Doctors now told Lauren she probably would miss a year of school because of her lengthy hospital stay. Returning to school was important to Lauren. Let's face it: she really wanted her normal life back. She was 15 years old and had been happy in her high school social setting. She really didn't want to be held back a year, and thus be different from her friends. It was so important to her to graduate on time with her class of 2008.

But it wasn't looking good.

Then a blessing and opportunity came Lauren's way. Laura Knoop, a friend from Stage 1 Theatre, who taught at Newark Memorial High School, offered to home-school Lauren. Laura taught Lauren while she was in the hospital, and later when she returned home. After a full day of regular high school teaching, Laura would drive miles in heavy traffic to Santa Clara Valley Medical Center. She would then work around Lauren's hospital schedule. It meant so much to Lauren and our family that Laura would volunteer this. She was a main component in one of Lauren's accomplishments of graduating high school with her class in

2008. Many Stage 1 members supported not only Lauren but our family as well. Debbie Otterstetter, a Stage 1 board member and my mom's good friend, would show up at the hospital on her lunch breaks with meals and gifts for my mom. The many people who supported our family helped us rise again. I learned that without the right people in your life many dreams aren't possible.

While Lauren was in the hospital she met Molly Hale at a spinal cord injury support group. Molly was telling the group that, with the water therapy she was undergoing, she was able to stand and walk again. This was music to Lauren's ears. Lauren wanted to know everything Molly did to get back on her feet. Molly took Lauren to the Betty Wright Swim Center. Pool therapy was the answer. Lauren had to get over her fear of a swimming pool. She decided her drive for recovery and independence was more powerful than her fear. She was introduced to therapist Vladimir Choubabko. He trained Lauren and pushed her in many ways in the water. Lauren did this therapy for years. The result: she regained a lot of functions.

Another hospital patient with whom Lauren made friends was Dan Dumas. When Dan was released from Santa Clara Valley Medical Center, he headed to Project Walk in Los Angeles, a full-time recovery center that specialized in spinal cord injury. After completing Project Walk, Dan had regained so much function that he and his wife Annabelle organized their own spinal cord injury fitness gym in the Bay Area. They called the gym Sci-Fit. They hired trainers who were knowledgeable in spinal injuries and who knew how to use specialized equipment. This would help Lauren become stronger and regain function not possible with any other therapy. It was always Lauren's goal to walk again, but more importantly to do the best she can with what she has at that moment. More therapy and more hard work gave her more movement and function. The stronger she got, the easier things became for her and the more independent her life became.

Therapy was expensive. Later, Lauren balanced time with her college classes. Dad continued working years past his planned retirement date, just to pay mounting medical expenses. Mom would take care of Lauren. Lauren and mom always had a great relationship. Mom would always reinforce the fact that she loved taking Lauren to therapy, school and doctor appointments. But Lauren and I knew this routine was wearing on mom. Some days she was worn out because she always put Lauren first. They always had to synchronize their schedules so that Lauren could attend everything she needed to. Mom would have to break the wheelchair down and put it back together six to eight times a day. Day after day she'd wait hours for Lauren to finish her classes, medical appointments, therapy and everything else.

Boy, I thought, if Lauren could someday drive on her own, she and mom would both become less dependent on each other.

Of course, Lauren was constantly dreaming of driving her own car. What teenager doesn't? Year after year she had the vision of driving — and each year it didn't happen. If anything, she was sad seeing all her friends driving their own cars. We learned that a modified car would be costly. A car tailored to Lauren would need hand controls, a motorized ramp and special doors to allow Lauren to enter and leave. With therapy and school taking all her time, Lauren had no time to get a job and save money for the car of her dreams. Therapy and school were her priorities, but she craved independence. We all knew that if she could drive on her own she'd be less dependent on others. Lauren didn't want to rely on others every time she had to go somewhere.

This went on for years.

Sharing a dream

ON JUNE 20, 2011 — six years after the accident — Lauren and I took a three-day cruise to Catalina Island and Mexico. I was working as a firefighter. She was a college student. So we really didn't get to spend much time together. The cruise would give us a chance to catch up and spend some quality time with each other. The middle of the cruise also marked the anniversary of Lauren's injury. Once on board, we quickly encountered our first problem: Lauren's wheelchair wouldn't fit through the stateroom doorway. Whatever the problem was, we learned to not let it ever stop us. I always told her to never let anything limit her vision.

When you are in a bind there is always someone to help you — usually a firefighter only a phone call away.

The cruise was exciting. We swam with fish, we made new friends, we enjoyed tasty dinners, we saw new sights, and we even saw a blowhole in Mexico. But like any brother and sister, we had our ups and downs. Add alcohol to the mix and it's easy for emotions to run the wrong way — and run high. For instance, we had an argument over something meaningless, and it ruined one of our nights. One thing was different on this trip, though. We were able to break the childhood habit of not speaking to each other. In the past, an argument may have lasted six months or maybe even a year. Now, as difficult as it was, I apologized for what I said, without requiring an apology back. People can grow. This allowed time for Lauren to reflect and apologize to me when she was ready. This also would allow us to have some serious conversations about our lives.

Next morning, the cruise ship arrived back in Long Beach. We had an eight-hour drive ahead of us to talk about life in general. As we drove, Lauren began to open up to me about her struggles. To the normal eye she was the happiest girl around, and an inspiration to everyone. But deep down, she told me, she needed more. She explained how trapped she felt because she couldn't walk. She explained that for years she had wanted to drive. She made no progress, she said, and she felt trapped. She was finding it difficult to save money. How could she possibly get the car she dreamed of, she wondered?

I have always been the type of person to help people solve their problems. I told Lauren we'll get this figured out.

First thing to do, I said, was for Lauren to get her driver's license. We got home; the next day we headed to the Department of Motor Vehicle office. Worst case scenario: she pays $26, fails the exam, and gets to take it again, this time with knowledge of what she will be tested on. Surprise! She passed the permit exam her first shot! That night we talked, and Lauren thanked me for all I had done for her since the accident. We reflected on how we took the more difficult but higher road together, and how the higher road takes you to higher places in life. These are the things that define people's lives.

The Joy of Fitness

WITH ATTENTION-DEFICIT DISORDER I was hyper, and sometimes I showed compulsive tendencies. I needed to have a lot going on to stay stimulated and to be headed in the right direction. As I grew older I realized I had to keep my energy aimed in the right direction. That would be a big advantage. Becoming a firefighter was perfect for me. It was a job that allowed this excess energy to be used in many ways. Different disciplines make up the job of a firefighter. There are so many types of emergencies for which to be trained. With this career, fitness became an important factor. I was working full time by the time I was 21. I noticed early in my career that I spent many of my days off drinking alcohol. But I decided I wanted to change my life. I wanted more.

This decision soon led me to sign up for my first triathlon. What a way to use my energy!

I bought a used road bike for $60. It was an old yellow Specialized bike. It did the job. I got into riding and I became addicted to my progress. On each day off from my firefighting job I would ride my bike, run and swim. I was lucky because California's central coast, where I lived, had many places to train. Each month I would increase the challenges, going further and signing up for tougher races. I first did a short sprint course, then several Olympic courses, then a Half-Ironman.

On Oct. 29, 2011, I remember saying that I could do anything I put my mind to.

I said in two days I will run a full marathon. I mapped out 26.2 miles in Nipomo. Two days later I woke up and began running. I hit the first 14 miles with no problem. The last 10 miles were a challenge because I developed tight muscles, but I still finished with a time of 5:27. I received great feedback and support. On the last mile, my mom called to cheer me on. I talked with her through the last mile.

Anything now seemed possible. I just had to believe in myself and find others who believed in me.

I THEN TOOK MY bicycling to another level. I created a fictitious race that I called my Three Day Full Ironman Triathlon. I rode my bicycle 112 miles the first day, I ran 26.2 miles the second day and I swam 2.4 miles the third day. I was again surprised at what I was able to accomplish. I kept telling myself that anything was possible because I believed in myself and listened to my inner voice. I learned that people tend to think within limits and boundaries, and thus hear all the reasons why they can't do something. If you can visualize your goals it is amazing what you can achieve. I was at a high level of fitness and mental strength. I was open to what the universe had to give me. I was using my energy for good.

A Trip with Dad

A FEW MONTHS AFTER my special three day triathlon, in July, 2011, my father and I traveled to New Jersey to celebrate his retirement. It was a memorable father and son trip. Once we arrived in New Jersey we made tracks to the Jersey shore, where my dad was born and raised. Our first stop was to the beach at Belmar. We met my godfather, John O'Heney, and the three of us caught up on the latest news. We were staying at the home of Billy Emmons, my dad's cousin. We spent time with a lot of relatives, many of whom I had never met. I was startled to learn I had somewhere near 112 second cousins. I was meeting new relatives every day. We had a lot on the agenda. It would be an exciting visit: concerts, fishing trips, visiting bars, such as DJ's in Belmar and The Stone Pony in Asbury Park, a New York Yankees baseball game, trips to Philadelphia and New York, and a load of family get-togethers. To top it off, my dad told me that, since I was showing an interest in bicycle racing, I could participate in a local triathlon right there in Belmar, his home town. Andy Meuerle, one of his best friends, was organizing the event. It sounded great, but I didn't have a bike for the race. We visited Andy on our third day. My dad hadn't seen him for years. As I said earlier, Andy was the person who introduced my mom and dad back in the day when they were single. While we were visiting, Andy showed me a photo of the first construction project he and my dad worked on back in high school. They talked about their love for local singer Bruce Springsteen. Andy started talking about the triathlon, because he served as public works director for the town of Belmar. I told Andy that I would have loved to participate, but I came to New Jersey without my bike. Andy listened, then walked into his garage and came out with this Ironman winning white Kuota Triathlon bike. It was the nicest bike I had ever seen. Andy said the bike was big for him, but should fit me perfectly.

He urged me to take it for a spin. If it works, he'd arrange for me to enter the triathlon.

I was wearing flip flops — I mean, I was hardly prepared to go bike riding — but I took Andy up on the offer. Andy added small platforms to the pedals to allow for my flip flops. I headed onto Ocean Ave. The bike was sharp, light and fast. It was a 20-speed model: a basic frame with hand brakes, but no fenders or lights. It had aerodynamic bars and wheels, and the gear cables snaked through the frame. The bike was made of carbon fiber. It was extremely light. I had never ridden a bike even 1/100th as nice. Here I was visiting New Jersey. I couldn't believe I'd be bike racing the next day. I eventually returned to Andy's house after taking an enjoyable lap adjacent to the beach. The only thing to do was to make a minor seat adjustment. Not bad, I thought. Andy went over the course with me. My father and I then headed back to Billy's house, where we were staying, to prepare for the race.

That night, like most summer nights at the shore, we all visited the local bars for their live music — and to hoist a few, of course. It was a pretty awesome atmosphere. Here I was hanging with my dad at a bar he used to hang out in. It was getting late as the band began its last set. We headed home and I was asleep sometime around 2 a.m.

Next morning I woke up to my alarm, quickly dressed, grabbed my gear and headed to Andy's house. I was excited as I picked up my race number and walked the bike to the transition area. This would be my first ocean start.

We all stood in silence ready to go. The air horn sounded. I was off. I raced into the water and, with my excitement and size 15 feet, I swam like a fish. I was so fast I was the third or fourth person out of the water

Andy Meuerle, left, me and 'the' bike at Jersey Shore triathlon. I nailed
second place and decided then that bicycle riding was for me.

ahead of the 600 competitors. I ran to the transition area and mounted
my bike. Like the pleasure ride the day before, today I flew. It was like
the bike had a motor on it. I was hitting about 25 miles an hour. My
legs felt like horse legs. I kept a pretty good lead with maybe only three
or four racers passing me. As I crossed the point to get off my bike, I
grabbed the bike, held it over my head and ran to the transitional area.
Andy watched as I did this. He later said he was amazed. Something we

will both always remember. I got to running and pushed myself hard for the run. I kept a great pace and finished strong with a big smile. After the race, I joined Andy, my dad and my Aunt Grace, who had come to cheer me on. I think I surprised them all, but mostly my dad, because he knew we were at a bar until 2 that morning. So much for training!

Then came the awards ceremony. Believe it or not, yours truly took first place in the Clydesdale division. That's the division for racers who weigh 200 pounds or more. I was surprised and elated. After the awards Andy told me he couldn't get over my performance. He said he had never seen anyone carry a bike like I did. He even took a photo of me holding the bike over my head. I was thankful to be involved in the triathlon, and I felt lucky to use such a top performance bike. I spent the night thinking about the law of attraction and how you can bring so many great things into your life with your energy and thoughts.

The Joy of Volunteering

WHEN I RETURNED HOME to California, my best friend Mike DeLeo asked if I could possibly help him operate a summer camp for youngsters with cancer. He was a counselor and he needed an Emergency Medical Technician. As a firefighter I was an EMT. I jumped at the opportunity. Mike volunteered across the country at AIDS camps and cancer camps. He also gave his time to any organization he felt he could help. Before this trip he shared some touching stories. This particular summer camp was set up to give families a vacation from their everyday situations dealing with cancer. On the final night of my stay, we sat around the campfire. It was a local native American tradition for each of us to write a wish on a piece of paper. We would read our wish out loud, then burn the paper to release our wish into the universe. I was so touched hearing the wishes of adults and children who were battling cancer. Volunteering at this camp was rewarding. It made me feel good. I now realized how important it was to give back.

I decided there and then that I would become involved in something bigger than myself. I just didn't know what it would be.

Gift of a Lifetime

THAT NOVEMBER IN 2011 my father called with bad news. My godfather John O'Heney suffered a heart attack and died. The funeral would be in New Jersey the next day. I quickly decided to do what I could to get off from work and fly to New Jersey. Mike DeLeo found coverage for me. I took the red eye from San Francisco to Newark, New Jersey, arriving in time for the funeral. My godfather did so many things for me. He had a big heart, and he lived life to the fullest. I heard story after story about how he loved his family and how he lived such an adventurous life. No one I had ever met had such a big heart.

After the funeral, I called Andy Meuerle. We planned to meet for lunch the next day at an oceanside restaurant. We talked and talked to catch up on things. I laid out my goal for the coming year. I told Andy I now wanted to ride my new bicycle 200 miles in one day.

"Is that so?" he replied. Then he said he had something to tell me.

"I was going to wait until Christmas to do this, but since you're here I'll to do it now," he said. He told me he had friends who were trainers and who had seen me in the race. They were impressed with my riding ability, he added

"You have a gift, John," he said. "So I'm giving you my bike, the one you rode in the race. Who knows? Maybe you'll do something great with it."

Wow! It was a $5,000 bike. The bike I owned back home was worth less than $100. I didn't feel worthy of such a gift. But Andy insisted.

His bike was now mine.

Next morning we went to a bike shop where we took a photo with the bike. The bike shop technician broke down the bike so it could be shipped cross country by train. A few days later Andy sent it on its way to California!

As I flew home I kept wondering why I received this bike as a gift. And I wondered what I would ever do with it.

A Ride to the Golden Gate

TO HONOR ANDY, I DECIDED I would attempt to ride my new gift bike to the Golden Gate Bridge from my house in Nipomo, a distance of about 300 miles. I had completed several triathlons, but had never ridden consecutive 100-mile days before. I made a Facebook post about the crazy idea. Soon, my buddy Dave Lienemann told me he would join me for part of the ride. Dave, a fellow firefighter, always supported my crazy ideas.

After my post, many of my friends started voicing concerns about me doing the ride. The objections included rain, dangerous road conditions, limited cell phone service, lodging and how poorly prepared I was for the ride. But nothing would stop me from this ride. I was nervous, but I'm a stubborn person once I make up my mind.

I packed a few items in a backpack — and I was ready for the ride.

Dave and I began the ride on Feb. 29, 2012. It was so cold we had to stop to buy gloves. The only gloves available were garden gloves. I knew they had to work, so we bought them. We headed north along the coast on Highway 1. We stopped at our Cal Fire command center in San Luis Obispo, where we talked with Capt. Damian Juarez, another of my good friends. He pointed to radar that showed rain was forecast along our route. Rain or not, we filled up our water bottles, shoved off and kept heading north, hoping we'd beat the rain. We didn't.

Our next stop was at our good friend Teddy Borja's house. Teddy was a Cal Fire apparatus engineer paramedic. We went in, warmed up and dried off from the rain. We were both freezing. Teddy's wife Marlisa prepared food and dried our wet clothes. Teddy quickly realized how unprepared I was for this ride. I had 250 more miles to go. I didn't even have a flashing red light or rain gear, just to name a few things I was missing. Teddy went to his garage and gave me his only red light. Teddy and Marlisa were concerned for my safety, and they tried to talk me out of continuing. I appreciated their sincere concern, but I was still set to continue.

This was Dave's turning point. He would now leave me and head back home.

I was on my own.

I worked hard the next hour peddling north to Cambria. Head wind was strong and rain continued. As I entered the city, I got my first flat tire. I was soaked and cold. I tore my backpack apart on the side of the road and repaired the tire. Then I headed four more miles to the Cambria Bicycle Outfitters. I was about 55 miles into my trip, and so far it was tough. I walked into the store and explained my situation: I had only one extra tube, and I needed a few supplies to be able to complete my trip safely. The shop provided what I needed. I warmed up and continued up the coast.

I was heading into the mountains as I was approaching Big Sur. As much as everyone was concerned about dangerous roads, the roads didn't seem dangerous as I pedaled. It was a scenic, but foggy, view. I could hear cars approaching. Fortunately, the sharp turns and steep climbs seemed to keep cars from going too fast. Finally, the rain subsided. I climbed, climbed and climbed until I arrived at Ragged Point Inn. The next resting area was miles away, and it was getting dark. So I decided I would break for the night here at the 80-mile mark.

I checked in and placed my wet clothes in front of the fireplace. I cleaned all the dirt and grime from my bike. I had a tasty dinner, then took a warm bath. I called my mom for the tenth time that day, then reflected on what I had accomplished so far. Today was a big victory for me. I laid out all my clothes for the next day and in minutes fell asleep.

Next morning I quickly got back on the road because I felt I was behind schedule with only 80 miles out of the way. Within the first 10 miles, trouble again. This time, the gear shifter cable broke. So now my gears wouldn't change. I had to manually change them. Not ideal for riding in the mountains. The nearest bike shop was more than 40 miles away. After a good push I stopped for lunch at a restaurant on Highway 1.

While there, I remember a lady asking, "so what are you riding for?"

"No cause," I answered. "I guess I'm just crazy."

After lunch I continued north until I reached the bike shop. They squeezed me in for service to install a new cable. The repair took about two hours. Then I was back on the road again. I got lost after leaving

Highway 1 heading to Monterey. I used Google Maps to get back on track. I kept heading north and made it to the city of Marina. The air was now cold and the sun was setting. I covered 100 miles today, so I figured I'd call it a day. I was concerned about reaching the bridge the next day because I still had 120 miles to go. The most I had ever pedaled in a single day was 112 miles. Can I do 120, I wondered?

On day three of the ride I shoved off at 6:30 in the morning. Surprisingly, I wasn't sore. My bike shift still caused a problem, but I decided to press on even though I could use only half the gears. I rode through Santa Cruz and was making great time. I stopped for lunch after pedaling about 50 miles. When I continued, my shifter problem worsened. I stopped at a bike shop in Pacifica. The staff dropped what they were doing to help me out. This stop was much shorter. I used the down time to hydrate, as I was feeling dehydrated. Vehicular traffic got heavy as I approached San Francisco. Somehow I was now on a freeway. I now had to bicycle across exit lanes to illegally stay on the roadway, almost getting hit by cars that were exiting. After one close call I decided to get off the freeway. I was exhausted and found myself climbing steep hills. I was 20 miles from the finish, I was lost and I was racing to beat the sunset. But I kept pedaling, dodging cars as I pedaled. Then, in a distance, I spied the Golden Gate Bridge. What a pleasant sight! At that point I realized I would complete the ride. Sight of the bridge gave a second wind. I realized I was about to achieve something big. Before long I hit the 301-mile mark as I reached the center of the bridge.

I pedaled an average of a hundred miles a day for the past three days. I overcame challenges along the way. I couldn't believe it. I took a photo of myself holding up the bike, just as I had done at the end of Andy's triathlon. I sent Andy the photo, then called him. I explained what I had just done with the bike he had given to me. It was such a physical accomplishment, and it further supported my theory that anything is possible if you believe in yourself. I excitedly called my family, then posted the photo online. I had done it! I took a cab to my parents' home. I felt so high on life. Next morning I headed home to get ready for the academy. I learned so much about myself and what's possible if you believe in yourself and surround yourself with people who believe in you.

I now realized it's important to believe in your dreams and follow your heart.

A FEW DAYS AFTER THE BIKE RIDE I began classes at the Cal Fire Officers academy in Ione, Calif. I was on a high after pedaling 300 miles. Imagine that, I kept thinking. I just pedaled my bike three hundred miles! A few people had heard about my bicycle journey, and it was a topic I excitedly talked about. The academy staff had a positive image of the department which they would convey to me as a student. We were all on our way to becoming permanent employees of Cal Fire. This six-week course would do it. Instruction at the academy went well. I graduated and was now a permanent Cal Fire engineer. An engineer drives the apparatus and operates the pumps at a blaze. I felt blessed and fortunate to be where I was in life. Seven years of hard work paid off. Most of my post high school days were aimed at accomplishing this goal. I wasn't sure what the next chapter of my life would include. But I knew one thing: I focused on becoming a Cal Fire engineer. And I reached my goal.

Being a Big Brother

NOW I LOOKED AT GOALS I had chosen a few years earlier. At this point I realized I had a great family, great friends, good health and so many other things for which to be grateful.

So I decided the next goal in my life would be to somehow give back.

I recalled Arnold Schwarzenegger talking about how important and fulfilling it was to give back to the community. Working with Mike at the summer camp for people with cancer showed me how rewarding it was to help out. I looked at various ways to give back to the community, then decided I would volunteer to become a big brother with Big Brothers Big Sisters of America. I struggled with a learning disability and low self-esteem as I grew up. I figured if I was able to turn my life around, then I could surely help others with similar problems. I applied to the organization. Before long, Madge from the Big Brothers office in San Luis Obispo called to tell me I was accepted. Next step, she said, was to come to the office to complete a routine questionnaire. This way the group could match me to a young member.

The Post that Changed It All

A FEW DAYS LATER I was working at Cal Fire's San Luis Obispo County Station 22 in Arroyo Grande, with Capt. Dave Latham. While talking one afternoon, I told him that my life was progressing nicely, and that I had just become a big brother with the Big Brother Big Sister program.

But I felt that I still needed to do more for my paralyzed sister, I said.

"Let's think of what you could do to help her" Dave offered.

We talked about a bunch of things. Then I routinely mentioned the three day bike ride from Nipomo to the Golden Gate Bridge and how people had asked me why I was riding.

As we were discussing the bike ride, I thought, maybe I could somehow ride my bicycle to raise the money needed for a special car.

Dave looked at me, then slowly asked a question.

"How about riding across the United States for Lauren?" he asked.

I thought and thought about it all afternoon. Then, around 6 p.m. I opened my eyes wide with excitement.

"I've got it," I said out loud. "I'll ride my bicycle from the Golden Gate Bridge to the Brooklyn Bridge."

I MADE A POST on Facebook at 6:53 p.m. on April 20, 2012.

> "I have an idea and am looking for advice. I would like to ride my bike across the United States in 30 days. I would like to do so to raise money for my sister so she can get a car that has hand controls. I would like to stay at fire stations across California to be cost efficient for travel. Anyone have any ideas or how long it would take to organize????"

The response was instantaneous.

Within ten minutes Lyn Bratton, a friend of my mom's who I knew through Stage 1 Theatre, answered my Facebook post.

"That is an excellent idea!!! I can help. email me."

We spent about an hour back and forth as I shared my vision for a ride for Lauren from the Golden Gate Bridge to the Brooklyn Bridge and how something like this could happen. Friends and family members quickly posted ideas, messaged me and wrote comments. By midnight, about five hours after I posted that original message, I was exhausted and needed rest. I was lying in bed, my head spinning. I thought I'd doze off, but I kept coming up with question after question. I wondered if my idea would work.

Could I physically ride that far?

Could I get that much time off from work?

Could I raise enough money?

Was my idea even possible?

The Planning Begins

I WOKE UP NEXT MORNING to find an email from Lyn telling me she had already created a website based on what we had discussed. She explained she had purchased laurensride.org, .com, .net and .info. She added photos and all details I had shared with her the night before. She explained that it turned out great! (You can take a break from reading to check it out right now at www.laurensride.org.)

I couldn't believe how fast she worked. I was thankful, but not sure if I could even get the time off from work, let alone ride my bike that far. I logged onto the website. It had everything. The first page was a story about Lauren's Ride and how I planned to ride a bicycle across the country to raise money to buy Lauren a special car. It explained that I would stay nights at fire stations. The website contained a section about the route, a media page with all links, a section that explained who Lauren and I were, a page for blogs and a place for comments from visitors. Most important to me was a section that listed donor names. Lyn had stayed up all night to create the website!

I spent the next few days discussing my cross-country plan with my family and friends. I called Lyn. I was thankful for everything she had done. A hundred things were bouncing around in my head.

So I created a list of items that needed to take place first to see if this ride would even be possible.

First on my list was to talk to Mike DeLeo. He knows me better than anyone and he was my mentor. He always provided insight to my problems.

"Mike, I want to ride my bike to New York from California to raise money so I can buy a car for Lauren. A friend has already made a website and I already have three weeks vacation," I said.

He looked at me in silence. For a long time!

"John, why couldn't you just do a ride through California?" he finally answered.

Mike was someone who always kept his expectations low and was happy when his hard work paid off and he accomplished a lot more. On the other hand, I was someone who always set the bar higher. We comfortably balanced each other. By now, I had made up my mind. I was set on riding between the two bridges. I explained to Mike that a man named Darrell Sales did something similar years prior. So we discussed the general idea and our concerns. Mike knew the struggles my sister had because he was close to our family when Lauren had her accident. He watched her overcome so much over the years.

I gave Mike a lot to think about.

"John, I'll support you under one condition: that you allow me to make sure you plan a safe trip," he answered. "I know that what I tell you won't matter because your mind is already made up. You just have to allow me to make sure your trip is safe."

We talked for a few hours about what we had to do to pull this off. We needed a team and we needed approvals. We needed a route. We needed supplies. We needed dates. We had many needs. More importantly, I needed to talk with Lauren and my family to make sure this idea was something they were comfortable with.

That evening, I posted this on my Facebook page:

> "I am beside myself right now. Thank you. Four days ago, I had an idea about a fundraiser to help my sister. Within 24 hours it started to become a reality. A web page was designed, and many people have called, texted and emailed me with ideas. I would like to especially thank Lyn Bratton for making this become real by publishing the website, which should be available soon.
> Do we do the ride?"

NEXT DAY I HEADED HOME to discuss the project with my family. We all had our fears. Lauren was concerned because she didn't want people to feel bad for her. My dad didn't want people to feel he couldn't provide for his family. My mom was worried about my safety. She reminded me that she grew a few gray hairs during the three-day bike trip I had taken a few months earlier. I was worried because the year before I bought a car for myself. Would people wonder why I didn't buy Lauren a car first? I had other concerns that we didn't discuss. I explained and assured Lauren that she was an inspiration, and the ride would be a light in people's lives. We talked about how people would look at us. We agreed that Lauren's injury was expensive, and that most people didn't have the additional medical expenses we did, which made purchasing a $50,000 modified car more challenging.

As a family, we decided to go forward with what we would officially call Lauren's Ride. It was a big day for our family.

Lauren's Ride was now a reality.

We had just taken on an enormous endeavor. We decided to use the fire department Incident Command System, a system used for emergencies, to break things down with a chain of command and duties for each position. Lauren and I would be unified incident commanders. If there was something Lauren or I didn't like, we had the final say.

Lyn said she would manage the website and oversee the donations. She would be our finance section chief. She would also spread the word to groups and organizations. Lyn had a lot to do.

Mike would take care of logistics, and he would function as safety officer. Mom decided she would put together a dinner to raise money for the trip. I made it clear that I wanted all donations from individuals to go directly to Lauren. Operating expense would come from somewhere else. I didn't know where, but from somewhere else.

We decided to go public in the next week or so. Lyn then told us we already received a $100 donation from Stephanie Dininni, an engineer I worked with. Lyn also posted a message on our page:

> "The first essential element of success is to have sufficient confidence in one's self to brave the criticisms."
>
> — Thomas Stevens
> The first recorded bicyclist
> to ride across America.
> March 22, 1884

That night I went to a Coldplay concert with my friend Bernie Gallizio. Chris Martin sang "Yellow." What a song! Later that night I did some research and learned the song was about brotherly love. Chris said that it was about a love where someone would do anything for another person. It was a sign we were on track in what we were doing.

May

May 3. I prepared for the Wildflower, a half ironman. That night Corrin Lee, a Cal Fire communications operator, called. She told me she was touched by what I was doing. She offered to help. I invited her to be part of our team. She would organize a fundraising dinner in Nipomo, where I lived. Mom was organizing a dinner. Now Corrin would organize a second dinner. It was great having our team come together. Corrin had never met my sister, but she was volunteering her time to help her get a car. I was touched by her offer to help my family.

The following day, Amy Jones, a secretary with our department, called. She, too, was excited about my plan. She said she was trained as a public information officer, and she could write, too. We needed someone to get the word out correctly...so Amy became our public information officer.

May 5. Today was race day. Excitement of the ride had worn me down, and now I felt a cold coming on. I told myself that I might get sick on the cross country ride, so this ride would be an important test. The swim went off without issue. The bike ride segment became challenging because I fought for air and energy. Near the end of the 56-mile bike ride segment I came across a cyclist who had fallen off his bike and was injured. I treated him and helped load him into an air ambulance. Then I got back on my bike and worked even harder to finish the race. Being sick made everything more difficult, but it made me realize I could push myself if this happened again.

May 7. We went public with Lauren's Ride. Today 230 people shared our Facebook post. Friends I had not talked to in 10 years were sharing the posts to get the word out. Every supporter who shared or liked our website made our story grow larger and brighter. I received messages and phone calls from hundreds of people. I was inspired by all the activity. There was no turning back now, I reasoned. Thankfully, I had a great team to help me plan the ride.

Donations began to pour in. We raised about $4,000 in the first two days. Major media outlets were now contacting me. I had to figure out what I would say and how I would say it. Although this was a private trip, I hoped to stay overnight at fire stations. I didn't want to misrepresent Cal Fire, and I wanted to avoid any possible conflict of interest. Amy Jones emailed our unit chief Robert Lewin to explain our conflict of interest concerns.

Chief Lewin responded quickly that he supported the project. He then moved to get official support of Cal Fire and our fire union, Local 2881. He told me that I was a wonderful brother and a great role model to my fellow firefighters. I can't put into words how important his support was.

Every day we saw more wonderful things happen. We now raised $5,000! Lyn, who had already created our official Lauren's Ride website, added a Facebook page. Facebook offered a great avenue in which to share photos, videos and messages about the ride. We quickly got up to 144 likes on Facebook. Donations now reached $5,470.

May 13. I spoke with my mother and Corrin about their fundraising dinner details. They were both excited about their huge undertaking. My mom designed thank you cards so that Lauren could acknowledge donations. We had now raised $6,821 — in just six days! We had loads of details to figure out. Mike and I decided we would set priorities. For example, a lot of things were in limbo until we established the route I would take. That evening I called Andy in New Jersey. He didn't seem surprised when I told him about my plan. He was excited about what I was doing. I told him that I wanted to ride through Freehold, N. J., if I could. My grandfather, after whom I was named, had been a volunteer firefighter in Freehold. Andy told me he would start making calls. I also asked if he would ride with me as I pedaled through New Jersey.

Absolutely! he said. That day I received an email from Bobby Williams, my mom's first cousin, in Staten Island, N.Y. He was a member of the Staten Island Lodge of Elks. He said last year a bike ride, called the Brotherhood Ride, rode from Florida to Ground Zero in New York City, and that he helped plan its arrival in Staten Island. He gave me the telephone number of a contact person at the Brotherhood Ride. Then he told me that when I reach New York I can expect a super duper New York welcome! It was just another exciting day.

May 14. I woke up to an email from Cal Fire Capt. Tony Hernandez.

I met Tony on a fire assignment about a year earlier. He was one of the grumpiest men I had ever met. So I was surprised at his message:

> John: I received an email from Lori about your fundraiser. You're taking on a challenge that is enormous, but not impossible. Just reading the email moved me in many ways. I want to help you any way I can. If you want, I will try to get one of the rental car companies to donate a car to use as a chase vehicle, unless you have other plans. I'll drive the car for you, if needed. Whatever assistance you need, let me know. I want to help you reach your goal. Call me on my cell and we can discuss further.
>
> Thanks,
>
> Capt. Tony Hernandez

Battalion Chief Lori Windsor, a good friend, had emailed all her friends and co-workers about my fundraising ride. Tony was a recipient. He didn't know me at all. And here he was offering logistical support that I certainly would need on the trip. And he'd have to take off work for six weeks to do it. He never met Lauren. He just decided to offer his help.

I couldn't believe what I was reading. Tony Hernandez might have been grumpy when I first met him, but that night I fell asleep thinking about this guy and his really big heart.

May 15. We had to figure out a cross-country route, so we decided to contact Race Across America, or RAAM, a bike race that goes from

San Diego to somewhere near Washington, D.C. We figured we could follow its route. The RAAM website showed stops with elevations and distances across the country. I called RAAM and explained that I needed a route to New York City. RAAM explained they stayed off all major freeways and highways and that I needed no special permits to follow its route. I received permission to follow the RAAM route. We figured we could use major sections of the RAAM route. So we saved a lot of time in this area alone. We were making traction.

May 20. Mike sent an email to support team members, including Tony, highlighting each role and explaining everyone's responsibility. He first mentioned that we had already raised $8,000, which was a testament in itself. He identified timelines and action items. We still had more things to figure out, such as tax liabilities and the exact route to New York. Yes, the plan was slowly and carefully coming together!

May 21. Tony Hernandez sent word: he was in. He'd follow me in a chase vehicle for the entire 3,600 miles and 36 days. I couldn't believe that someone else would make the same commitment I did. But here he was.

Tony Hernandez

Tony Hernandez was a Cal Fire training captain and Type 1 logistics section chief in San Diego. What this meant was that Tony oversaw all logistics at a large fire. He was the guy who moved firefighters and emergency equipment around. With the increase of huge brush fires sweeping California, the blazes were drawing firefighters and special equipment from many other states. Logistics, in fact, boggled the mind. Tony was so good at his job that after he retired from Cal Fire he joined the Federal Emergency Management Agency's (FEMA) national response team — as a logistics section chief.

He'd be the perfect guy to help me get from San Francisco to New York City in one piece.

Tony was 57 years old. He lived with his wife Sandra and four children on a two acre ranch with three horses, two dogs, 11 cats, 10 chickens, 12 ducks, a few doves and cockatiels, a tortoise and a pot bellied pig. He is president of the Norwegian Elkhound Association of Southern California. You can see he liked animals.

Tony is a member of the board of the Canyon Little League in Rancho Cucamonga, and has been a longtime San Diego Chargers football season ticket holder.

So it looked as if Tony and I would become a team with one goal in mind: to get to New York City safely in 36 days!

AFTER HEARING FROM TONY, I learned that my vacation request was granted. That night I again talked with Bobby Williams in Staten Island. He said he had talked with officials in various agencies and they all agreed it's possible to end the ride in New York City — as long as we arrive on a Sunday. I couldn't believe it. He said New York City would provide a police and fire escort right to the Brooklyn Bridge finish line. Things were falling into place — and we hadn't event set the route yet!

Then he asked me a question. Would I consider writing a book about the cross country ride experience? It sounded exciting. But I was hesitant. Write a book? I told him of my struggle with having a learning disability and having to take English in college three times to finally pass. How could I possibly write a book?

"John, you'll experience something that very few people in this country will get to experience," he said. "In the next few months, as you bicycle across the country, you'll see things that no one will ever see. When a person writes a book, the reader gets to share that experience."

That did it. I was inspired because what I was experiencing so far was taking my breath away. Bobby explained that I should go back to write down everything I could remember, and to just take clear notes. For the ride, he'd give me a pre-printed form that I'd complete at the end of each day. This way, he said, I could record such items as the time I awoke, weather conditions, temperature, miles covered, etc. Items I probably would forget after the ride ended.

May 23. I went to the Seaside Cafe in Shell Beach, Calif. I told the cashier about my planned ride. I was excited and my energy was showing. A customer behind me overheard our conversation and asked me if I could sit down and talk to him about the ride. I gave him all the details. I went into more details about the ride and he told me that years ago a man he knew had kayaked to Hawaii from California. The first week at sea the man lost his two navigation devices, he said. He ended up being weeks late, while everyone thought he had died at sea. After weeks and weeks at sea he made it to Hawaii. He stood up onto the shore and collapsed instantly and was taken to the hospital. Nevertheless, the guy had made it. He just kept going in the same direction one paddle at a time. The guy in the café said he looked forward to following Lauren's Ride and hoped I could stay on track unlike the kayaker. He then gave me a check for $150.

May 27. Amy Jones wrote our first press release. She sent it to our Cal Fire union, hoping for support. Good thing I had a team member with writing skills. Two days later our union president, Bob Wolf, expressed interest in our cause. He decided to buy Cal Fire riding jerseys for me and for other riders who joined the ride along the way.

That day I learned that the San Luis Obispo County Firefighters Benevolent Association would allow us to use its not-for-profit tax identification number for our cause. The group explained that our ride met the intent of their mission statement. Thus, we could have donations to Lauren's Ride go through them. This would allow donations to be tax deductible.

May 31. Mike was busy sending email after email for support and donations. Every donated dollar would reduce our operating cost. He received interest from Fluid and Power Bar. Fluid was a company founded in San Luis Obispo by a Cal Poly graduate. It had different products for different parts of the workout. By today we had raised $9,320. We couldn't believe it! I was happy, but I knew there was still a lot to do if we were to pull off this ride.

June

June 1. Mike DeLeo called to tell me that Target Solutions became a ride sponsor. By now help was coming in from every direction. I emailed our team with goals with timelines. We had 15 Sundays – or about three months — remaining until the start of the ride, which we decided would be Sept. 9, 2012. Everyone had a ride responsibility, yet everyone was still working their day job. For our team this was also a full-time job. Our team worked night and day answering emails, making telephone calls, and thinking the unthinkable while doing a hundred and one other things. As we would complete projects, I would cross them off the list — then assign more tasks.

June 3. I decided to interrupt my planning and continue my riding. I had to get the practice miles in. I did an aggressive ride in the heat to the home of my friends Damien and Trish Juarez, in Creston, Calif. We spent time talking about the ride. They wanted to help. Later that day I rode home. I was feeling strong on the bike.

June 6. I rode my bike to San Luis Obispo and back. During the ride, Lyn called to tell me she received a $1,000 donation from a person at Stage 1 Theatre. This brought our total to $10,435. My fire station donated $400. That's when I decided to use corporate donations for logistical costs of the actual Lauren's Ride. Additional money would come in through sponsorships. I'd use the money we received from fundraising dinners for Lauren herself. We decided that every dollar donated would go directly to the ride. I felt strong about this.

June 8. I worked with Mike at the Nipomo fire station for two days. At night, we reviewed the RAAM data as it applied to elevations and distance between cities. We decided I'd begin the trip at the Golden Gate Bridge, then work from there. It was crazy having a map of the whole country in front of us. I then decided to cut the states out that we would not travel through. I put in pins from all the cities RAAM had on its time stations to get a better visual of where we were going. We plotted things out with T pins and started a route excel sheet. This wasn't an exact science. I never planned a ride like this before. We determined we needed to leave on a Sunday and arrive on a Sunday primarily because of heavy weekday traffic in San Francisco and New York City. It looked like it would take 36 days to pedal about 3,600 miles. This meant an average of 100 miles biked each day. I figured on days with steep hills I would probably cover fewer miles. On flat routes I would make up those miles. Using this theory, when entering Kansas, a relatively flat state, I would set 11 consecutive days of 100 miles or more each day. A rest day would only add miles to the total, so a rest day was out of the question. By the end of our planning we came up with a starting route for the first few days. Phew! I began to feel some weight lifted off my shoulders.

June 12. I continued my riding to Creston, Calif., where I stayed overnight. Now, my practice rides were getting easier and more routine. The more I rode the stronger I felt. The ride to Creston had wind, heat and slopes. I climbed the Cuesta grade. The next day on my return home I got back-to-back flat tires. I was out of tubes and didn't carry a patch kit. Who gets two flats on one ride? I had about a five mile walk ahead of me to reach a bicycle shop. I began the walk. Before I walked a hundred feet a guy pulls over and has me put my bike in the car. He drove me to a bike shop in San Luis Obispo, where I got new tubes and then continued my ride home.

June 15. I spoke with Jeanie Watkins of Tax Girls. We had to figure out how donations to the ride would affect Lauren's tax liability. We didn't want to raise thousands of dollars to find out later we would all be in jail. We realized we needed professional advice. We discovered that, if handled correctly, the car would be gifted to Lauren from our not-for-profit organization. Jeanie agreed to handle our tax paperwork at no cost to us.

June 20. I received a message from baytobrooklyn2011. I had emailed this group the night we got the idea for the ride. I had read about Darrell Sales, who had ridden his bike to New York from the Bay Area, arriving at Ground Zero on the 10-year anniversary of 9/11. Now I was excited hearing from him. Who knows more about what it is like to plan a cross country bike ride than someone who had already done it? Darrell saw our Facebook page and offered to help. Mike and I were doing our best to establish routes and call fire stations. We realized early on that it was really a lot of work. After talking with Darrell for more than two hours, we decided he could help break up the route and work on the second half of the ride. He understood what we were doing, and he became a team member. He offered suggestions to make sure everything would go as planned. Meanwhile, *tempus was fugiting.* We now had only 50 days to get our planning done.

June 30. We were making good progress. We had received four confirmations out of 36 for overnight lodging. Many overnight stays were in desolate towns. The majority of fire stations were staffed by volunteer firefighters, so making contact with them was challenging. Mike told me that in one town, for instance, the only person he was able to reach was the postmaster. By now we had several sponsors. Our emails and phone calls were paying off. Amy Jones worked with a friend who was a designer. Now we had an official Lauren's Ride flyer. My mom hit the pavement planning her dinner, seeking donations for the silent auction. Many people were willing to help her. Corrin gathered a team as well and was planning her dinner. Meanwhile, Tony was contacting businesses for donations, and was looking for a chase vehicle to suit our needs…Amy was contacting the media…Lyn spent hours each day updating our website to make sure each donor's name was listed…Lauren had planned to practice driving modified cars, but many times it didn't work out because of cancellations or the car not fitting her needs. Our team handled a lot of tasks so that I would be free to focus on getting into shape. We were heading in the right direction — but we still had a load of detailed work ahead of us.

July

July 1. As summer moved into high gear, an unusually high number of wildfires broke out across California. I was dispatched to the Grass Valley command center to help with the Roberts fire. Everyone was busy. I worked long hours. A few days into the fire, Chief Tom Webb, who headed the command center, told me he had heard about the ride. So I explained details about it. He made a few telephone calls and things took off. He sent me to the base camp, and who did I cross paths with? Tony Hernandez, who was handling the fire's logistics. Eventually we were allowed to distribute Lauren's Ride flyers to everyone. My supervisor even changed my shift hours to help make the flyer distribution smoother.

July 6. I handed out more flyers and constantly talked about the ride. The strike team from Monterey made a $70 cash donation. I was told to talk to Capt. Matt Streck. He asked me what I wanted as an advisor, and what I was looking for. I told him I was planning a cross country bicycle ride and, although the ride wasn't sponsored by the fire department, I would be wearing a Cal Fire jersey. I told him I wanted to represent our department correctly. I wanted to make sure I wasn't crossing any lines if and when I talked with the media. He asked me more about Lauren. Later I learned that Capt. Streck had worked as a public information officer for California Governor Arnold Schwarzenegger. In the brief time I spent with him, I could see he had a big heart and that he was figuring out how he could help me.

My mom called to tell me so many people were donating to Lauren's Ride on our website that the server crashed. Lyn told us that she contacted actor Wil Wheaton. He posted about the ride on Twitter, asking his fans to donate a mere $2 each. Bingo! Eighty eight fans responded. Donations totaled $1,200 for the day. As donations poured in from our website, the server crashed repeatedly. We were having what I called good problems. Chris Brown, a friend of Amy Jones, donated a larger server to handle increased website volume.

July 18. Tony told me he met Bob Shuster of Shuster Oil. After Tony's chat, Shuster Oil donated $500 to Lauren's Ride. When the Roberts fire was extinguished, and I had returned home, I was happy to think about what we accomplished with the ride. The interactions were exciting.

My days off were given to practice bicycle rides. One day, while out on a ride, I met Jennifer Best, a newspaper reporter. We talked about Lauren's Ride as we rode. She wrote a great story. Her story went to a lot of newspapers, with a few giving the piece front page exposure.

July 31. Trish Juarez joined our team. She would put together a packet with facts that we needed to know about the towns and areas we would pass through. We had 40 days before the start of the ride. I could see a lot of things finally coming together. We confirmed a few more overnight locations. By now I was balancing work, training and planning. Each was important. I knew I had to stay focused.

August

August 6. We reached 500 Friends on Facebook and we had now raised $15,000. Joel Fitzpatrick, a good friend and bicycle mechanic, helped me order the correct bicycle parts for my cross county trip.

August 7. I set out for a two day training ride from Nipomo to Long Beach, a distance of about 200 miles. I left early in the morning and would stay that night with my friend and fellow firefighter Dan Hagstrom at the Carpinteria Summerland fire station. I finished the ride the first day at 106 miles. The fire crew made a few contacts, and they donated money. Not a bad training day.

August 8. My plan today was to stay with friends in Long Beach. The weather was nice and it was an enjoyable ride. I had not traveled through this area before. I was riding on the Pacific Coast Highway. In Malibu, bicyclists were everywhere. I bought lemonade at a Hot Dog on a Stick stand in Venice Beach. I continued my ride, but I missed a turn that would have kept me on the Pacific Coast Highway. Instead, I wound up in downtown Los Angeles. What congestion! I was lost. So I decided to head in a general direction and hoped it would be the correct way. At one point, a car pulled out right in front of me. I jammed on my brakes and fell off the bike. Here I was on the ground – yet no one stopped to help me. I was bleeding from my right arm, knee and hip. My bike had minor damage. I walked my bike two blocks and bought first aid supplies at a 7-Eleven. I decided to continue the ride. I had never before fallen off my bike so I was pretty shaken up. I had only about 25 miles to go. I wasn't pedaling a mile before I rode through water. The bike slid, and I fell again. This time I bent my hand back, so I decided I would call it quits for the day. I called a cab for what I thought would be a short ride — and ended up paying $75. To this day I don't know what hurt more: the fall or the cab bill. I walked into my friend's house looking like I had been beat up. I decided to rest and nurture my injuries. I was set to ride back home to Nipomo a few days later. I hoped I would feel better by then.

August 9. I spent the next two days in Long Beach, feeling better each day. While there, I relaxed on the beach doing yoga, made new friends and went for a light run. Having a few days to myself was a pleasure.

August 11. I started out for home. As I was riding I received a telephone call telling me I was needed at work for a fire. I was riding my bike and I was far from home. But eventually I arrived home and quickly reported to my fire station.

At work, I made sure I got my workouts in. We were now less than 30 days from the start. Tony called to say he met Greg Vermeulen, whose firm wanted to donate to the ride. We had a conference call with Greg, and I explained what had happened to Lauren and why I was riding cross country.

Greg startled me by saying he would donate a dollar for every mile I completed. Even after we told him the trip was 3,600 miles, he said he was still on board.

I talked to Battalion Chief Julie Hutchison, Cal Fire public information officer. A few donations came from companies we were working closely with, and I wanted to be certain there was no conflict of interest. She said she would run everything through Sacramento legal. She got back to me. Everything was okay. No conflicts. I wanted to be up front and honest about everything we did. I didn't want any gray area. I felt it was important that everything be done correctly.

That same day I heard from a caller who asked to remain anonymous. He wondered how the donations were being handled. In our discussion, I told him that just today someone had donated a dollar per mile. He said he liked that idea. Then he said he'd donate $1.50 a mile! I couldn't believe it! Wow! We raised $9,000 in one day. What a great day! We were quickly getting closer to our goal, — and I hadn't even begun the ride.

August 21. Over the next few days I was dispatched to several Northern California fires caused by lightning. Total donations to date were $18,025. I then heard from my mom that Stage 1 Theatre raised $1,040 for Lauren by sponsoring a fundraising event. Just like that we were at $19,065.

August 24. I returned to my home fire station. Mom told me that two customers where she works offered to help her with the fundraising dinner she was planning. Kevin and Lori Orweller volunteered to scout for donations. They also donated their camper as an auction item. Kevin told our ride story to everyone he met. He customized a jeep with a Lauren's Ride display that was to participate in the annual Newark Day parade. On one of my visits home, mom brought me to meet them, and we took pictures around the camper they donated. I was moved by their kindness, love and support.

August 25. I biked to Davies Appliances to thank them for contributing. It was important that we recognize each and every donor. On my way there, I got a flat tire. My CO_2 cartridge refill broke. So I was out of luck. Rick Schoephoerster saw me walking and carrying my bike and stopped his car to help. Luckily he had a bike pump. After a few minutes I was good to go.

Seems like every time I needed help someone showed up to help me.

We now had 13 days left to put things together. Several cities still had not confirmed overnight lodging. So we decided to look at other options. We still had so many things to do. I was feeling a lot of pressure. Next morning, I went for a bike ride to help clear my head and to help me prioritize. When I returned, the chase vehicle was there to greet me. It was a brand new black 2013 Chevrolet Suburban. I called Joel who was outfitting my bike. He explained that parts were still on order. I would spend the next few day tracking things down.

August 30. KSBY, a local television station, aired a story about Lauren's Ride. Immediately, our Facebook page shot up to 700 likes. That day a friend of Lyn's created a radio advertisement. I met with Richard from Fluid to review the electrolyte products he was donating. These products would give my body proper nutrients and recovery as I bicycled 36 days in a row. That night I attended a meeting of a local running group, of which I was a member. The group gave me a care package of riding gear, a care package for Tony and $341 for Lauren's Ride. At this point we were eight days and two fundraising dinners away.

August 31. Joel and I worked on the bike. We weighed it in at 20 pounds. Joel saw I was nervous, so he offered key advice. He told me that at this point I was as physically ready as I would be. Nothing I could do now would change it. The most difficult part of planning was completed. I now needed to believe that I was physically ready. This gave me a confidence boost.

Joel said the bike would be ready in a few days.

September

September 1. We were greeted with another front-page story about Lauren's Ride in the *San Luis Obispo Tribune*, our local newspaper. Although we were making progress, I was still asking myself a lot of questions.

How do I put GPS coordinates into the Garmin?

Would my bike be ready?

What am I forgetting?

Darrell Sales told me it took him 18 months to plan his ride. Here we planned our trip in a third of the time. He found that hard to believe, he said. But I told him ours was a team effort. Mike reported that overnight accommodations had now been confirmed for our first 15 nights. Darrell was nearly done with finding places to stay on the second half of my route.

September 4. My friends Angie and Mike Leeper gave us Lauren's Ride glow-in-the-dark fundraising bracelets. I wore one on the ride, and when I rode at night the glow reminded me that others were with me.

September 5. I continued to have frustrating issues with my GPS. The coordinates were supposed to give me a turn-by-turn notification along the cross country route. But we couldn't figure out how to upload the information to the Garmin. Later in the day I accepted a donation from Home Motors.

September 6. Tony and his wife arrived. We began to outfit the chase vehicle. I continued to work on last minute details. Joel reported in that my bike was ready to go!

September 7. We finished outfitting the chase vehicle. We decorated the vehicle with magnets from some of our sponsors. I wasn't able to get the GPS coordinates into the GPS. I decided not to spend any more time on it. I'd wing it. My friend Victor Carrillo, a helicopter firefighter, gave me a lucky shirt. He said he wore the shirt on days he was nervous. He said it kept him safe. So he gave it to me for my journey. The special shirt gave me a sense of security as I rode from coast to coast. That night, before we headed to the fundraising dinner in Nipomo, I picked up my Cal Fire riding jerseys that had just arrived at the post office. The Nipomo dinner was held at the Edwards Barn. Corrin had done a wonderful job organizing the event, which included a silent auction. On hand were volunteers, friends and relatives, co-workers and our special guest — my sister Lauren. We raised about $3,000. It was an exciting night. Lauren and I spoke, thanking guests for their help.

September 8. After breakfast we drove to Fremont, Calif., for yet another fundraising dinner, this one put together by my mom. The dinner sold out. Our friend Belinda Maloney made table centerpieces. Guitarist Carl Rosenblum supplied background music. Denise Watson printed dinner programs with photos of Lauren and me. My daily schedule appeared on the back cover. So many people made the dinner event come together, including the Stage 1 Theatre, friends and family. Mom even had help from the local firehouse. Firefighters helped set up tables, and they even cooked! You could feel the love in the room. Their salad and lasagna dinner was delicious. After dinner, Belinda served as mistress of ceremonies for the silent auction of about 200 items that included the camper trailer, vacation trips and other high value gifts. My mom had done an incredible job. Lauren and I spoke, and we surprised Lyn with an airline ticket to New York to meet us at the end of the ride. Lyn was elated. Guests had tears in their eyes. Kevin and Lori presented Lauren and me with sterling silver bracelets. It was an event that I didn't want to end. But we knew it had to end, because tomorrow I would begin a once-in-a-lifetime cross country bicycle trip.

We had completed months of preparation and planning. Now we were only one night away.

After dinner, Tony and his wife, Mike, John Reynolds, Trish, Damian and I drove to San Francisco, our official starting point, to get a few hours sleep before the kickoff. We arrived at the Hilton, checked into our rooms, then got together to shoot the breeze about tomorrow, our kickoff day.

It didn't seem real. I felt blessed because for the past few months people donated their time, their money and their skills. I knew it would all add up to help Lauren live an independent life.

Now it was my turn. I said I'd bicycle 3,600 miles across the United States for my sister Lauren. Tomorrow, Sept. 9, would be the beginning of the greatest and most exciting time of my life!

September 9. Surprisingly, I woke up just before my 5 a.m. alarm. The *big* day was here. There was no turning back. We took turns showering and getting our bike gear on. We admired the great design of the Cal Fire jerseys we were wearing. Jeffrey Foy had designed the jerseys a few months earlier, and they were ready just in time. I called Tony and Damian to make sure they were up. After we dressed, we grabbed our gear and went to the lobby to wait for our vehicles.

I tried to stay calm. I was experiencing such a high: it was a feeling I never had before. I was feeling so ready to begin this journey. I had dedicated the last four months of my life to this day. Everything I had done was in preparation for this ride. I had no idea what was ahead, but I had the confidence, the support and the faith that it would all work out. I had no fear. I honestly didn't know what I would be up against. I felt that if something bad happened to me on this ride, there was nothing I would rather be doing with my life than what I was doing. I had a few minutes to wait outside with my special friends: Mike, John, Dave, Tony, Trish and Damian, who had supported me so much in my life.

As we drove toward the Golden Gate Bridge, I couldn't believe how clear it was outside and how majestic the bridge looked as it came into view. I remember thinking: I rode 301 miles to get to you a few months ago, and now I leave from you with aspirations of New York. The sky could not have been any clearer, and the sun had not yet risen. There was no one on the road. We pulled off at the Vista Point rest area just north of the bridge. We were the first to arrive. I was not sure who would be showing up to see us off. After a few minutes of taking it all in, I quickly got organized while I had time, and set myself up for the start.

John Reynolds went right to work and set up the GoPro. He mounted it to my bike with all the equipment Matt Streck had given me. Dave and Mike checked their tire pressures. Tony organized food and drinks, and he rearranged the chase vehicle so we could easily find items when we needed them. As we prepared to leave, people arrived to see us off. John Reynolds explained how to use the GoPro to me, "So you hit it once to video, twice to stop and this button changes it to photo." I had

Lyn Bratton joins me and Lauren at Golden Gate.

never used one before. Why not wait till the morning of departure to learn, right?

My little brother Tyler from the Big Brother program arrived with his mother. Two engines from Marin County Fire Department arrived. Capt. Aaron Jarvis arranged for them to come after we had worked together on the Roberts Fire. Next to arrive was a limo from Red Eye Limo, donated for the cause. Lauren and my family and friends were inside. More and more family and friends arrived. Lyn Bratton came too; she was responsible for making the idea a reality. Emotions ran high. Darrell Sales arrived. It was the first time I met him in person. He was going to ride this first day with us. Knowing he had done a ride to New York for the 10-year anniversary of 911 gave me confidence. Rachel Burns, a high school friend and neighbor, came out to ride making the total number of riders five that first day: Mike, Dave, Darrell, Rachel and me.

A man I met when I got a flat tire months earlier came out to see me off. Co-workers from past and present showed up, and so did people who had heard about the cause but never knew our family. We took many photos overlooking the bridge and the city with our friends and family. It was a sight to see. Finally, the sun rose over the city on such a special life-changing day.

As 7 o'clock approached, we started making our way down to the bridge. We gathered at the north end of the Golden Gate Bridge and bowed our heads in a prayer for a safe journey. Mike DeLeo opened up for prayer before we left: "Dear God, thank you so much for this day, for all of your wonderful blessings, for the gift of friendship, for the gift of family, for the gift of support and strength, for the gift of hope, thank you so much, please keep us safe, please keep Lauren in your thoughts and prayers, and everyone who has entered this ride. Thank you so much. We accept your will for us, and thank you all." After the prayer, we took a final photo of the five riders and were ready to begin Lauren's Ride — which was to become the adventure of my life!

Lauren rolls with us right to the kickoff.

Here I Go

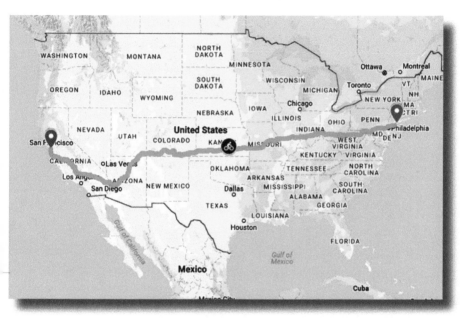

My route from bridge to bridge – or from sea to shining sea.

NOW YOU KNOW what makes me tick. And by now, you probably understand why I believe I can pull off this unusual undertaking.

It's still early in the morning. I'm ready to get rolling. And I'm really glad you're with me. So let's go.

PART II

Day

1

Sunday, Sept. 9, 2012

California: Golden Gate to Watsonville
Miles to pedal today
106

I FELT THE SPAN BELOW as we moved across the bridge. I now realize the enormous journey ahead of me. Today's goal is to get to the Cal Fire Pajaro Dunes fire station in Watsonville, Calif. It's about 100 miles away. One hundred six, to be exact. The sun cast our shadows on the side rails of the bridge, while I felt the sun shining on me through them as I passed. It seemed as if I had the whole country ahead of me. In fact, I did. Darrell pulled up on my left, and we talked. He gave me a pep talk and explained he knew I could do this as he had done it before. "Are you ready for this buddy?" he asked. I responded in the affirmative. "Yes, I am Darrell." We talked about how fast the day had approached for his ride as well as for mine. He shared with me that his biggest fear of his ride was being chased by dogs. I told him my fear was to not finish on time, being hit by a car, being injured, and even dogs. My biggest fear was not raising enough money for Lauren to get her car. As we crossed the bridge, I told Darrell how I got the bike and about all the events that led up to this moment. I explained to him that hearing about his ride gave me the idea of it even being possible.

As we rode, we had to dodge runners on the bridge because we had begun the ride on the wrong side of the bridge. We were supposed to be on the west side. When I planned the route, I didn't know this lane wasn't for bikes so we decided to just go for it. After we crossed the bridge, we pulled off making a wrong turn. In the first three miles, we had gone the wrong direction and made a wrong turn. I told everyone we were getting the kinks out early. It was good for a laugh. We turned around to the right direction to the coast in San Francisco, and even passed Tony in the chase vehicle.

My friend Rachel rode the first 10 miles with us, as she said she would do. It was so awesome she came to see me off and ride with us. I was feeling strong on the bike. It was such a beautiful day. Much of the city was rolling hills, and there was little traffic as we started. It helped that we left on a Sunday morning. With the tune-ups we made, I never rode as fast and felt so strong.

As we rode on, we were met by fellow Cal Fire workers on the coast. Jamie Norton, a battalion chief with the Cal Fire Santa Cruz unit, had organized with one of his stations to make us lunch out on the coast at Pescadero State Beach. This was about the half-way point for the day. Lauren, mom, our friend Denise Watson and my high school teacher Barbara Williams met us for lunch. It was emotional for mom because this was the last time she would see me before we would meet again 36 days later in New Jersey. She was concerned for my safety. After our goodbyes, we were back on the road. A few miles later, Darrell's gear changer snapped in half. He called his family, and they came to pick him up. He said he would catch up with us down the road. We rode down the coast seeing many bicyclists heading south as well. They were heading to Los Angeles for an organized ride for cancer. As we passed them, they asked us where we were heading. They never expected to hear we were going to New York. As we made our way to Santa Cruz, we got lost again. Mike said we should go one way. Dave said we should go another way, and Tony wasn't even with us. I decided to take us in another direction, which ended up being the wrong way. We headed about three blocks in the wrong direction to a main road in Santa Cruz, and we ran into Darrell on his bike who was backtracking to find us. If we had not made a wrong turn, we would not have met him that day.

Firefighters from Pajaro Dunes station welcome us after first hundred miles.

Luckily, his bike had been repaired. I had only driven to this point the week earlier to scout it out, but Darrell was familiar with the route to get us to Pajaro Dunes.

We headed down the coast realizing this was the last time we would see the ocean for many weeks. We continued south taking several stops to hydrate and take in the view. Kite surfers were surfing; wind was blowing from the south.

We rode and rode that first day. After a long day, we reached our destination. We had ridden 106 miles. We took photos with the fire station staff. There was no room for us to stay at the station because extra fire engines were brought into the firehouse for the wildfires throughout the state. We went to a nearby station, ate dinner then made adjustments to our bikes. We showered and did our best to get a good night's sleep. Before we went to bed, a firefighter tried to see if he could load the route onto my GPS. He couldn't get it to load. We talked about the best routes of travel for the next day — and then got some rest.

Miles pedaled so far
106

Day

2

Monday, Sept. 10

California: Watsonville to Coalinga
Miles to pedal today
135

NEXT MORNING, WE PACKED OUR GEAR and headed back to Pajaro Dunes. We figured we had about 120 miles ahead for this second day. Today it would be only Mike and me on bikes, with Tony in the chase vehicle. Mike and I rode off while Tony readied the vehicle. It was nice and cool with the fog. We headed down the roads we had thought we should be on — and were quickly lost. We ended up on a rocky dirt road as we tried to get on the road we thought we should be on. The road wasn't for a road bike, but we had a lot of miles to get in and no time to stop.

At 8:45 a.m., after riding about 15 miles, I stopped for a phone interview with Lesley Lafferty of a Bay Area radio station. She would interview me every Monday to update radio listeners on our progress. As we rode, I would get news updates about donations by phone from Lyn, Lauren and the rest of my family. I'd usually share this information with people we met. Now only in our second day, the consistent problems we had were figuring out the route and where we should be. We also had challenges with determining which roads were ideal for bikes and which ones were not. The day warmed up. Tony caught up with us and planned our route. We took a break for water, more sunscreen

Mike DeLeo and I on break. Mike rode with me the first few days, returned home, then came back to accompany me the final six days.

and a few snacks. Then we pushed forward. Mike and I talked most of the ride because the roads were mostly empty. As we pulled up to pass Highway 101, I nearly fell off my bike while making a turn because my tire all of a sudden went flat. I made a quick repair. We were back on the road in minutes.

We were now heading east. It was just about noon when we arrived at the Cal Fire Bear Valley fire station. Capt. Josh Campbell came out to help us. He was excited to find out what we were doing. He had no idea we were stopping by — because we had no idea, either. The company invited us to lunch, and later even topped off our ice supply. The guys made telephone calls to the stations we were planning to pass, giving them a heads up that we were coming. A few people even donated to our cause. We ate lunch, and the guys pointed out the hills that were just a few miles away. One was Mustang Hill. After lunch, we gathered around a helicopter for a group photo, then headed on. We still had a long ride ahead of us for the day. I punched into my phone Coalinga,

Tony tried to carry everything we'd need for 36 days in chase vehicle.

Calif., and it told us we still had about 70 miles to go. It was now one in the afternoon. Mike and I made a decision to take this leg of the trip 10 miles at a time.

Before yesterday, Mike had never ridden more than 40 miles in one day. As we rode, Tony pulled up to a school ahead of us. He began telling the teachers what we were doing. From far away, we were not sure if they were going to pepper spray him and call the police, or believe what he was telling them. Luckily, they believed him, and then they posed for a photo with us. We handed out fire prevention material and flyers that our department hoped we could share along the way.

Up ahead we could see the hills. As we approached the bottom of the grade, Mike and I each had different thoughts about how to get over them. I thought it would be easy, but I could not see the whole trip ahead. Mike liked to plan for the worst, thinking that many hard challenges were around the next bend, and he would feel better when they turned out not as bad as he thought. I hoped for the best. He planned for the worst. Together we worked our way up the grade. Tony kept our spirits high sharing comments and taking photos of us as we rode. Every ten miles or so we would stop, cool down and hydrate.

We spent a few hours pedaling up the grade. By this time the sun was starting to set. We flew down the grade. It was about 8 p.m. when we arrived at the bottom. We had traveled about 110 miles today, but still had about 20 miles to go. We stopped at a Starbucks for food and drink. We were beat and tired. We put on our safety vests and knew we had about an hour of riding left on busy roads. Tony positioned behind us, staying close to avoid any vehicles passing him and not seeing us. We finally arrived at the Cal Fire Coalinga fire station around 10 p.m., having traveled 135 miles for the day. Neither Mike nor I had ever bicycled this far in one day. We took our finish photo at the station and were then greeted by the crew. They had prepared dinner for us, and they were keeping it warm. The day was much longer than we had anticipated. I was exhausted, but talking about our ride with the crew kept me energized. Tony decided to reorganize the chase vehicle; firefighters helped him wash it. That night we talked with the crew about the route ahead and it sounded like a much flatter day and a few less miles.

Miles pedaled so far
241

Day

3

Tuesday, Sept. 11

California: Coalinga to Bakersfield
Miles to pedal today
100

BY THE THIRD DAY we realized we had a pretty straightforward flat route ahead. As we dressed, the station tones went off for a moment of silence for the men and women who had lost their lives on 9/11. That's right. Here it was Sept. 11. We paused for a moment to think about the sacrifices they made. Sitting there, I knew we would make it to Ground Zero in New York City in a month or so. My battalion chief, Bill Fisher, and his daughter showed up to meet us at the fire station around 6:30 a.m. It was nice to have the support of my coworkers and supervisors. Bill was planning to ride the first few miles with us that day.

We did a morning video blog. We would be doing morning and evening blogs for our followers. This was the last Cal Fire station where we would stay overnight. We took a few photos in front of the station. Then we started our ride nice and early. Like always, we didn't know what was ahead of us, but we had faith to know we would make it to our next destination.

As we rode, Bill told me how proud everyone at the station was of what we were doing. He thanked me several times for allowing him to ride with us. I was so honored that he came out to ride with us. We rode through orange fields on nice flat roads with no wind, or maybe a soft tail wind. We were averaging about 20 miles an hour. When we reached 30 miles in about 90 minutes, Bill was ready to leave. We talked for a few minutes about what we faced, and he said, "John, don't worry about work back home. We're all proud of you. We know you'll make it to the Brooklyn Bridge." With that, Bill and his daughter turned towards home and rode out of sight.

Today's ride was easy compared to the two previous days. For one thing, the chase vehicle was better organized. Tony had drinks and food ready for us every 30 miles, so we really didn't even have to stop. Many days, Tony would drive ahead to a McDonald's to buy lunch. Then, as we rode alongside, he would hand cheeseburgers to us out the window. Things were now really coordinated. By 3 p.m., we had knocked out 90 miles. So we took a break and were feeling pretty good because we had only 10 more miles to cover that day. My shifter was out of line, and I was having trouble staying in the correct gear. So I knew it was time for a tune up. Plus, my back tire was rubbing against the frame. Besides the bike, my back was tight from all the riding, so I figured I would need to have something adjusted. Tony called around to see what he could find on such short notice.

A few years earlier on a fire assignment, I worked in the Kern County Fire Department dispatch center for a series of fires in that area. While I was there, I got to know the people who worked in headquarters as well as out in the field. One of the people I met back then was Sylvia Coronado. When I discovered I would pass through Kern County, I gave Sylvia a call. She was influential in contacting her union and department staff. She made a lot of arrangements beforehand that I only found out about when we rode into her area. Tony informed the Kern County Fire Department we were about half an hour away. Up to this point, our welcomes were small. Not today. As we arrived after completing our 100-mile day, news crews from three television stations greeted us. This was our first major news coverage since we began the ride. They got great footage of us arriving, and they interviewed Mike and me. They covered the story well. It was exciting. Sylvia was there with people I had worked with during my earlier assignment. After our

One of many detours we faced.

television interviews, we went into the station to meet more staff. They had an assortment of food for us. Tony went into logistical mode washing our clothes and figuring out what we would do for the night.

Tony called the Action Sports bike shop and explained our project. Our next stop would be the Mojave Desert, so this was our last chance to get an equipment tune up. The owner took us in and went right to work. He raised my handle bars and made other adjustments. He donated all his time and sold us the bike parts at cost. He changed my rear tire with a tire that was a bit smaller so it wouldn't rub the frame. He even took a few of our promotional flyers and hung them up in the shop.

Then we headed to Tony's Pizza. Sylvia had talked to Tony Martinez, its owner who also worked for the Kern County Fire Department. He set up a fundraiser for us. Twenty percent of all sales would go to Lauren's Ride. Many Kern County employees came to support our cause. About 30 employees showed up, including their chief. Some were on duty and some were off duty. Many people gave us cash donations. One

The press is on hand as we arrive at Kern County fire station.

of their captains drove home and returned with his spare bike tires and tubes for us, and wished us a safe ride. We ate a lot of pizza that night. We definitely earned the calories we were eating. I got to share our story and the exciting things that had happened. Kern County outdid itself. Because of television coverage when we arrived, donations went up significantly. I realized that people do watch television news. Looking ahead, Tony reminded Mike and me that we faced a huge uphill grade the next day, and it would be a hot day, so we needed to get some rest. We headed back to the station, charged our devices and talked over the route for the next day. Stephanie Dininni said she was coming out to ride and would be at the station in the morning. Our plan was to leave around 5 a.m. to beat the heat.

What a day our third day had been! We couldn't believe what this fire department had done for Lauren's Ride. It was a first class department!

But will tomorrow be as rewarding, I wondered?

Miles pedaled so far
341

Day

4

Wednesday, Sept. 12

California: Bakersfield to Mojave
Miles to pedal today
73

WE WOKE UP, THEN WASHED AND DRESSED before the sun came up, knowing we had a hot and hilly day ahead. We went out to the back of the engine bay where we had parked the chase vehicle. It was now time to change batteries on the GoPros, put on sunscreen, pump our tires to the proper pressure, fill our water bottles with Fluid mix, load up on snacks, check the planned route and do our morning blog — just to name a few items. As we were checking out our bikes, the firefighters came out with coffee. A few off-duty firefighters arrived with the department chaplain. Stephanie arrived, excited to be there. The smile on her face was bigger than I had ever seen. In the station, we did our morning blog. Then the chaplain offered a prayer for our journey. It was the one moment I could slow down and just stop what I was doing. I remember thinking that we had so much of the country ahead of us, including a pretty big climb, and I prayed for a safe journey. After our prayer, we left for the desert — while it was still dark outside. We knew the route we would be taking. We had about 30 miles of flat land and then that long upgrade. No getting lost today, we reasoned!

Now we were out of the major traffic areas, so riding was looking to be much safer. Up until now we had only a few close calls with cars.

Some drivers could not understand why Tony was driving so slowly, and others were pulling out in front of me. Tony did a great job of protecting us from impatient drivers. Stephanie decided to ride with us all day. She then spent time helping Tony with his chores. I knew he would enjoy the company and help. With the adjustments made to my bike by Action Sports, my bike was now riding much better. My handlebars were raised slightly, which resulted in less stress on my now-sore lower back. Actually, every part of me was sore! The three of us rode together down the empty streets of Bakersfield. Two miles later, bingo! I got my second flat. But we were back on the road in less than five minutes. I was getting better at changing tubes.

We left the city and were now covering nice flat land. By 7 that morning we had pedaled about 20 miles. After a pit stop at Starbucks, I again adjusted my tire pressure. We ate, applied more sunscreen and hit the road. Stephanie had loaded her bike into the chase vehicle, and she continued driving with Tony. We had reached 1,000 Facebook followers that morning! It was amazing to think we had so many people following the ride. One thousand people! Each day more and more people were following us. Our blogs were becoming more interesting because Tony would add facts about local fire departments or towns we were passing through. We were getting a lot of messages and posts supporting us. So we spent a few minutes at Starbucks reading some of the daily posts in response to our blog.

Tony and Stephanie rode ahead of us to scout. Mike and I followed. After about 15 minutes, Tony and Stephanie let us know there was a road closure ahead. This detour would now take us about 15 miles out of the way. Fortunately for us, bikes were allowed to go through. At first the road closure seemed like a bad thing, but then we realized it meant we didn't have to share the roadway with any cars and trucks. I was able to take my helmet off for a few minutes and cool down. We passed a construction site where a huge portion of road had been taken out. We walked our bikes through the area talking to the construction workers about our ride. We handed them flyers and took photos. They said they would look up our ride online and post news of it in their union hall.

Among unusual sights is this windmill field in middle of nowhere.

About 30 miles in for the day, we were all together again. We looked at the map and we saw we were pretty close to Kern County Fire Station 11. The weather was hot, so we headed for Kern to see if we could ice up our drinks, reapply sunscreen and take a break before the upcoming grade. My legs were getting sore now. We got to the station and knocked on the door. The guys were happy we stopped, and some of them even made donations. We went about our business, and pushed on. We had a climb ahead of us. Mike, Stephanie and I started up the grade. Mike and I again began our routine talks when we hit steep hills.

I kept saying we just have to get over this hill, and then it's all downhill. He wanted to plan for the worst; being happy when the next hill wasn't as bad as he thought it might be. We joked that we both had opposite ways of getting through the grades. We were drinking as much water as we could, but staying hydrated was difficult. We made a few stops to stretch our legs. This was necessary to avoid cramping. Aside from the cramping, I was feeling strong.

We had a beautiful view behind us as we reached the Tehachapi Loop. The Tehachapi Loop is a complete circle formed by railroad tracks to climb the Tehachapi grade. We all joked that we could go straight up the hill and didn't need to do a stinking loop. In reality, I wanted to ride as little as possible. At the end of the day each mile mattered, and we still had a lot of miles to go. As we made our way into Tehachapi, we were greeted by Kern County Fire Department Station 12. They escorted us into town and took us to Subway Sandwich for lunch. As we walked into Subway, the owner caught wind of what we were doing. Before Kern County Fire could buy our lunch, as they had planned to do, the store owner covered our meal, and he even wrote out a check to Lauren's Ride. He told us a story about a man from India who had a spinal cord injury. That story inspired him to give, he said. He explained to us that we are all connected in so many ways. How true, I thought.

It amazed me that everywhere we went, people offered to help.

WE CONTINUED TO THE TOP of Tehachapi Pass, reaching an elevation of 3,800 ft. We had more than 5,000 feet of ascent for the day so far. Ascent is measured by elevation gain. If you go up a hill 200 feet, then down 200, then back up 200 feet, you have 400 feet of ascent. The good news was it was still early in the day, and our ride would be mostly downhill from this point on.

It was beautiful sight seeing all the windmills. We flew down the road at record speed. We were going so fast I honestly didn't know how I would stop if I had to. We rode in the middle of the freeway because there were no cars on the road — other than Tony driving the chase vehicle behind us. We eventually stopped to take photos of the windmills.

Owner of a Subway Sandwich shop near Tehachapi,
Calif., donates to Lauren's Ride.

Then we kept flying down the hill.

We flew down for another 30 minutes, then came across Juan, a stranded motorcyclist. We made sure he was okay and gave him water, snacks and flyers, took a few photos of course, then hit the road again. At one point, I was moving at 44 miles an hour.

Before long, we arrived at Kern County Fire Department Station 14. We were now in the Mojave Desert. We arrived much earlier than we had planned (it was all that downhill speeding!) Early arrivals always made things a lot better.

Fire company members began making us dinner and setting us up to take showers. Of course, before we ate and showered, Tony decided to make a few recovery drinks for us. We were nutritionally stripped. I drank a few bottles of water and a few Fluid recovery drinks. We took showers and just rested on their cool, comfortable recliners. It was nice to have a quiet night. I dozed off for about an hour. Meanwhile, Tony and Stephanie organized and cleaned the chase vehicle. I woke up — and it was time for dinner. It was nice being able to eat whatever I wanted to eat. I was burning thousands of calories each day and needed as much as I could to keep my body going.

After dinner, we did a night blog. Tony talked about how difficult it was for him to watch us climb the hills from the comfort of his vehicle. We could not believe how much Kern County Fire continued to do for us. We joked about just riding the rest of the ride through Kern County, making stops at each station. The next day, we would be going into San Bernardino County. We were getting into our blogs more and describing what we were seeing and experiencing along the way.

The highlights of our long trip were the encounters we had with the people we met.

Before we hit the hay, Mike told me he would head back home in the morning. He would follow the ride online, and he wished he could go the whole way. Seems Mike volunteers every year for a cancer camp called Camp Keepsake. It was now time for him to go back to help at the camp. When camp ended, he said, he would fly out to meet me somewhere on the East Coast and continue riding with me to the finish.

Imagine that! I was sad he had to go, but I understood that people needed him at his camp. What a guy! I felt a lot better when he told me he'd return.

Miles pedaled so far
414

Day

5

Thursday, Sept. 13

California: Mojave to Newberry Springs
Miles to pedal today
94

WE BEGAN OUR BLOG early to beat the heat. Kern County Fire was up to make sure we had a hot breakfast before our journey. Tony now decided he would wear a different hat for each blog post to add a bit of entertaining value. In our blog, we let everyone know what Lyn Bratton, my sister Lauren, my mom Judy, Darrell Sales and Amy Jones were doing back home.

Lyn was keeping track of all the donors, updating the website with our blog posts and photos and routinely calling to check on us. She was contacting every group that wanted to help. At this point, she had put in hundreds of hours to make sure everything was running smoothly. Lauren by now was beginning to look at different cars that she thought would suit her need. At the same time, she was going for her driver's license, following news of the ride, and even attending college classes. Mom was nervously following the ride while making sure everyone who donated received a thank you card from Lauren. Darrell Sales was helping Tony contact fire stations that we planned to visit in the next few days, and he finalized a few more stations. Amy was busy making a lot of media connections. She would edit my writing for proper grammar and spelling.

We wanted to continue the ride through Kern County because of the way the department and the people had treated us. I mean, they were great! We had raised so much money for Lauren in our time in Kern County. Mike told me how honored he was to have ridden this far, and he said that what we were experiencing was amazing.

We ended our blog, thanked the guys from the station and got on the road to unfamiliar territory.

The nice part about today was that we only had two main freeways on which to travel. It would be a relatively easy day. We just had to start east on Highway 58 and then we would travel east on Highway 40. No turn-by-turn route for the day like we had before. We left at dawn. A rare view as the sun rose ahead of us. We saw nothing but flat road before us. The three of us headed out on our bikes with Tony behind us. We were riding about 15 miles an hour. As we rode, there was enough room for all of us to ride together, even though debris appeared on the side of the road. We rode for about 30 miles till we reached U.S. Highway 395. This was Mike's last stop before he left us. So we decided it was a perfect time for an early lunch. Mike's wife was on her way to pick him up. We loaded his bike onto the chase vehicle and headed in for lunch. I would keep his bike as a backup in case I needed it. Meanwhile, it would be there for him when he rejoined us. Having completed a third of today's trip by 10 a.m. made me feel good.

We ate, we took a few photos together and said our goodbyes. Mike told me to be safe. He also said he'd see me before I knew it. We were both sad he had to go. But a lot of people back at the camps were depending on him.

Stephanie, Tony and I continued heading east. The temperature warmed up; the sun was beating down on us. Stephanie would ride a few miles then hop in the chase vehicle to help Tony. We were making great time. There seemed to be a light tailwind pushing us. Believe it or not, every semi truck that passed me helped to push me down the road. Sometimes I felt as if I was so close that they pulled me in a little bit, too. By noon, we had reached Barstow, Calif., and had completed 60 miles. Now it was Stephanie's time to leave us. She had planned to

How would you like to have this thing growing in your yard?

board a train with her bike at Barstow to head home. We said our good-byes, then Tony and I made our way onto Highway 40. Good news: only 30 miles left for the day!

I was feeling strong, making great time with a fast cadence. Tony and I were having good handoffs for food and water. It was nice not having to stop every time I needed to eat or drink. I was becoming pretty good at throwing empty bottles into his car as I passed it. We made our way into Newberry Springs before 3 p.m. Unlike our other stops, mostly at fire stations, we would be staying at the home of a Newberry Springs firefighter. We made our way to the headquarters, and three miles later reached the station. There we met Candice Robertson and Daphne Lanier, who worked for the Newberry Springs Fire Department. Actually, we arrived about five hours ahead of schedule. What a day! Man, we were kicking ass! The women told us that they had planned a special dinner at the place we were staying, and that everyone from their department — and their families — would join us.

I fueled up with Fluid recovery drinks, as I did after each ride. Then Tony and I decided to head back into Barstow to buy supplies we needed, since no major cities were ahead of us for miles.

I was surprised that we had now ridden more than 500 miles! It was nice having time to reflect and get ahead of things. We found a store. We bought duct tape, sharpies, a power inverter and more bottles of water. We decided we would make signs and take "official" photos when we reached milestones, such as hitting 500 miles. We were learning that it was a struggle to keep our electronics charged. The power converter we just bought would be a big help, we reasoned. Now I was resting, and I realized I was really sore. I may have pushed it a little hard at the end and had not done any stretching. I think I had forgotten I had another 3,000 miles ahead of me when I was racing to get to Newberry Springs. So we came up with a plan to take an ice bath to help recover. I had never taken an ice bath, but I knew a few marathoners who swore by it. They told me that it strongly aided in recovery. Tony placed a call to James Schwartz, the firefighter with whom we would be staying, to see how we could accomplish the ice bath. Mr. Schwartz said we could use his bathtub, and he would bring ice home. With that, we headed to the Barstow train station to record a blog for the day.

As we prepared for our blog, a car pulled up and passengers tossed trash at a trash can. But the trash missed the can. This sparked a conversation among all of us. Here we were, about to start our blog, so we invited them into it. The car passengers turned out to be Kathy Guley, her daughter Chelsea and her friend Olivia, all from California. The more people we met, the more people would help spread the word of our cause. People we had already met on the road had donated, shared our cause and created so much support with likes on Facebook, emails and comments of encouragement making sure we never felt alone on the road. After our blog, we headed to Starbucks to upload our blog for the day. After coffee and uploads, we headed back into Newberry Springs to the Schwartz residence.

We arrived at James Schwartz's home, where we met the host and his wife, Holly. They were so gracious to have everyone over for dinner and allow us to stay the night! They were beginning to prepare dinner, and they asked us what we needed. They showed us their home and explained that they would sleep on the couch. Tony would get the spare bedroom. They wanted me to take their room so that I got the best sleep I could. We tried to talk them out of it, but they insisted we were visitors and were staying in those rooms!

BRRRR! BEFORE GUESTS ARRIVED, I decided to take the ice bath and clean up. After a long day of riding in the heat, I would usually smell, to put it mildly, not to mention that my legs would be covered with grease and dirt. James poured the two big bags of ice into the bath he had started. I decided to wear a shirt to avoid hypothermia. My body wasn't as warm as it was hours earlier. I never knew what I was doing when it came to doing most things. I just did them and hoped for the best. As the tub filled up I wondered if this would help me at all, but figured it could only help. As I put one foot in, I had no idea how I would get my whole body in, so I just went in fast. I was freezing. I figured I needed to do it at for least 15 minutes. I started to clean off the dirt and grease from my legs. It seemed like the dirt and grease were stuck on. I did what I could to make it through it all. I think I realized then that my marathoner friends were just crazy. After nearly freezing to death, I let the water drain and took a quick shower. While I was still in the bathroom, I heard people arriving. One firefighter after another arrived, each bringing trays of food or desserts. More than 20 people joined us for dinner. I was certainly getting the required calories for the next day's ride. Over dinner, I explained to the guests what we had encountered so far and how the ride actually came together. We gave thanks for everything that everyone had done for my sister. Calvin, who coordinated our stay, said they had organized a fund-raiser, and that their department would make a donation, too. After dinner, we went outside and watched the sun set.

As Tony was showing the chase vehicle and how he had organized it, a 12-year-old boy named Kaden came over to me and said he, too, wanted to help Lauren.

He handed me a quarter.

What a nice gesture of kindness at such a young age. His mother, Candice Robertson, told us that after hearing about Lauren at dinner, Kaden said he wanted to help her get her special car.

I walked Kaden over to my bike, and I taped his quarter to the bike frame. I told him that I would ride his quarter all the way to New York, and that I would give it to Lauren in person there. Having the quarter visible to me as I rode across the country would remind me that Kaden was there supporting me.

As the evening wore on, and before anyone left, we recorded a blog with everyone participating. Kaden added to the blog, "Well, I didn't have much, but I gave him a donation to help him out with his sister." It was a special blog for me to have everyone in it who shared the evening with us. Tony and I just kept asking each other how could this day be any better?

That night we stayed up pretty late having deep conversation about life and about dreams. We eventually went to bed not knowing what tomorrow would have in store for us. We did know that we would leave early. Weather reports called for another really hot day.

Extra heat could mean bad news.

Miles pedaled so far

508

Kaden Robertson points to 25 cent coin he donated. I taped it to bike frame.

Day

6

Friday, Sept. 14

California: Newberry Springs to Needles
Miles to pedal today
127

TONY AND I AWOKE AT 5 A.M. To our surprise, a hot breakfast was ready. We ate, took a few photos and left for the fire station, where we had ended the day before. It was different riding on my own now. I put on a good playlist composed of mostly Coldplay songs, and then started off. One advantage to being on my own was that I could leave when I wanted and could go at my own pace. The more people with you, the more coordination is necessary. There are a lot more advantages to having people with you, but I always tried to see the light in every situation, just as Lauren would.

As we got on the road, I knew I had 127 miles ahead of me on what would turn out to be a scorcher. It was going to be a hard day. Some days were easier and some were difficult. I wasn't an expert at the plan I had made. I just made it. If I had a good pace, I would miss the heat of the day, I reasoned, so that's what I focused on. We had a straight shot to Needles, Calif. Today is our sixth day. Before shoving off, I looked at Tony. "This is our last day in California, Tony," I said. We were on the road before sunrise and were traveling east. The ice bath must have provided some recovery because I was feeling strong. I had the option to get on the freeway or take a side road that, for as far as I could see, ran parallel to the freeway. I went with the parallel road. That was my first mistake for the day. Although it went in the right direction, the road was poorly maintained, especially for my bicycle. After traveling five miles, I decided I would ride on the side of the freeway. The bumps I hit on the crappy road jolted my bike, and the jolts went up through my arms to my shoulders. They hurt. The only problem I had getting to the freeway was trying to find an entrance. I looked on my Google Maps and it was miles and miles away. I wasn't going to ride five miles back to the start of the day either. My other option was climbing over a 3-foot high barbed wire fence and walking 800 feet through marshland. I decided to climb over the fence.

I carefully raised the bike over the fence to avoid punctures or penetrations. I went about 30 feet down the fence line and carefully stepped on the first line of wire next to the metal T post and swung my leg over, straddling the fence. I thought of all the things that could now go wrong and felt vulnerable. I carefully balanced and crossed over the fence. Luckily, I made it over without any scrapes or tears to my riding shorts. I grabbed my bike and walked through the muddy area. Mud covered my shoes. Not the ideal way to start the day. Meanwhile, Tony drove back to enter the freeway, and would eventually meet me. I got onto the road and used my water bottles to spray down the bottom of my shoes so the cleats could connect to the bike. Finally, I was back on the road. No big deal. Just wound up with wet feet and muddy legs.

Tony caught up with me a few miles later. The road was flat. The sun was rising. By 7:48 a.m. we made it to Ludlow. We had completed about 30 miles. Now we had less than 100 miles to go before we'd call it a day. Getting up early paid off. At this rate, we'd have another early day. We stopped for a break and took photos. I stretched out on the grass for a few minutes to relax. But only for a few minutes. Then it was back on the bike, and I was off again. I tried to remind myself not to overdo it. We had a good pace, but I was having some tightness between my shoulders. As Tony followed me, he made a few phone calls to set something up ahead. He pulled ahead of me. Things had been going smoothly. Then I saw Tony pulled over and out of the vehicle. He was not taking photos. He was on the ground next to the rear right side of the vehicle.

The chase vehicle had a flat tire.

Besides the flat, there was body damage. Something on the side of the road had kicked up and damaged our vehicle. I was able to dodge most things on the side of the road, but it was a lot harder in a vehicle. The body damage was minor. It looked like cosmetic damage only. No big deal, we thought. After all, we had a spare tire. As Tony cleared out the vehicle to get to the jack, I offered to help. He suggested I keep riding. But I figured this would be a good time to take a 10-minute break inside the vehicle. I mean, how long would it take to change a tire? About 10 minutes I figured. Tony gathered all the equipment and dropped the spare tire. After I rested and hydrated, I got out of the car to help him. He jacked up the vehicle to the proper height, and we removed the flat tire. We were ready to put the new tire on, but the vehicle wasn't high enough. So we gave the jack a few more turns and tried again. Still too low by about a half-inch. We turned the lever to raise the jack a little higher — and *badda boom*. The vehicle slipped off the jack and crashed to the ground.

The jack had snapped in half.

Rats! We couldn't believe what had just happened. Here we are in the middle of the desert. And we're stranded.

Luckily, we had cell phone service. So Tony calmly called AAA. As he was on the phone, a California Highway Patrol car pulled up. Ah, ha. This is our lucky day, I thought. The police officer was sure to have a jack. We told him what had happened and we gave him details about our ride. He took a Lauren's Ride flyer and headed back to his vehicle to grab his jack. But his jack was smaller than the jack we had used. So it didn't work.

Tony stayed on the phone with AAA — getting transferred five or six times.

After about 30 minutes on hold, Tony was told a tow truck was on the way. That was the good news. It would reach us in about three hours.

That was the bad news.

We still had about 70 miles to go for the day. The temperature was now into the 90s.

We sat in the vehicle and tried to relax. What else could I do now but conserve my energy during the wait. Then we decided to come up with a new plan of action.

We decided to update our followers. Subsequently, at this difficult time, John Reynolds created a video and had posted it on our Facebook about the start of Lauren's Ride. He had music, and he had the storyline from the beginning. We watched and watched. Then, half way through the video, Tony jumped up. "I got an idea," he said.

"Grab the sharpie out of the glove box," he said. He took a cardboard box from the rear of the vehicle and drew a sign that read JACK! in large letters. Tony got out of the vehicle and held it up pointing to the vehicle as cars flew by. The main problem was we needed a floor jack. We were on the bottom of a downhill grade, so it would be hard for a commercial truck driver to stop. But, what the heck. We had no other option.

We got a lot of honks and waves. Within 10 minutes, though, Jeff Klingoffer pulled over in a truck hauling jet skis. Yes! Jeff had a floor jack!

Eureka! We were saved from being stranded!

Tony and Jeff lifted the vehicle and positioned the spare with no problem. Everything looked ok. Phew. That was that. We took photos with Jeff and thanked him for helping.

I NEEDED TO GET BACK on the road because we had been sidelined for almost 90 minutes. The temperature now was touching 100 degrees. Before leaving, Tony and I decided that, because Jeff had helped us, we would stop for any motorist we came across — to return this favor.

Not long after getting back onto Highway 40, we saw two motorcyclists who were on a fundraising cancer ride across a good portion of the country. Like us, they were broken down. They told us they had AAA on the way and didn't need our help. It was great to see other people on the road for another cause. We offered them snacks and drinks, and we were again on our way. By 2:30 that afternoon we were making

Car jack broke, so Tony advertised. Sure enough, within
minutes motorist stopped to offer one.

good progress. It wasn't just hot out. It was hotter than hot! It was now
hotter than any time of the ride so far. We came upon a rest stop for
the Hi Sahara Oasis where Route 66 and Highway 40 crossed in Essex,
Calif., a town I had never heard of. After pedaling 80 miles I figured I
could use some real food, so we pulled over. The town of Needles was
still about 40 miles ahead of us. We ordered a few cheeseburgers. Tony,
as usual, drew a lot of attention telling other customers what we were
doing. Gathered around him and listening were two Federal Express
overland drivers, travelers from China and Spain, and a few others.
Each and every listener donated to Lauren's Ride.

The further we traveled the more of an accomplishment it was. We
took a lot of photos. I ate my food quickly because I wanted to get back
on the road.

A few miles down the road I passed a road sign on the ground that
read EAST. It was a strong reminder of what I kept telling myself as I

rode. If I keep riding east, I will make it to my destination. I realized I had a lot of miles ahead of me, but if I looked at things in simple terms it would be obtainable. Two hours later we arrived at Needles, which would be our final stop in California. So far we had completed 635 miles. Today was a 127 mile day. I had been on the road for just over 12 hours. Sure, we ran into several problems and struggles, but we were 6 for 6.

Here we were in Needles, greeted by firefighters of San Bernardino County Fire Station 31.

Captain Kelly Lambert Anderson was the first person to welcome us. Tony had been in touch by phone with her most of the day planning the evening. We took photos in front of their station, and she told me that Dr. William Lansford of Action Chiropractic would remain open to give me an adjustment. He not only stayed open, he donated his service. My back was extremely tight, so he had some work to do. While I was being treated, Tony bought a new spare tire and a new jack. After my treatment, the fire engine crew, Tony and I headed to Denny's restaurant for dinner. Kelly gave us history of her department and of the town. She said that just a few days earlier bad weather hit the path we had just traveled. We finished dinner. I was exhausted. The firefighters wouldn't let us pay for anything; it was their treat, they said. Kelly paid for a hotel for us. It was within walking distance. It had been a tough day. But at least we had fewer miles to complete tomorrow.

We went to sleep with the satisfaction that California was just about under our belts. A few more miles tomorrow, and it's on to our second state.

What's ahead now, I wondered?

Miles pedaled so far
635

We just keep heading east day after day. Notice how barren the countryside is.

Day

7

Saturday, Sept. 15

Leaving California: to Kingman, Arizona
Miles to pedal today
63

TODAY WE DECIDED WE'D SLEEP IN. With only a 63-mile day ahead of us, and little elevation, it would be an easy day. It would have been nice to have an audio-visual person on this trip, what with all our devices: GPS, cell phones, GoPros, computers and cameras. At least the power inverter helped with charging devices while on the road. Uploading the videos from the GoPro and the cameras every night was also a major task. I was eager to finally be in another state. California was a great state, but we had spent such a long time in California that it felt like we were not really traveling across the country. Now we're ready to attack our second state: Arizona. We drove to the fire station at about 7 a.m., thanked the crew for its hospitality, then got on Highway 40. About 10 miles into the ride, we stopped at a place called Pirates Cove, a recreational area with a restaurant and store. It looked like a pretty fun place to spend a weekend — but, of course, we didn't have a weekend to hang out. We browsed a little, then were back on the road.

Now, on our seventh day of the ride, another milestone: we made it to Arizona at exactly 8:36 a.m. It was a huge milestone for all of us. Not sure how many states we had to go, but we had one down. We celebrated! We made a few phone calls and Facebook posts. Then we quickly were back on Highway 40, making record time. Today, I felt like I was in a race. I was feeling strong. After 30 miles, we stopped to eat snacks. While pulled over, we were greeted by an Arizona Highway Patrol officer. He was making sure we were okay. He donated money and accepted a flyer. That was our only encounter on the road the entire day. No flat tires on the chase vehicle or on my bike. We arrived in Kingman at 12:30. It was a 63-mile day. Years ago, that would have been a long day on the road, but today it was a piece of cake, completing the journey in just a few hours.

The fire crew was surprised to see us so early. They were having lunch. It was hard to know with so many variables what time we would finish each day. We met Chief Chuck Osterman, Capt. Curt Schrade and Engineer Dan Winder. The crew helped us unload our gear in their living room. I plopped onto the recliner and put my feet up. Chief Osterman explained arrangements for the evening. He had given us a gift card for a steakhouse in town, and the crew was making us lunch. Chief Osterman pointed out that firefighter Winder had completed a ride from Arizona to Kansas for an anniversary of Sept. 11. Dan and I talked most of the day about his ride. He looked at the route we had planned and told us about his experiences on his journey.

By late afternoon we washed and went into town for that steak dinner. We came back to the fire station — and called it an early night.

Miles pedaled so far
698

It feels good to finally enter another state. We're cookin' now!

Day

8

Sunday, Sept. 16

Arizona: Kingman to Williams
Miles to pedal today
116

WE RECORDED OUR MORNING BLOG POST with the crew. On the blog, Tony told the story of the Kingman explosion on July 5, 1973, a massive explosion and tragic fire. It was the worst firefighter disaster in history at the time. A propane explosion at a train station killed 11 firefighters and a state trooper. They had been setting up hose lines when the explosion occurred. It was a sad day for the fire service.

Tony went on to describe how he got involved with Lauren's Ride. "I received an email from Battalion Chief Lori Windsor," Tony told blog viewers. "Something about the email just kind of touched me, so I felt compelled to help.

"I think you'll need somebody to travel with you to support you, and I think I'm that guy, if you would have me," he had told me. "I would be happy to help out."

The crew then added their stories.

We were back on the road for another fairly short, easy day to Seligman, Ariz. It was only a 70-mile day with little elevation gain and perfect weather. We stayed on Highway 40 and on the old Route 66. We would be going through some neat places.

Starting off the day, I got flat #3. Believe it or not, I was actually

How'd you like to eat here? We did — and survived.

beginning to enjoy some flats because it allowed me to take a break from pedaling. Today, with only 70 miles to cover, I really wasn't in a hurry. This flat tire was a simple fix. Tony pulled up and grabbed the pump. As I got the tire pumped back up, I noticed a spoke was also broken. Luckily, I had spare wheels from other bikes that fit. I took one of the wheels off Dave's bike and removed the tire from it. I then took the tire off the wheel I was riding on. I made the exchange. I was back on the road. No big deal.

Today's route had a lot more hills and elevation gain to it than I had anticipated. We were starting to climb the Rockies. We definitely were no longer crossing a flat desert. We arrived in Seligman around one in the afternoon. Today was yet another early day. We ate lunch at the Roadkill Café.

I asked Tony, "What do you think about continuing to the next town today? I'm feeling strong, and it's early." We looked on the map and saw that Williams, a nearby town, was within traveling distance. This would give me a partial rest day tomorrow. Even though my body was feeling strong, I began to feel a cold coming on. Or maybe it was allergies. After lunch and a few milk shakes, we decided to go for it. It was one of the few days we didn't have arrangements set up.

Come up with your own caption for this photo. We
saw sign and just had to stop for a picture.

As I pedaled, I noticed that hundreds, maybe thousands, of grasshoppers had lined the side of the road. It was strange. I did my best to avoid crushing them. Somehow, one ended up on my handlebars. It stayed there for some time. I figured it was a good sign, like someone was there watching me on this journey. It just looked at me as I rode at 20 miles an hour. I wasn't sure if it was too scared to jump, but I figured it was like a person in my life who had passed away and was communicating with me in this form or something. I didn't start talking to it or anything. After about 10 miles, I stopped, and the grasshopper hopped into the grass. It wound up getting a nice ride.

A few miles ahead I came upon Tony stopped at a disabled truck with a coolant problem. Tony was pouring five gallons of water into the truck's radiator so it could reach a gas station. We joked that maybe we should open a roadside service center. I kept eating and drinking and struggled sometimes to find the balance of proper nutrition. I would hit "walls" of energy depletion throughout the day. So many hills.

After being on the road for 10 hours, gaining 7,423 feet of ascent and traveling the unplanned 116 miles, we reached Williams, Ariz. Williams had a volunteer fire station. Tony hadn't been able to contact the fire station, but he was able to contact the dispatch center. While on the road, Tony contacted a motel that we could use, since the station couldn't help us. We made our way to the Williams fire station. I took a photo and met their dispatcher at the dispatch center. Before long we were off to the motel to unload and clean-up for the day. We recharged our electronic devices and unloaded everything onto the computers and external hard drives. Tony and I showered and went back to town for dinner. Although we were ahead of schedule, I was beat. A lot of tour buses were parked in town, and we noticed a lot of older buildings and stores for shopping. We enjoyed a nice leisurely steak dinner before heading to the motel for a good night's rest.

Miles pedaled so far
814

9

Monday, Sept. 17

Arizona: Williams to Flagstaff
Miles to pedal today
38

IT'S ONLY OUR NINTH DAY on the road. I'm already getting sick.

I woke up with a runny nose, watery eyes and a slight sore throat. Since we only had a mere 40 miles to cover today, I figured I'd go back to sleep for a few more hours. Rest and time were always competing with each other. We were ahead of schedule, so it was time for more rest. Of all the days to get sick, I lucked out because a 40-mile day was a good day to have it happen. This was our shortest day. Fortunately, Tony was ready for whatever I ran into.

While I slept, he contacted a doctor's office in Flagstaff. He woke me up at 10:30. The vehicle was ready. I just needed to get riding. I started down Main Street, USA. The town had a traditional American feel to it. Although I slept a lot last night, I was still tired. I knew I didn't have a long day ahead and could get through this. I was thankful I had pushed the day before.

In Flagstaff we would be in a populated area again. Tony told me the city had an International Association of Firefighters (IAFF) motorcycle escort set up for our arrival. As I pedaled, I felt really weak. I had some climbing to do as well. Our first stop came about 10 miles into the day. It was a disabled vehicle, but they had a tow on the way. We talked with them for a few minutes and gave them food and water. Like always, we gave them a Lauren's Ride flyer.

I was anxious to have the day end. I continued to ride at a slow consistent pace. I had to keep wiping my running nose. I sprayed my throat and took cough drops that Tony had picked up. It was not physically ideal for riding a bike across the country, but the weather was perfect — a sunny, warm day in the 80s, with no wind — and Tony was encouraging me. Around noon, we were 15 miles in, and we decided to stop for lunch. Within a few minutes Arizona State Trooper Justin Shelton pulled up to check on us. Joking, we asked him if he had any cold medicine with him — he didn't — then told him about our journey. We took some photos and gave him a flyer.

Every mile we traveled from the start became more and more of an accomplishment in the eyes of the people we met. We were now more than 800 miles away from our start at the Golden Gate Bridge.

Tony and I talked about going to a doctor, and about the escort into town. We were still ahead of our estimated schedule. I asked him if he could call ahead to find a bike shop because my gears were beginning to skip. After lunch we crossed the Arizona Divide at 7,335 ft. I didn't show that much excitement, but I was happy to cross it. Every foot we gained in elevation felt like less oxygen. I was not sure if this feeling of having less air was because I was sick, or it was just a mental thing. Nevertheless, each small feat kept me charged to move forward. The good news was, if this was the Divide then it was downhill from here.

We reached Flagstaff city limits at 1 p.m. We took photos, loaded the bike into the vehicle, then headed to Flag Bike Revolutions, a bicycle repair shop. The bike was performing pretty well, but, as I said, it would occasionally skip gears. We were greeted by CJ and Jeffrey. It was a busy bike shop. I asked them if they could squeeze in a tune up because we had only three hours. We told them about the ride, and they tuned up the bike right away

We decided it would be a good idea for me to visit a local doctor while we waited for the tune-up. The doctor evaluated me, and he was surprised to hear I was in the middle of a bike ride going to New York from California. He prescribed medication for a cold. He also prescribed

Arizona Divide
ELEVATION 7335

Pedaling uphill is certainly a physical challenge.

medication to help with the symptoms while I slept. The doctor and I took a photo together as I left the office.

It was nice of the doctor's staff to squeeze me in. I never had seen a doctor so quickly in all my life! Somehow, I wasn't even charged for the visit. Now we were off to the pharmacy for the prescriptions, then back to the bike shop to collect the bike.

After we got my bike we headed back to the city limit sign to take a picture. Before long we would meet the IAFF motorcycle riders. I thought to myself that things were still running smoothly, and we managed to get a lot taken care of in town.

Wes Forblock and Grant Bradley pulled up on motorcycles. We talked for a while about the IAFF motorcycle organization and our bike ride. They ride for many firefighter funerals and special events around the country. I was honored to be escorted by them through town to Flagstaff Fire Station 6. We received a warm welcome by the Flagstaff firefighters, who were excited to have us there. Firefighters Chad, Phil and Eric were on duty. They helped us unload everything and set us up with a room in their barracks. The staff had placed an order at their favorite pizzeria. As we finished eating pizza, salad arrived. It was all you could eat rules.

Two members of the International Association of Firefighters escorted us.

The staff told us they would put our cause in their union newsletter, to help us get the word out — and it was so nice that they also made cash donations. We enjoyed good conversations and talked about what we had encountered so far. We also talked about the route ahead into the Navajo Nation. We were no longer just staying on Highway 40.

After dinner we did our evening blog. During the blog Tony told viewers, "John is in good shape. He's like the Energizer Bunny." I recapped the day and explained that on this trip we were meeting the best people in the world!

Finally, still suffering from the cold, and with a big day ahead, I took medication and went to bed.

Miles pedaled so far
852

10

Tuesday, Sept. 18

Leaving Arizona: to Tuba City, the Navajo Nation
Miles to pedal today
78

I WOKE UP FEELING a lot better than I had in the past few days. The medication was certainly helping. I mean, when you ride, little things, like a runny nose or watery eyes, wear on you.

We began our day as usual with breakfast and the morning blog. We recorded the blog from the fire station engine bay, with the crew standing around the fire pole. As I started talking, Tony slid down the pole during his introduction. Some guys know how to make an entrance! It kind of added to the blog. It was common to have fire poles at all firehouses back in the day. A brass fire pole wasn't seen as a safety concern as it is today. Over the years, injuries discouraged the use of fire poles, so more and more departments eliminated the brass fire pole during new building construction. This particular fire pole, in fact, came with a lot of history. Station 6, this station, is a newer fire station, but the fire pole was an original from the 1800s. When they tore down the old fire station, they saved the pole and installed it in the new station. There is a lot of neat history with different fire stations. This was really awesome to be able to carry that history to their new station. For years, firefighters had been sliding down the same pole to calls.

Actually, a brass fire pole allows firefighters in multiple story fire stations to get to the main floor fire apparatus in seconds — much faster than having to race down flights of steps, in many cases tripping and falling on their way.

After completing the blog, we hit the road. Engine 6 escorted us through town to the city limits. The day was turning out warm and nice. There was no wind, and I was feeling strong again. I was getting better. We had about 70 miles to our next destination. We were actually leaving the United States of America and going into the Navajo Nation. Our stopping point tonight would be Tuba City. I had never heard of Tuba City, so I really didn't know what to expect. As we headed northeast, we saw very little around us. I passed a warning sign with a photo of an elk on it. In California, we have deer signs. I had never seen an elk warning sign. It was funny. Maybe I would be lucky to even see an elk. The topography was fairly flat, covered with trees. And the view was nice. I was also riding strong again. It seemed like there was always a constant challenge to have proper nutrition for a day's ride.

But, before long, the scenery changed. It seemed like we were in the desert again. Not a tree in sight.

At 10 a.m. we entered the Navajo Nation, the largest Indian reservation in the United States. More than 150,000 people live on the vast reservation, which stretches 27,000 square miles across Arizona, New Mexico and Utah.

I couldn't see anything for miles ahead of us except highway and hills. I continued pedaling, and we reached Tuba City a little past noon. We were sure not to forget to take a photo of the city limit sign. It was always a huge relief when I reached a city limit sign. I would stop, hold the bike up, pose for a photo and be thankful that we made it that far safely. Tony checked the map to find out where the fire station was. We had a few more miles to go to reach it. It was always a victory lap to the station from the city limit sign. We pulled up to the Tuba City fire station 20 minutes later and were welcomed by Lt. Hebert Manheimer. It only took us four and a half hours on the road. We covered the planned 78 miles in that time. We had a slight decline in elevation, which was a nice change. It turned out to be another easy day. We found Lt. Manheimer staffing the station by himself. He helped unload our gear. The

Plaque marks entrance to the country's Navajo Reservation.

station was a combination of paid and volunteer firefighters. There were three beds in the back of the station, and I kept thinking it was crazy that I was in another nation.

Actually the Navajo Nation is more like a separate state or U.S. territory, similar in a way to Puerto Rico. The Navajo tribes do precede the existence of the U.S. government and, as such, get certain different legal frameworks. The tribal land is held in trust by the U.S. federal government.

Putting the trip together, I guess I didn't realize this. I said to Tony, "Hey, if nothing else, I rode to another country." Being in a different country didn't change their need to have all the same required equipment on their engines. It didn't matter where you were a firefighter; we all shared what we do in our communities. The common sentiment was that we all joined our departments to help people in need. As members of this firefighter society, we take calculated risks, and at times risk our lives for life and property. We have a brotherhood and sisterhood that cannot be measured.

The lieutenant noticed that I had a cold and asked me if I needed anything for it. I told him I should be okay and that I was still feeling sick, but didn't feel like I was getting any worse. I think it's difficult to get better when you are taxing your body so much each day.

The department dispatcher, Richella, and some volunteer firefighters arrived at the station after the lieutenant called them. We got there earlier than we had expected. We sat around and talked about our bicycle trip and what was ahead, and the type of calls they had, and their equipment. They told me they would contact the chief of the tribe to see if he would allow us to attend a ceremonial sweat lodge. I couldn't believe what they were telling me.

They said that Tony and I were worthy of this special Navajo ceremony for what we were trying to do for Lauren. About an hour later, they excitedly told us the chief had granted permission for us to participate in the ceremony.

I knew little about what happens in a ceremonial sweat lodge. I just knew it was a rare honor. I was a little nervous. Lt. Manheimer explained the Navajo Nation to me and how fire protection was divided among different areas. Tony and I had question after question about the history. After dinner, about an hour before we were set to leave, Kevin, a firefighter, explained the honor of the sweat lodge. I asked Kevin if he would explain this in a blog. So we opened the blog by telling of the day's ride, and then introduced Kevin. This is what he said: "It's good to have you guys here. Good to be part of this endeavor that you guys are partaking. I am sure the creator will bless you and your journey. Thanks for having us be part of this.

"The significance of the ceremony tonight is for a cleansing. It's what our warriors would go through in every tribe in every nation. It was spread long ago throughout different tribes and different people. This ceremony is to cleanse you of your stress and clear your mind. The ceremony will also show the great spirit, the creator, that you're worthy of what you're asking for. When you get to the lodge you can pray and let the creator know what's really in your heart and on your mind. You will come out a better man. You'll come out a stronger person. You will see the future; you'll see everything that's ahead of you that you need to get done. Your journey along this way, your endeavor and your path will be blessed after this is done. We are happy you are part of this."

Around 6 p.m. we headed to the ceremonial location. We followed Hebert in the fire engine. When we arrived at the lodge, others started a fire just as the sun was setting. It was exactly 7 p.m.

The lodge was about 12 feet in diameter and only about five feet high. Its entrance faced the east where the sun rose. The fire burned hot. We felt really connected standing together watching the fire burn and talking about the warrior's journey. Tony and I were feeling so honored. Who ever thought we would be standing in this special setting? We spoke in disbelief how honored we were at this moment on our trip. We took a few photos in front of the lodge and in front of the fire. As the fire burned down, it was time to get ready to enter the lodge. They moved the hot coals into the center of the circle. We lined up, and the lieutenant explained that we must enter in a clockwise manner. There was no leaving. We would be the last ones to enter. If the temperature got too hot, we could exit by walking in a clockwise circle around the fire.

Five of us entered the lodge in clockwise manner. Hebert, the lieutenant, began the ceremony and explained that it would be getting hot. First, there would be four rounds of four songs that were passed down from generation to generation. Warriors who went out centuries ago sang the same songs as they sing today. Sure enough, the lodge warmed up as the first round began. Three participants sang as the lodge got warmer and warmer. The fire was stoked with a material that had a strong smell. I felt like it was opening up my lungs. The songs were loud. It got hotter and hotter. The first round of four songs lasted somewhere between 10 and 20 minutes. Then we talked about our journey. The others asked us questions about our mission and what we wanted to gain. I told them how Lauren was injured and that I wished she could live life like everyone else.

Then the second round started. The air was much hotter. The songs became louder and stronger. The fire glowed down below. I was really sweating. I sipped water I had taken with me, and crouched as low as I could to the ground. There was a pause between each song. By the end of the fourth song, I was feeling overheated. We finally came to the end of round two, so we talked again about our special bicycle ride to New York.

Tony was hot, too. Tony had been in fire service for more than 30 years. I had been in fire service now about seven, and we both had never been this hot in our lives. We talked about the heart and spirit of a warrior, which was the focus that needs to take place to clear out everything else. They explained that things in our lives that hold us back or cloud us would be set behind us. We were being released of everything.

We had a warrior's journey ahead of us and the creator would be watching over us, we learned.

Hebert left the circle to get more coals for the fire, and when he returned the third round began. By the second song, I had my head to the ground breathing for cool air. At this point I was feeling spiritually connected to God. I was listening to the songs, and I was praying for Lauren, Tony and myself.

The fire burned hotter. The singing grew louder. There was a splash into the fire and more steam and more smoke filled the air. By the fourth song, I was close to leaving, but I didn't think I would have the energy to get up from the ground. I just prayed for strength. At the end of the fourth song, things quieted down. Phew, I thought, a needed break for all of us. The Navajos spoke among themselves and decided to give us warrior names. They said the warrior names would protect us.

The warrior names were not to be shared with anyone, they instructed, because if someone knew our warrior names they would know our weaknesses. These names protected each of us. They allowed us to work better together. The names were animal name-based and strongly related to our journey.

Now the last round began. This fourth round was by far the hottest. I laid down and prayed to be strong and to allow my body and mind to be healed. The songs seemed to run longer, and it took everything I had to make it through the last few songs. At the conclusion, we said a few prayers out loud. Tony started the prayer, and we moved in a clockwise circle, eventually leaving the lodge. We walked to the fire engine and drank water. By now, we were dehydrated and depleted. But I'll tell you, I felt great! We took a photo in front of the engine, thanked the Navajos

Richella Tracey presents me with Navajo warrior blanket.

for allowing us to participate in their special ceremony, then drove back to the fire station. It was now 10:30 p.m. We had spent a little over 2½ hours in the lodge. We climbed into our beds.

OMG, I thought. I can't believe what we had just experienced. A rare Navajo Nation ceremony.

I fell asleep in minutes.

Miles pedaled so far

930

11

Wednesday, Sept. 19

The Navajo Nation: Tuba City to Kayenta
Miles to pedal today
62

I SLEPT IN TODAY, feeling more rested than I had the entire trip. I had a deep sleep and didn't feel sick anymore. My mind was clear and focused. Richella, the dispatcher, arrived at the station. We took our time getting up. After dressing, we went into the apparatus bay to get ready for today's trip. Richella presented us with a Navajo warrior blanket. Again, I was honored to receive such a great and powerful gift. Tony, Hebert and I sat down and did the daily blog. Tony and I told them how honored we were. Hebert wished us a safe and powerful journey. Hebert, Richella and I went to the fire engine and took a few photos. By 9:30 a.m. we were on the road to the next Navajo Nation stop — Kayenta Navajo Nation. We had about 62 miles ahead of us. The sun was out, the temperature was comfortable. Now we were riding into a desert, with neat rock formations all around us. I gave Darrell Sales a call back home, and we talked about everything that was happening. He wasn't surprised at all. He said the same things happened to him in different ways on his ride, and he, too, couldn't believe it when it happened to him. He told me that he would get done riding each day and have the energy to stay up all night meeting everyone from each station and tell stories until the late hours of the night, then get up early the next day and ride another 100 miles.

I called Mike DeLeo to catch up with him. He was now at his camp, and things were going well, he said. I told him about our last few days, and I could tell he wished he was still with us. He said he would be seeing me soon. I couldn't wait until he rejoined us. It gave me something to visualize. I called dad to give him the same update. He couldn't believe what I told him about the Navajo Nation either. Now, I was two hours and 42 miles into today's ride. There wasn't much scenery on the road, so I talked on the phone most of the day. Before I knew it, I was approaching Kayenta.

Tony had called ahead to let them know we were getting close. We arrived in Kayenta at 2 p.m. Today I had ridden four hours and 29 minutes to cover the planned 62 miles. My total mileage since I began 10 days ago was 992 miles. Almost 1,000 miles! Ascent for the day was 2,936 ft. Today would be a fast, strong day. Temperature was a comfortable 76 degrees. Sky was clear. Road surface was smooth and road conditions were ideal. There was hardly any traffic.

We pulled up to the station, and Capt. Odie Peshlakai met us. Members were in the middle of working on their fire engine motor. A few minutes after I arrived, Rob Lewin, my unit chief back home, called me to check on my progress. It was a phone call I'll never forget. He told me how proud everyone back in the unit was and encouraged me to keep going. I told him a few of the things that had happened, which he later shared with coworkers back home. He said, "John, you're my hero." This was coming from someone I thought so highly of throughout my whole career. He was a great fire chief and did so much for so many of his employees, and here he is calling me a hero! He kept me focused and driven, and I felt so supported by him. I hope someday I can be a leader like he is.

Capt. Odie arranged for us to stay at a local hotel. He told us that the fire company had planned a routine drill that night. And that we could watch, and meet the volunteers. That sounded great to us. So we went to the hotel to shower and to get everything charged up. We hadn't done any charging the night before. Capt. Odie told us that Monument

Monument Valley, between Tuba City and Kayenta, Ariz.

Valley was only about 30 miles away, and that if we had time we should check it out. Since we arrived ahead of schedule, Tony and I decided to do just that. I had no idea what Monument Valley was, but it sounded like a neat place to see. We showered, then hit the hay for an hour. Then it was off to Monument Valley before dinner.

On the way to Monument Valley, Tony noticed a few stray dogs on the side of the road. He pulled over, fed them and gave them fresh water. I could tell Tony was missing his pet dogs back at home. Monument Valley was an unusual sight. The sun looked over these huge rock formations that must have been formed thousands of years ago. We walked around for quite some time taking photo after photo of these incredible views. We watched the sun set, then headed back to catch the fire department drill.

We arrived at the station to find most of the members ready to begin their meeting and drill. That's when we met Torrence Jones. Torrence was a high school student and a member of the fire department. He was excited to meet us. Two other members gave me a set of arrowheads, one for Lauren and one for me. We sat through the meeting. Then the drill began. They trained with a breathing apparatus and practiced deploying the fire hose. After the drill, we introduced them in our blog. We had them relate their department history and talk about the area they served. After the blog, we talked with Torrence. We decided to return to Monument Valley in the morning for sunrise. It was getting late. So we made tracks to our hotel for a good night of rest.

Miles pedaled so far
992

Day

12

Thursday, Sept. 20

Leaving the Navajo Nation: to Cortez, Colorado
Miles to pedal today
116

WE AWOKE AT 5 A.M. and went to the Kayenta fire station. Who was there to meet us but young Torrence Jones. Torrence was holding a jacket. He told us his mom had been making it for him over the past few months, that it was to be ready in a few more months, and that he would receive it as a gift after he completed a retreat. When his mom heard about Lauren's Ride, he and his family put their heads together. She stayed up most of the night to finish tailoring the jacket. And now here was Torrence in front of us holding the jacket in his hand.

He presented it to me as a gift.

WE ARRIVED AT MONUMENT VALLEY before the sun had risen, and we shot many photographs as the sun rose over the valley. What a sight! At some point in your life, I urge you to come here and see this sight at sunrise! After taking photos, Tony, Torrence and I walked to the area where the movie "Forrest Gump" was filmed. We found the exact spot where Forrest Gump ended his run as he ran across America. We shot a few funny videos and photos, then headed back. After all, we reasoned, I had 116 miles to cover today. We took Torrence back to the fire station and returned to the hotel.

My family was dumbfounded when I called to tell
them I was touching four states at once.

Tony and I did our morning blog. In it, Tony said it would to be sad to
leave the Navajo Nation. Each stop we made was special. We were meeting the best people in the world. Tony swore that I got my energy back
from the special Navajo sweat ceremony the day before. I explained
how Andy had given me the bike a year ago, and how inspiration comes
from acts of kindness. How we affect others can be greater than we may
ever know.

We had milestones ahead of us today. And I was getting excited to
move on.

We left for Cortez, Colo., at 8:45 a.m. It was a sunny day. The ride
looked to be flat. Another simple route. I would be riding on Highway 160. I was now eight miles away from the 1,000-miles mark. I was

Torrence Jones gives me a Navajo jacket.

excited. I called dad, excitedly told him about the last two days in the Navajo Nation, and that I was about to hit the thousand-mile mark in a few minutes. I watched as my GPS said five miles, six miles, seven miles and then eight. Bingo!

Eight miles. That made 1,000 miles completed! I'll say it again: I had completed 1,000 miles. Tony pulled up, I got off the phone, and we celebrated this huge accomplishment. We took 1,000-mile photos and then shared our progress with our followers.

BACK ON THE ROAD, there wasn't much around to look at. It was just a valley. Our next stop was the Four Corners. This is the only place in the country where you can stand in a single spot — and be in four different states at once. I remember learning about Four Corners when I was in elementary school. As I pulled up, it looked like a neat place — but in the middle of nowhere. Of course, vendors were all over the place selling gifts and flags from the four different states. People from all over the world were visiting. We shared flyers with the people we met. Tony and I took loads of photos of the area, and Tony even did some gift shopping.

I called Lauren and told her I was in Arizona. "How do you hear me?" I asked. I walked a few feet over to Colorado and asked if she could hear me better there. In New Mexico I told her I might get roaming fees for the call, then finally I walked over to Utah. It was funny. It took me six days to ride through California, yet only 10 seconds to cross these four different states.

It was now about 3 p.m., and we still had miles to cover. We got back on the road to head for Colorado — and into a new time zone as well. Now we lost an hour. "Boy," I said to Tony, "if we had planned the ride from New York to California we would have gained three hours instead of losing them." Tony agreed.

The topography changed noticeably in Colorado. I now started climbing. The headwind was increasing. I was a little over half-way done for the day. Yet I still had about 60 miles to go. The climb was not steep, but it was steady. Now I was beginning to climb the Rocky Mountain range. I wasn't feeling that great, so I stopped for food from the chase vehicle. Whenever I felt drained, I made sure I took Fluid and food. I was usually behind on my nutritional needs anyway because I was focused on riding and knocking off the miles.

I wound up pushing myself through the day. After each set of miles I sat in the van and tried to talk myself into pedaling yet another ten miles. It worked. Before I knew it, I hit 100 miles.

Tony and I looked at our map and figured we had about 20 miles still to go today. Every mile after 100 seemed longer than the mile before it.

I mean, much longer. We made it to Cortez 90 minutes later. We took a traditional photo at the city limits sign. We were now at an elevation of 6,200 ft. We made our way to Cortez Fire Station 1. The crew was outside to greet us. It was 6 p.m. Mountain Time. I had completed the required 116 miles with an ascent of 4,424 feet for the day. I also burned 9,993 calories according to my GPS. I realized I was not eating enough, which is why I felt stripped and tired. Tony made me a Fluid recovery drink. We took some photos with the fire crew, then went inside. We had accomplished a lot today. Inside, I instantly fell asleep on a recliner. Then dinner was ready. The crew was doing Emergency Medical Service training, and they told Tony the history of their station and the community they served. They cooked a delicious homemade dinner for us — pasta with a huge salad — and I felt refreshed after a short snooze. Then it was time for our evening blog. Tony and I realized that I had a rough time completing the day. I was fighting for rest, so I went to bed real early.

I sensed the ride was getting tougher. Tomorrow I'd be climbing the Rocky Mountains.

Climbing all day tomorrow.

I was beginning to feel it.

Miles pedaled so far
1,108

13

Friday, Sept. 21

Colorado: Cortez to Pagosa Springs
Miles to pedal today
100

I WOKE UP FEELING groggy and weak.

I had now developed a slight cough, so I decided to sleep for a few more hours. A few hours later I felt worse. Tony got up and got everything ready to go. I finally woke up around 9 a.m. I had 100 miles to ride today. The stop chart showed we had about a 1,000-foot gain for the day, which didn't seem too bad. We met with Cortez Chief Jeff Vandevoorde and recorded a brief morning blog. We were on the road by 10 a.m.

The day started by me climbing a few hills. It was another nice day, sunny — with little to no wind. I powered through the first two hours at a constant pace, climbing and descending. We hit a stop for road construction. This was another good time to take in some food and drink. We chatted with the construction crew and shared our cause. I enjoyed saying we rode here from California! The area we were riding in was beautiful. The day was filled with much more climbing than I had expected, but the sights kept my mind focused on other things. My legs were tired. We were crossing different little rivers along the way. We made it to Durango, Colo., by 2 p.m. Four hours into the ride we completed about 50 miles. This was a perfect time for a break. I was traveling an average pace of 12 miles an hour, with stops.

I sat in the chase vehicle and closed my eyes for a few minutes while Tony prepared water and food. While we relaxed, Tony showed me some of the recent Facebook responses, posts and photos from our blog. Then he read me this:

> *Please send John thoughts/prayers today.*
> *Riding 93+ Rocky Mountain miles with a cold.*
> *Take care of the cold, John!*
>
> Judie Hagstrom, Josh Campbell
> Angela Magario, Judy Blalock
> Sandra Gray Jones

Each photo we posted would receive overwhelming response, likes and comments. People back home, and those along the way, were cheering us on and telling us of the changes we were making in their lives. As bad, tired or sick as I felt at times, their support touched my heart and made me realize I was not riding alone. I had thousands of people pedaling with me. As the harder times came and steeper hills were ahead, I was never alone. I had so many people with me. Tony did a perfect job of sharing what we were doing each day. He passed on what he was seeing as he followed me.

After I was done eating and being inspired by the messages, I got back on the bike. There was still another 50 miles to go for the day.

No sooner had we hit the road, when I got another flat tire. I was heading downhill about 20 miles an hour. So I carefully leaned forward and braked lightly until I could safely stop. It was a rear tire. Although Tony was following a few miles behind, I had what I needed to repair the flat. I was counting, and this was my fourth flat tire. It wasn't bad for having biked more than 1,000 miles through all the debris and crap on the roads. I pulled clearly off the roadway into a rocky area. I turned my bike upside down so I could take the rear wheel off and allow my bike to stand up on its own. I released the brakes, moved the chain and took off the wheel. I took the old tube out of the tire, then felt inside the tire for whatever punctured it. It was smooth. I put the new tube in the

Fixing one of many flat tires that interrupted cross-country journey.

lining of the tire and added air. That's when Tony pulled up. I told him I was okay, that I just needed the hand pump to pump the tire to the correct pressure. As I put the wheel back on the bike, I could see that the tires were showing a little wear. Tony took a few photos of me putting the bike together, and then posted them. I pumped the wheel up to 110 pounds — and we were on our way.

I don't know exactly what it was, maybe the cold, the elevation or not having a rest day, but I was really tired and weak today. I knew I just had a few more miles to go. I decided I would take a rest after every 10 miles. I figure with the shape I was in I could comfortably go 10 miles. Anyone can go 10 miles, I told myself.

So when the 70-mile mark hit on the GPS, I took a break.

When 80 miles hit the GPS, I took a break.

The same for 90 miles. Each time I stopped to rest Tony refilled water bottles and read to me more responses and likes to our posts.

Now, we set off for our final 10-mile stretch and made it to the Pagosa Springs city limit sign. Reaching that sign seemed to energize me. We were at a 7,079 ft. elevation mark. We made our way to the fire station, completing 100 miles for the day with an ascent of 6,400 feet. It was a lot more ascent than I had been ready for.

The fire crew booked us into a hotel for the night and made dinner arrangements at their favorite restaurant. Tony then told me that one of our online followers, Nancy Rosenblum, had paid for a sports massage for us that evening. Wow! I think Tony and I really needed a massage. We were really sore. He sat in a car for 12 hours a day while I was riding a bicycle for 12 hours. I don't know which was more difficult.

We sat and talked with the crew for about an hour, then went to dinner. Later, back at the hotel we showered, washed our clothes and prepared for the next day.

Marcus Hughes from San Juan Sports Massage Therapy showed up at the hotel. I went first and it felt good. I talked with him during the massage. He said he had done massages for athletes on similar journeys across the country. Then it was Tony's turn. We did our blog during his massage. It brought a bit of humor to a long, hilly day. We were both so thankful. Marcus finished, then left (he wouldn't even take a tip). Tony and I both felt great and ready for the next day.

The Continental Divide was only 30 miles away.

We slept so well that night!

Miles pedaled so far
1,208

Day

14

Saturday, Sept. 22

Colorado: Pagosa Springs to Alamosa
Miles to pedal today
95

WE AWOKE AT 7 A.M. I was feeling much better today. We dressed and went to the station, but no one was there. After a few minutes, Chief Manny Trujillo arrived. We did our morning blog together thanking everyone who was helping us on our journey. I took time to talk about the good things Kevin and Lori Orweller did back home to support our cause. For instance, before we began the ride, they had donated several items they hoped would raise money. One item was a camper trailer. Its raffle raised several thousand dollars. They were following our progress every day. Today, while I would be pedaling, they would be driving Lauren in a vintage car in the local community parade, while spreading word of Lauren's Ride.

Tony pointed out that we were almost over the Continental Divide, with about 30 miles and 3,000 feet of elevation to gain, and then it would be downhill from there. Chief Trujillo said he was happy to have supported us, and he thanked us for stopping in Pagosa Springs.

Another day. We put the wheels to the ground and began the climb to the top of the divide. Tony veered off into town to buy some logistical supplies while I continued to ride. It was a constant grade to climb, but knowing that I was so close made it easy for me today. I found that I could talk myself through most of the challenges I encountered. One pedal down, one pedal up. One pedal down, one pedal up. Over…and over…and over.

At one point I hit a really steep climb. I stood up and powered through it, focusing on the road. I was maybe 20 miles away from the mountain top when my foot slipped forward: the bicycle chain had broken. Tony was still in town, and I didn't have adequate cell service to reach him. The chain looked as if it simply gave out from tension. I was worried because I wasn't sure we could fix a chain with the tools we had. I had no idea where the nearest bike shop was.

Man. This would set us back hours. Tony would have to catch up to me; then we would have to find a bike shop.

As I coasted to a stop off the road, a man wearing a yellow riding jersey, bicycling in the opposite direction, saw I was stranded. He made his way across traffic, introduced himself as Larry Christine and asked what was wrong. I found it common in the riding community to help each other, but this wasn't the common flat tire. I showed Larry my broken chain. He noticed my jersey with the Cal Fire logo. He told me he was a retired firefighter and, get this, a retired *bike store owner* with the tool to remove a broken chain link and fix the chain.

Oh, baby! I couldn't believe this! I hadn't seen one bike rider all week. The moment I break my chain, someone appears to help . . . someone who used to own a bike store and has this special tool. His wife Dorothy pulled up to help us as well. We removed the chain. Larry removed the bad link, strung the chain back through the proper channels and reconnected it. He explained this was a temporary fix because I would not be able to use all the gears since he had shortened the chain.

About then, Tony arrived. Larry said he would head back with his wife, then meet up with us and ride to the top of the grade to make sure I made it.

What an unlucky situation — then lucky situation — that was! Could you believe it?

Someone was definitely watching over me!

Back on the bike I powered up the steep grade. I guess I was stronger

A retired firefighter, owner of bicycle shop, stops to help me fix broken chain.

than the bike. My body and mind have been close to breaking down many times on this trip, but I am not broken. I was blessed with an amazing view and a huge team by my side. The fall colors on the mountains were beautiful, very green and yellow. I even passed a few waterfalls as I was climbing.

We were about five miles from the top when Larry, the guy who had just fixed my broken chain, pulled up in his van, stopped and brought out his bike. He said he could do a tune up on my bike if I wanted him to. He had contacted a bike shop in Alamosa that would put on a new chain and tune the bike if needed. So Larry joined me on my ride. His repair job was holding up just fine!

We rode our five mile victory ride to 10,806 ft! We had reached the Continental Divide. The top of Wolf's Pass was more than two miles above sea level. I called my mom, dad, sister, Lyn, Mike and Darrell to tell them I made it to the Divide. We stopped for photos and shared our story with families who were there. After celebrating, we still had about 50 miles to go, but it was almost all downhill. We thanked Larry and said our goodbyes. Boy, was it downhill! It was the ride of a lifetime! I put on some Coldplay and just flew downhill. I mean, only once in the 20 miles of zooming downhill, at 30 to 40 miles an hour, did I have to tap the brakes. At times, I felt I was going a little *too* fast.

We quickly reached bottom. I guess I had made my personal record. We stopped at a diner for lunch. Now, Tony and I were in high spirits. I guess you could say our trip was filled with mountains and valleys. While getting food, Tony called ahead to Randy of Kristi Mountain Sports in Alamosa to arrange bike repairs when we arrived.

We calculated we had about 20 miles left for the day. The weather was still nice, the road was in good condition and we faced a bit of rolling hills ahead. I think I even had a bit of a tailwind behind me.

At 4:40 that afternoon we reached a total of 1,287 miles from our start at the Golden Gate Bridge. And we now had 1,287 followers on Facebook. We decided to take a photo with a sign saying 1,287 miles and 1,287 followers. The more followers we had meant the more word spread and the more support we would have. We reached Alamosa at 5:30 p.m., covering 95 miles for the day. We took our traditional photo at the city sign. We were now at the 7,544 ft. elevation mark. Looking at that sign made me realize we still had a few downhill days ahead.

Our first stop in Alamosa was at Kristi Mountain Sports — which was already closed for the night. But Rand, the owner, was there wait-

Beautiful scenery helps take my mind off pedaling through the Rockies.

ing for us. He replaced the chain and aligned the wheels. Just in case, since we were there, we bought two new tires and a few spare tubes.

Randy charged us only for the parts and wished us a safe trip. He was a nice guy. I was thankful he had helped us out.

We covered 95 miles for the day and an ascent of 4,797 ft. We had now traveled a total of 1,303 miles. Next stop was the fire station. The department was staffed with paid-call firefighters who came out to meet us. They pulled out their rig for a photo with us, and they gave us their challenge coins. We met in the engine bay, where the fire engines are parked, and we did our night blog. The guys gave us some history of their department, and we chatted about events of the day.

It was an uneventful night. We ate burgers for dinner, then went to bed.

Miles pedaled so far
1,303

Day

15

Sunday, Sept. 23

Colorado: Alamosa to Trinidad
Miles to pedal today
108

WE SLEPT 11 HOURS — 11 hours! — woke up and did our morning blog. Then we hit the road. I had about 125 miles ahead today. What I had in my favor was a lot of downhill riding. Tony now had a cold, and it was getting worse. My cold was getting better. I was sore from the climb the day before, but I figured as I pedaled I would work some of the soreness out. I took Ibuprofen to help with the swelling and pain. I had a lot of miles and a long day ahead. So I really had to be focused. Off we went towards Trinidad

We started with a bit of a climb up to La Veta Pass at 9,413 ft. After this pass we had another good downhill ride. I just flew at a good pace of 30 to 40 miles an hour. Tony pulled ahead to scout the roads and find a place to eat. A few more miles down the road I came upon a stranded motorist. While I was stopped, another person stopped to help. I took a photo of them. They seemed to be ok, so I pushed on. Eventually Tony joined me and said there wasn't much ahead. So we stopped and had some snacks from the chase vehicle. We completed a little over 50 miles today. I had been flying for the day, and it felt great! As we ate, I looked a little closer at our route and noticed that if we took a different road, we could save about 25 miles. We weren't sure if we'd be allowed to ride

Cruising downhill is always an enjoyable part of bicycling.

a bike on that road. We decided to take the chance anyway.

The shortcut took us on a main road — with traffic. The road had rolling hills, and I was still feeling strong. I was knocking the miles out. Tony and I played a game where I would throw water bottles in the vehicle as we both rode, and I would grab full bottles without stopping. Nice game. It killed time.

Before long Tony waved me down and said that Lyn had called him with good news: we had hit the $45,000 fundraising mark. We raised $45,761 in donations. Tony made a $$$ sign, and a bit later we took a milestone photo. We arrived at Trinidad city limits at 4:46 that afternoon. Elevation: 6,017 ft. We covered 108 miles today. Total ascent for the day was 3,222 feet. Most of the ascent was early in the day.

We pulled into Trinidad Fire Station 2. The station was a paid station

I receive word by phone that donations top $45,000.

staffed with two career firefighters. The department was established in 1864, and today had 15 paid members. The surrounding area was given to coal mining. Trinidad Fire Station 2 was Colorado's oldest paid fire department, we learned.

The guys told me a resident of Trinidad, whose son I had worked with in California, had dropped by to make a donation. We took a few photos in front of the station and went inside. The men ordered Chinese food for us; they made personal donations. My fortune cookie read: "Others appreciate your sensitivity." During the evening blog, Aaron, a firefighter, gave us the town and fire department history. And that was that for the evening.

I retired early. Tomorrow would be a day of pedaling less than 100 miles.

By now I needed an easier day. These 100-plus mile days were kicking my butt.

Miles pedaled so far
1,411

Day

16

Monday, Sept. 24

Colorado: Trinidad to Kim
Miles to pedal today
71

WE BEGAN THE DAY recording our morning blog with the on-duty crew. Today, we had a mere 71-mile day ahead of us. Phew! These long days on the road were beginning to catch up with me. I was really sore and tired. I was so mentally tired that I had to talk myself up each day. I was looking forward to this shorter day. Looking at the schedule, today and tomorrow are both shorter days. After that, at least 100 miles or more a day for 11 days lay ahead of me. To stay on track after the Rockies, I had to cover longer days on the flats. I'm not really a bike ride planner, so putting this schedule together was more of an educated guess.

Tony seemed a little tired today. By now, it's been two straight weeks on the road, with Tony constantly watching out for my safety.

We left Trinidad. Now there was nothing around us. Along Highway 160, power lines were on the right. Barbed wire fence ran along both sides of the road. I could see for miles ahead. There was nothing in any direction. Just empty fields and the road — and us. My map showed no cities along the way. There was just 70 miles of plain roadway ahead. I put on some Coldplay music and tried to focus on pedaling to Kim, the town at the end of today's journey. It would be a short, but challenging

Talk about a flat countryside. Here I roll along on a nice level plane.

day for me. It was a partly cloudy day, neither hot nor cold. The challenging part was talking myself through the ride and not letting soreness overwhelm my thinking and attitude.

Riding now became more and more challenging. I was tired. I had so few miles to go today, compared to most days, and I didn't really understand why I was having so much difficulty. I kept a pace of about 15 miles per hour. Tony stayed in town for awhile, and I had cell service if I needed to reach him. I noticed I was again passing hundreds of grasshoppers on the road. So the goal today was to focus on not running them over. Grasshoppers were all around. The road was flat and slightly down in elevation. I just took it easy. I had little motivation today to push hard, but I kept focused on not running over the grasshoppers.

I went the whole day without eating. I did only one water exchange and wanted to finish the ride for the day. I simply wanted this day — Day 16 — to be over. I loved what I was doing, but there are great days and there are difficult days. Today was a tough day. After riding for nearly five hours and pedaling 71 miles, I arrived at Kim at 2 in the afternoon. Overall, I had a small amount of ascent, about 2,328 ft., and lost about 2,000 ft. of elevation for the day. Many riders would say it was an easy ride.

Dinner and shootin' the breeze with townsfolk at Kim, Colo.

I held my bike up in front of the Kim, Colo., sign and took a photo. Kim is a small town. By small, I mean it had a population of 70 people. I had more than 70 people living on the street I grew up on back in California. You couldn't miss Kim though, because there was nothing else around until you hit it, and nothing for many miles after.

I rode to the fire station, which locals call the fire shed, and met Chief Harold Unwin. Glancing around, it was clear that we wouldn't be staying overnight at the fire shed. The building was nothing more than an apparatus bay with a bathroom. So Tony went to find lodging. Harold told us we could stay overnight at the community church and shower at the local school. The next town was about 50 miles away. I wanted to stay here in Kim but Tony wanted to head south. He felt we would rest better if we stayed at a motel. I was exhausted and just wanted to rest. I really didn't want to travel anymore for the day, not even in a car. I simply wanted to shower and rest. The only store in town was the Kim Outpost and it would be closing at 4 p.m. If we needed anything, like dinner and snacks, we had to go now.

I rode my bike a mile to the store. We decided to eat dinner at the store where we met local residents. The Kim Outpost was a friendly family-owned store and restaurant. I sat down at the table joining other diners as though I was part of the community. We ate dinner and took a few photos. And we bought snacks to hold us over till morning. As we sat there, Tony was trying to figure out arrangements to stay in nearby Springfield. He said he was looking out for my best interests. But I said I wasn't going. I was ok with him going, but I just wanted to stay where I was and rest. So we were headed to Kim High School. Harold introduced us to the school secretary, telling her that we had ridden here from California and needed to use the locker room showers. We told her about the ride — then it was off to the locker room for a shower.

After showering, we went to the Kim Baptist Church. Harold arranged for us to stay in the church basement. At this point, Tony was becoming pretty agitated. We had been on the road now for more than 14 straight days; we were both really tired, I mean really tired — and it looked as if we were about to have our first disagreement. When we finally got set up, Harold headed home. Tony started organizing the chase vehicle, pulling out many items. Incidentally, we brought our fire helmets with us, thinking at some point in the ride we would take photos wearing our helmets. As he took the helmets out, he said that it was a stupid waste of space that we brought the helmets. He was pissed off, and I was getting pissed off, too. I organized my stuff and headed downstairs.

I needed space away from Tony.

When Tony was done outside, he came downstairs and prepared dinner. I rested. Around 7 p.m. I walked to the chase vehicle and called Darrell. I was venting and I wanted to get Darrell's advice. He said he could tell that Tony and I were having a little bit of a difficult time. Darrell said that on his ride to New York the same thing had happened with his chase driver. It makes sense because you are with the same person during long hours and tough days. By now, a few things were bothering me with Tony. Darrell told me Tony and I needed to talk. Communication is important. Tony was doing a lot for me and for my whole family. Tony takes care of people. For sure, I couldn't have pedaled this far without him. But I refused to be treated as a child, and at times he made me feel that way. As Darrell and I spoke, it started to rain. I just hoped the rain would stop in the morning and we would have a good tomorrow. I finished the call to Darrell, went downstairs and hit the hay on a cot for a good night's sleep.

Tony and I went to sleep without doing our nightly blog. And without speaking to each other.

Hmmm, I thought. The end could be near.

Miles pedaled so far
1,482

Day

17

Tuesday, Sept. 25

Colorado: Kim to Walsh
Miles to pedal today
69

I WAS AWAKE EARLY. As I lay there, I realized I felt better than I had the day before. Tony was usually up long before I was. But now he was back sleeping. Who plans a trip without any rest days? I never claimed to be good at any of the things I was doing. I was still a little frustrated.

I know I can be a stubborn guy, and when I have my mind set on things, it's hard to change. That can be my strength and my weakness. For example, the ride wouldn't have happened if I had listened to many of my close friends and family members. Why, they tried to stop me a year ago from doing a three-day 300 mile ride along the coast from Nipomo to the Golden Gate Bridge. Too dangerous, and you're not prepared enough, they said. But I learned things about myself.

I don't like to be told what to do. I like to control my destiny and accomplish my goals.

When Tony and I finally got up, we packed the vehicle and Tony said something like, "Hey, let's go grab breakfast at Kim's Outpost." I told him that I was just going to ride.

I said it with an attitude. He got upset.

Then I let him know how I felt. Boy, did I let him know!

169

"**TONY, I'M NOT YOUR WIFE,** your firefighter, your inmate or your son," I yelled. "I organized this ride, and I don't need you always harping and telling me what to do, and treating me like I'm a child. I won't take it anymore! If you're not happy with that, take the next plane home," I screamed.

I mean, I had lived on my own at 20 years old, I was promoted to an engineer at 21 and I was not a child. I realized I wouldn't be on this trip without his help, and I believed no one could do the job the way he was doing it. But that part of our relationship had to change.

I understood why he treated me the way he did. He was a fire department captain. I was a lower rank. He was a lot older than I was. At major fires he was used to handling logistics as a profession. So, over the years, he felt he knew what was best.

I finished my venting.

Tony just stood there. We looked at each other in silence.

Then we began to talk.

I teared up a little as I spoke, probably because I'm an emotional guy, and I lead with my heart. We had cleared the air. Our talk ended on a high note.

We both agreed that we had been on this journey for more than two weeks. This was the first real argument we had. It's common at fires, when you work for a period of time with the same group. Everyone is exhausted and everyone is working hard. It's human nature: people start to get on each other's nerves.

I just wanted to be treated like an adult and not a child.

Sometimes you have to make things clear with other people how you want to be treated. People don't know what you think, or how you feel, until you discuss it with them. Tony said he thought I was narrow-minded at times, and he was right. I didn't like being told what to do. I asked him to help me with that by asking me instead of ordering me. I felt we would have a better outcome. For example, he could ask me, "Hey, do you want to wear the reflective vest?" Instead of demanding, "Put the vest on now!"

I felt much better after our talk. Tony said he did, too. We certainly cleared the air.

From that point on, our relationship changed. We both knew we had a tough schedule coming up. There were hundred-mile days ahead, and to complete them early would be great for each of us.

Tony headed to Kim's Outpost to buy our breakfast. I started to power through the miles for the day. I had another 69-mile day ahead.

As I pedaled I was beginning to feel better. Darrell was right. It was important for me and Tony to talk. We had to clear the air, and we did. I dwelled on the fact that I didn't like being told what to do. I get pretty steamed when I get fired up. Good thing Tony and I each realized that it had been a long, long trip so far, and events surrounding this journey were bigger than the two of us.

I felt good riding today. I didn't care that there was only a road, grass, a fence and power lines. I was flying. I quickly put in eight miles and reached the trip's 1,500-mile mark. I set my phone on video and took a video of myself with a sign showing 1,500. Hard to believe I had made it this far pedaling 1,500 miles! Wow!

Today I was wearing the shirt my buddy Victor gave me. It was a fire shirt he wore when he was a helicopter firefighter. A few days before the ride began, he gave me the shirt, telling me it was his lucky shirt. He said he would wear it when he had a bad feeling about the day. And it always kept him safe, he said. I was alone on the road that day, so I decided to wear it to keep me safe. I called dad and told him I had reached the 1,500-mile mark. I told him about the talk Tony and I had. He told me he was proud of what we had accomplished so far. He wondered why there was no blog last night, saying that he received calls from followers who had expected the blog. Beautiful, I thought. People were actually following our trip because it was exciting. I told him we'd be back to normal tonight.

Tony pulled up with the food, but I wanted to pedal a few more miles before I stopped to eat. I told him to head about 10 miles down the road and set us up for a blog. I would eat there. Before long I caught up with him. As I approached, I knew right away it was his car because there were no other cars on the road the whole day. The whole day! It was just us out there! Could you believe it? We ate breakfast and did an impromptu blog. We explained that Dana, a close friend who worked on the ambulance in my town, and Stephanie, a fellow engineer who was our first donor, were leaving from California today to meet us in Kansas. When an idea is first formed, the people around can quickly change the direction, and she helped build the cause. They would be driving through half the country to support me. Crazy!

I powered through the day like it was a ride in the park. I didn't understand why some days were easy while others were such a challenge. Now I had the wind at my back and the sun in my face. The tailwind was great. We arrived in Walsh at 11:30 in the morning. I had ridden 70 miles today in 3-1/2 hours. It might have been my fastest day. We took the city limit sign photo, then rode to the local restaurant where we joined Chief Everett Brisendine of the Baca County Fire Department for lunch. After I wolfed down a hamburger, we rode with the chief to his fire station. Chief Brisendine explained that the company of 15 or 16 volunteers served a wide area. The department had modern equipment and new gear they received from grants he helped write. He also told us he lived several miles away and that he and his wife owned a dry land farm. This was something very different from anything I had experienced growing up in the city. After the fire station tour we drove to his house.

He ran his farm, yet still had time to train an entire fire department and oversee other community functions. I could tell he was a hardworking man who gave a lot to the people around him. He explained that the difficult part about being a firefighter in his community is that he knows each person where he responds. I rarely had that happen back home. When it did, it was hard. I couldn't imagine on every call knowing the person as a neighbor and friend.

We arrived at the chief's home. It must have been hundreds if not thousands of acres of farmland. Farm equipment for different crops was scattered all around. We met his wife, Becky, who was happy to have us staying with them for the evening. She was preparing dinner and setting us up for our overnight stay.

After Tony and I showered and prepared our beds, Everett and Becky

Chief Everett Brisendine and his wife, Becky, with mechanized equipment. The couple took us for a tour of the farm.

took us for a tour of the farm. Dry farming, in case you're wondering, doesn't use water from the ground to water the crops. Rain would provide the necessary water. It had been a few dry years and the crops were not the greatest. In the last few years, farmers had been drilling deeper and deeper to reach water. The chief helped me onto a few pieces of equipment and showed me the complexity of the machinery. The tractors steered on their own and used GPS for precision. GPS steering, he said, was actually more precise than most tractor operators.

He had cows and bulls and lived off the land. He and his wife farmed hundreds of acres of land and sold the crops. Even the way crops were sold was more complicated than I imagined, similar to buying and selling stock on the stock market. The price was all based on supply and demand in the market. I had no idea what farms were all about. I had only seen farms from the air on my airplane flights across the country. As his tour ended we watched the picturesque sun set over the flat countryside, then headed back to the house. What a beautiful sight!

Becky prepared a tasty dinner, with brownies for dessert. We did our evening blog with the chief and his wife. In it we covered our day's events and then talked about the newest followers to the blog — Mr. Tindula's third grade class from Nipomo Elementary School back in

Nipomo, Calif. His pupils had heard about the ride. So he decided to get school approval. The class would watch our progress and study about the different states and cities through which I bicycled. Truly an educational experience, we thought. So we thanked the third graders in our blog that night. The experience with these kids was exciting for us, too. We then talked about the difficult schedule ahead. After our blog, we told the chief and his wife a lot about Lauren and her goal in life. I explained that she hoped to become a teacher, adding that, despite her handicap, she managed to live an active life. We stayed up shooting the breeze about life and what had happened so far on our journey. This was an interesting couple. I really wished we had more time to spend with them. Soon we headed to bed.

I lay in bed and prayed for strength. I knew I had a difficult 11 days ahead of me. I just needed strength to focus on one day at a time. At least I'd be traveling over nice, easy flat land.

Or so I thought.

Miles pedaled so far
1,551

Day

18

Wednesday, Sept. 26

Leaving Colorado: to Montezuma, Kansas
Miles to pedal today
108

LIKE MOST DAYS, TONY was up long before I was, and preparing everything that we'd need for the day. Coffee was on, and breakfast was ready. As usual, I was the last one up. I knew I had a lot of miles to cover today. There had been a long string of 100-mile days, but I still managed to make it across the Rockies. So this leg should be a lot easier. Our route today would be a simple ride east until we reached our next stop in Kansas.

Today would be a big day. The ride today would bring us into another time zone and into another state — and we'd reach the trip's midpoint. Kansas, here we come!

The conclusion of today would mark 18 days down and 18 to go. The point of no return, I thought. The place where the effort and energy would be greater to turn back than to continue ahead and complete the ride. I had a lot to think about as I ate breakfast. I felt better knowing we would hit some important milestones. The past two short days made me feel more rested than I had felt for most of the trip. Thank God for those easy days!

After breakfast, we drove to the fire station. It was time for me to begin yet another day of pedaling. Before we shoved off for Kansas, Chief

Brisendine took Tony to the town gas station, where he fueled our chase vehicle.

I wasn't pedaling long before I reached a sign proclaiming:

Entering Central Time Zone

Hey, another hour lost! Tony was right next to me, and so we took a few photos — of course. I had now made it through two time zones. But I was experiencing bike lag. The next stop wasn't far at all. It was a sign for the state of Kansas. Man, we made it! We had been in Colorado for days. Up and over the Rockies. It's easy from here, I reasoned. The route elevations were low for the rest of the trip. I could see for miles ahead. It was just flat. No hills or mountains. Yipee! After our photos, I pushed on. I had a lot of miles to cover. My cold had disappeared. I was feeling strong.

The sun brought a wind from the east. It dropped me from a comfortable pace of 20 miles an hour down to about 10 miles an hour. I felt like I was climbing a mountain again. I hadn't yet experienced wind like this. I had encountered sickness, restlessness, hills and mechanical failures. But nothing prepared me for the wind I would battle the next few days. I was listening to music, and decided to work my way through this. I put on the acoustic version of "Princess of China" by Coldplay and Rihanna, a song about a struggle in a relationship. For some reason I listened to the song over and over for hours. Probably because I was having my own struggle today. It was rough pedaling so hard only to be moving a mere eight miles an hour because of the wind against me. I had about 100 miles still to cover today. At least every now and then the road would go from heading east to heading a bit north. When the direction changed, I'd have a side wind instead of a headwind. And I could pick up speed.

My first stop was for water and food. I told Tony the wind was killing me. Who would have thought Kansas had wind? A constant steady wind. Maybe I should have watched "The Wizard of Oz" a few more times as a child. If I was heading west this would have been a great day. But no, I was heading east, and it was anything but. I just needed to talk

Entering another time zone – and losing another hour.

myself through this. It was another test. The hills here justified when climbing them because I knew that the slow, hard climb up a hill had a payout of an easy ride down. The wind didn't have the same return for me. I just needed to power through it. I did the math over and over in my head, eight miles an hour, 100 miles. Eight times ten is 80, which leaves 20 miles. Two more or so and that's about 12 hours on the road today. Yikes! I had shoved off this morning at seven just so I could arrive around eight tonight. That's with riding all day and stopping for breaks only a few times.

It began to frustrate me. I could hear wind blowing through my headphones and feel it in my face. I took my GPS, which gave me speed and mileage, turned it upside down and just rode. When I stopped, Tony encouraged me by cheering me on. I called my dad, but he couldn't hear anything because of the wind. It was that bad. I just needed to ride. My phone rang around 11 a.m. Dana and Stephanie were calling. They would reach me in about two hours. I told them I was excited, and I asked them to call Tony to get our exact location. After the call, I went back to listening to music and tried to enjoy what I had ahead of me. I was riding so that my sister Lauren could become independent. Every day she faced struggles that she managed to overcome. This was just one day of my life that I had to get through.

AS I WAS DAYDREAMING, I happened to glance back. Tony had been pulled over by the police. Now what? He was about a quarter of a mile behind me. I turned and headed back to see what was going on.

When I reached the car, I could see Tony hadn't been arrested, so that was a good start. As far as I knew, the road we were on was okay for bikes. If it wasn't okay, I didn't know another road that would work. I think there was only one.

Tony told me we had to follow the police officer back about a mile onto a side street. This sounded rough for me. Any mile the wrong way was really two extra miles. But, despite how I felt, I followed them. I wasn't exactly sure what was going on. There was not much around us. As we left the main road, we entered a little town. We made a few turns and arrived at the Stanton County Fire Station. We were now in Johnson, Kan.

Seems they had heard we were passing through and wanted to contribute to Lauren's Ride. So they sent the police out to intercept us. Phew!

The firefighters gave us a donation, then showed us around their station and talked about their community. They served about 1,500 residents and also responded to calls outside the city. This certainly raised my spirits. Here we were on Highway 160 with nothing around us, but somehow those guys managed to find us and donate. After we took a photo together, we got back on the road. We had a rough day ahead because the wind was acting up, and it would most likely be steady. It was actually a light day compared to our standard, so I guess I was lucky.

Back on the road, instead of being upset with the wind, I just rode

Dana Morton, left, and Stephanie Dininni take a page out of 'Wizard of Oz' as we meet in Kansas. Note 'tin' funnel on my head and red shoes on Dana. They brought Toto, too!

to enjoy it. Pedal up and pedal down. Seems as if I was climbing the Rockies all over again. But the road was flat. It was all about willpower. My body felt good, and I wasn't sick. I just needed to stay positive. So I just rode and rode.

Another hour went by, or about 15 more rounds of Coldplay and Rihanna, when a car pulls up behind us. It was Dana and Stephanie. They made it. We had traveled about 50 miles for the day. Close to the half way mark or so, and it was now about noon.

Dana and Stephanie came dressed as "The Wizard of Oz" characters. After all, we *are* in Kansas. Dana's bike had a front carrier for her little dog which she dressed to resemble Toto. It was cute. We hugged and took a few photos. Dana and I rode together while Stephanie drove their car. They later switched so that Stephanie and I rode together. We both couldn't believe how windy it was. I could feel it even more now with headphones off. It didn't matter though because I had so much to tell them. So much had happened since we had ridden together back in California. I told her story after story, and she said that everyone back home was so proud. They would tune in to television stations covering this story to see what had happened each day. That made me feel good. Stephanie would ride about 10 miles with me, then transfer to the chase vehicle with Tony. It was good for Tony to finally have someone to talk to. He had a lot of long days by himself.

The one thing that just didn't stop was the wind. If anything, it had increased. How would I make it through Kansas? I thought I better hit the road much earlier tomorrow to beat the wind.

After some challenging hours, we were about 80 miles in for the day. It was about 5 p.m., and we still had 28 miles to go. The wind didn't let up. I just had to keep pedaling. I took a needed rest to stretch my legs and took a few Ibuprofen. My body believed it was heading back over the Rockies. Tony announced there was a big community dinner planned for us in the park in town. I just kept pushing through, but it was difficult because I felt like I wasn't getting anywhere. I would get off the bike at times, and the wind was still blowing through me. It was probably a 20-mile constant easterly wind. I knocked mile after mile out for two more hours until we reached an intersection where a car was parked on the side of the road. In front of the car stood John and Amy Goossen and their children, Rylan and Lakin. A few bikes were in the back of their truck. They came to greet us and to officially lead us into their city, which was only a few miles away. Man, was it good to finally see that city limits sign! This, by far, was the hardest day of the ride for me. But we completed half the journey. No turning back now!

I took my photo in front of the sign, barely able to hold up my bike. I pedaled 106 miles today. And I still had two more miles to go. John and the kids got on their bikes and we headed into town. As we rode, we passed the Montezuma Bank. The electronic billboard proclaimed:

JOIN THE MONTEZUMA FIRE DEPT.
FOR A MEET AND GREET AND FUNDRAISER
AT THE CITY PARK
WITH JOHN BYRNE
AS HE BIKES ACROSS AMERICA

I always enjoyed people riding with me. Billboard signs like that would always blow me away. It's amazing the effect some people can have on others.

A crowd was clapping and cheering as we entered the park. We made it! The adults were preparing dinner; the children played. This was our biggest reception so far. About 50 people were there. Again, I reminded Tony we had made it to the half way mark!

By now I was so sore that I got off my bike and quickly changed into warm clothes. Tony made Fluid recovery drinks for me. It was night-time now — and the wind was still blowing. We enjoyed a great community-sponsored dinner. Interestingly, the children asked a lot of questions about the ride. A youngster named Kimble even came up to me, handed me a pen and politely asked for my autograph.

The people collected donations which they presented to us after dinner. This was such a friendly community! I could tell these people were really involved with their families and each other.

After dinner, we took group photos and a photo of me and the children.

I talked with Gerald, who wanted to ride with us as we left town the next morning. I was excited. He had been a rider for years. I got his information before we left for the Goossen home. It was only a mile away, so I bicycled and Tony drove. Dana and Stephanie, meanwhile drove to a hotel in the next town.

As I started to ride that last mile, I felt rain. I made it to the house. As I rode up the driveway I slipped and fell off my bike. I wasn't hurt, and it looked as if I hadn't damaged the bike. Actually, I had caught myself as I fell, and I slightly bent my hand back. I was lucky. This would have been a lousy way to end the ride. The rain started to come down even harder. We thought this should be good for the dry farmers. It can rain all night; it just needs to stop in the morning. We had been pretty lucky with our timing. We were half way through the trip. And one hundred eight miles in the tough, rough Kansas winds was behind me now.

If it wasn't for the support of so many people, I don't know how I would have made it through the day.

So many things are possible when everyone works together.

Miles pedaled so far
1,659

Children turn out for group photo. Tot on right insisted on posing alone.

19

Thursday, Sept. 27

Kansas: Montezuma to Pratt
Miles to pedal today
103

I WAS STILL IN BED and wondered if rain was still coming down. The few times I woke up during the night I could hear rain hitting the roof. Now it was about 6:30 a.m. I got out of bed and stretched a bit to test my soreness and to assess the damage I had done to my body the day before. I was a little groggy, most likely dehydrated, but somehow I was not too sore. I walked out to the living room. Becky and John were making breakfast for us. They poured me a cup of coffee. Tony was already sitting at the table reading the local newspaper and checking today's weather. He said it rained all night, but it looked as though the storm was around us and not over us. Our path looked pretty clear. We were lucky. The children woke up. We all had breakfast together.

After breakfast, we went to meet with Gerald, Stephanie, Dana and a few others. I rode my bike feeling happy that it wasn't raining anymore. It was a foggy morning. The wind was calm. Gerald was using a recumbent bike, one with a lower profile that was ideal for the Kansas winds. He was riding with us. We gathered for a few minutes then headed east together. As we rode, we noticed more traffic. A few days earlier, I may have seen one car on the road for the entire day. Not today. The fog made visibility minimal. Tony made sure to drive close behind us to protect us from traffic. Gerald and I talked about his community and about the ride. Having someone next to me made riding easier, especially when the wind came up as it did almost every day in Kansas. At one point, two dogs began to chase us. It scared the hell out of both of us. Luckily, they didn't get either one of us. It was a close call, and they chased us for about a quarter mile. I remembered Darrell telling me that a dog chasing him was his biggest fear. Gerald rode ahead of me to cut down the wind. We rode 25 miles together to Dodge City.

Our first stop for the day was at Cup of Jones coffee shop. Gerald's wife, Kara, and children met us there. This was Gerald's stopping point. His wife would be driving him back home. We all had coffee, and I had my second breakfast. Although my spirits were high, I was still feeling sore. Today was the second day of what I called the 100 mile sets. We managed to do a blog while we were at the coffee shop. We covered 25 miles so far today and are making good headway.

WHILE AT BREAKFAST, I had a chance to talk with Lauren by phone for an update. She had some big news from back home. The first thing she said was that Cal Chiefs President, Demetrious N. Shaffer, who met Lauren during the Newark Day Parade, put the Lauren's Ride story on the Cal Chiefs' website. The website went out to every fire chief in California. He also made a personal donation and went out of his way to support our cause in other ways. I thought, what were the odds Lauren and the president of Cal Chiefs would run into each other?

The second piece of news was that Lesley Lafferty, who had been covering our story on radio, and our family friend Belinda Maloney had set up a fundraiser dinner at Love at First Slice. They planned it around a karaoke night.

The third bit of news was that Lauren herself had a driving lesson scheduled for later that day. And I could tell by her tone of voice that she was really excited.

She ran into some obstacles trying to find an appropriate car to drive with her permit, so this was really big news. She had to have a vehicle with hand controls, and only a few cars are equipped with them. Every time she set something up with someone, the person canceled, or the car had an issue with it, and they couldn't meet with her. She was still working on a plan to get her license, and now this was becoming difficult. It was a huge obstacle. So having something lined up for the day was big news.

AFTER WE HAD BREAKFAST and spent time together, Gerald and his family left for home. Stephanie and I rode our bikes together while Tony and Dana tailed. The Kansas wind was blowing in our face again. After about 10 miles my bike got another flat tire. This was flat #5. Good news was that it was a front tire flat, which was easy to fix. There was no chain to slip over and no grease, so it was a simple fix. A flat tire was the least of my challenges with this wind. I changed the tire, and we were back into the wind in Kansas.

After Dodge, we passed Ford City then approached Greensburg. We were now on Route 400. We stopped for lunch at Cook's Deli and Mar-

Pratt firefighters welcome me.

ket, a local sandwich shop. We joined the community members having lunch. We learned that Greensburg had been completely destroyed some years ago by a tornado and was totally rebuilt. I was so sad. I couldn't image a whole town being destroyed at once. From riding on Route 400 it was hard to tell that a tornado had wiped out the town. We took a few photos after we handed out the flyers and kept on our route. Tony and Dana diverted through the town while Stephanie and I continued ahead. Inside the town there was a lot more evidence of the tornado. Some people just up and left, not rebuilding at all.

We rode and rode until we reached Pratt, Kan., our stopping point for the day. It was 5:30 p.m. We had been on the road for 10 hours. Most of the time spent pedaling. We took few breaks. We had ridden 103 miles for the day with an ascent of 2,100 ft. We had just completed two long days. Nine more long days were ahead. We rode to the fire station where firefighters were waiting for us. We met Chief David Kramer, and took photos with him and his crew. Dana talked with him. I didn't know it at the time, but Dana's mom grew up in Pratt. She and the chief went to school together. What a small world! Chief Kramer set up lodging for us at a local hotel. Our visit was enjoyable, but brief. We just experienced a long day. I was eager to rest.

We made it to the hotel, showered, then went to dinner where we face-timed into the pizza fund-raiser back home. It was really nice to see everyone who had shown up at that fund-raiser. It was the most interaction I had with my family since the ride began. People cheered me on and sang high-spirited songs. It was just what I needed. What an evening!

We made it back to the hotel and did our nightly blog. Tony was the Cowardly Lion, Dana was Dorothy, Stephanie was the Scarecrow and I was the Tin Man. They brought all the appropriate props with them. As we did the blog, we made references, of course, to "The Wizard of Oz." Tony was working on courage, I was a little squeaky and needed some oil to get ready for the ride the next day. It was our funniest blog so far. With the challenging days, I still had a smile on my face, and we were

Lunch with the locals at Pratt, Kan.

happy. The strong wind wasn't going to stop us from finishing this ride. At least I had hoped it wouldn't.

Miles pedaled so far
1,762

20

Friday, Sept. 28

Kansas: Pratt to El Dorado
Miles to pedal today
115

I WOKE UP AROUND EIGHT while everyone was sleeping. We were all beat. The past few days were long days in the car for Tony. Dana and Stephanie had driven more than 1,500 miles to get here. I was pretty sore. It was not until about nine that everyone was finally awake. I was anxious to leave, knowing I had 115 miles ahead of me. We decided to skip the morning blog. We made our way to the fire station and Stephanie and I began the morning by riding together. It was another foggy day. I usually disliked riding in the fog, but fog was much better than wind. I had never experienced wind like the wind here in Kansas. I remember back when I trained I was happy riding in the wind. Little did I realize I was training for this ride, but nothing prepared me for this Kansas wind.

As Stephanie and I rode, I told her about the effect she had on the fundraiser by making the first donation. We were not even officially doing the ride yet when she donated. She gave me faith that people would help us and that it was a worthy cause. I could say we had already raised $100 after the second day of the idea. She was sad about leaving, and I was sad about having her go. She was very good company and was so positive and supportive. We talked for a while. Around mile 20 we pulled off the road. This was their stop. They had many miles to drive back. I gave them both hugs, and we parted.

Once again, it was just Tony and me heading east on the yellow brick road. Fog began to lift and wind picked up. The weather began to wear me down.

I was so upset at this point, and I was alone out here in the middle of nowhere. Maybe this coast-to-coast bicycle ride wasn't such a good idea after all, I told myself. Maybe there's a chance I won't reach New York. Perish the thought.

It was torture because I was so sore. This wind certainly was making it difficult. I was moving slowly. I kept thinking I had so many miles to complete today, and it would take so long at this rate. The music was not making riding any better for me either.

I was at mile 32.2 and decided to start counting like I was an auctioneer auctioning out bike miles. Here it begins, folks — the mile is 32.2. 32.2, 32.2; oh there you are 32.2! Anyone for 32.3? 32.2 going once, 32.2 going twice! Oh we have 32.3! I did this for hours. 48.1, 48.1, 48.1, come on 48.2; I know you are there, 48.2! It kept me going and focused on something simple and achievable.

It was either this or lose my mind.

The roads began to get congested. We had no idea where we were heading. Tony checked the weather report which indicated rain ahead. Sure enough, before long it began to sprinkle. The roads were wet as we entered the city limits of Wichita. So much of Kansas is empty, and then you hit Wichita, a major city. The old "head east until you get there" strategy was the one I would have to go with. I didn't have time to not be riding. We had a long way to go. Now there was heavy traffic. We still had no idea where we were going. We headed about eight miles through city traffic and reached a toll center that led to the highway. Shit! Something's wrong!

We stopped and double checked the maps. Looks like we would have to backtrack miles to reach a proper route. Rain was coming down harder now. We put our heads together. We agreed to go through the toll, disregarding the sign that read **No pedestrians beyond this point.** I pulled my own toll ticket, and we went for it. The highway seemed safe and had a wide shoulder. But we knew we had to cross over each highway exit and entrance. That part was dangerous. The road was smooth and there was no east wind. It was cold, but I was feeling okay with the rain. I would take the rain over the wind at this point. Tony stayed close behind me providing excellent protection as we crossed exits. We really needed a sign in that proclaimed: **Caution. Bike Rider Ahead.**

After a few miles, our good luck ended. A Kansas State Trooper pulled Tony over. Well, we had taken a chance — and we got caught. I pedaled back the eighth of a mile. The trooper told Tony that it was illegal for us to be on the highway. He ordered us to load the bike into our chase vehicle and drive off at the next exit.

I was devastated at hearing this. I could feel my heart drop. I had ridden this far capturing every single mile. Tony, like always, knew what was important to me, and he explained to the officer that I had ridden this bike from the Golden Gate Bridge to this location and had ridden every single mile at this point. It was important to me that I was able to ride the whole distance. Simply, we had gotten lost in his city. Tony asked him if he would consider escorting us off the freeway. That would allow me to ride in front of him. The officer thought about it for a few seconds, then looked at both of us, and then looked at the bike.

"Okay," he replied.

Phew! I could now breathe easy again. The trooper escorted us to the next exit, we pulled off and then talked with him. He learned more about our ride and took a flyer.

He even made a donation.

He said he would post the flyer back at his station and share details of my ride with his co-workers. I took a photo with him, and he pointed out a good route to make it to our destination. Not bad for getting pulled over by the police, I thought.

Thank you, Wichita!

The rest of the ride that day was like the last few days — windy and challenging. It was a matter of will power and mental toughness. I arrived in El Dorado, our destination, at 7 p.m. It had been a long day, but

I managed to complete the 115 miles. To think the next day was going to be 133 miles. Hard for me to visualize and accept. I didn't think I had another 18 miles left in me for today. I took a photo in front of the city limit sign. That was me with the huge grin.

I had completed the third 100-mile series.

We rode to the fire station and met the crew. They were excited to greet us. Earlier, Tony had arranged a massage for me for 8 p.m. at El Dorado Massage. We ate a delicious meatloaf dinner with the fire crew. Then we showered, and I headed to El Dorado Massage.

Jody, the owner, stayed open for us. Boy, was this massage on the money. I really needed it. Every part of me was sore. She did her best to stretch me and move some of the lactic acid. I felt beat after the massage.

Back at the fire station we did our evening blog. I talked with Lyn back home who was maintaining the donor list and contacting interested people about the ride. Before we hit the sack the station set up a phone interview for us with the *El Dorado Times*. I spoke with a news reporter about what I was experiencing and what the ride was for. After the phone call, I called Lauren. More good news — the fundraiser back home had raised about $600, plus an additional 20% of the sales that day at Love at First Slice in Newark. Donations were beginning to pour in. We were on the road to success. No pun intended. Still, my biggest concern was that we would fail to raise enough money for the special car. But, so far we were on track. Tony and I stayed up talking with the crew for hours before going to bed. It was great to talk with others about the ride and to see them as excited as we were.

I had never experienced anything like this.

Miles pedaled so far
1,877

Trooper patiently listened as I explained that I'm riding to the
Brooklyn Bridge — then personally donated to Lauren's Ride.

Day
21

Saturday, Sept. 29
Kansas: El Dorado to Fort Scott
Miles to pedal today
122

THROUGHOUT THE ENTIRE 36-DAY journey I never worried about getting a good night's sleep.

I was usually asleep as soon as I hit the sheets. I needed at least eight hours sleep each night for my body to heal and recharge. Every day I planned to get an early start. We would talk about that the night before. But every morning we departed later than we planned. Fact is, I needed sleep.

I woke up about 8 a.m. Today would be the longest day of the trip: 133 miles. I went outside, and I could already feel the wind blowing. It was a hard realization. I came inside, and we began the morning blog. We were with fire crew members Rick, Troy and Tyler. They filled us in with community and fire department history. As was becoming routine now, we took photos together in front of the station, then hit the road.

Although we were meeting the nicest people I had ever met, this was probably the most difficult few days of my life. This personal struggle was due to the wind. I was experiencing a lot of pain in my hips, legs, back and IT bands. I tried to keep moving forward, telling myself that if I could just get through today, no following day would be as difficult. Then again, I was the guy who figured Kansas would be easy pedaling

— so I went ahead and set up a lot of long days. This will teach me! I hadn't counted on this constant strong wind. I really didn't know what to expect next, but as the day wore on I tried to focus on the fact that no day would have as many miles as today. I've just got to get through today, I kept telling myself. But, honestly, I didn't know how I'd do it.

After 30 miles of eastern wind, we arrived at a small restaurant. I was ready for lunch. It seemed like an ideal place to eat and rest. More importantly, I'd be out of the wind for a while.

Name of the eatery was Benny's, and it was crowded with families. Tony quickly explained to the diners what we were doing as he handed out Lauren's Ride flyers. They all became excited. Whenever I met wonderful people, like the ones here in Benny's who wanted to help, it really recharged me. It made the struggle seem not so bad.

We sat down to lunch and Tony shared more of the messages of support from our followers back home. This is what kept me going.

After lunch it was back on the road for hours. Eventually I came upon a road sign telling me that our destination, Fort Scott, was 62 miles away. Rats! 62 more miles! It was now 4 p.m. I figured that at an eight-mile-an-hour pace, the day and night would be long. But this sign was a sign of progress. Progress or not, however, I still had a long way to pedal. The wind today seemed to be unusually strong. As the day wore on, I kept my pace of about eight miles an hour. Every hour or so I would stop, sit in the car and talk with Tony. He would read me more messages that were coming in, and we would try to figure exactly how many miles to Fort Scott. What a torture!

I finally reached a point where I had only ten miles to go! Darkness was now setting in. I was completely drained. I felt so tired. I was beat. I really didn't think I'd finish the day.

FACED WITH THESE NEGATIVE thoughts, I decided to call my dad for support. I told him I had about 10 miles to go, and I was having a really difficult time. The sun was now setting but the wind was still blowing into my face. Mom got on the phone, too. Dad told me that mom was planning a huge celebration dinner at the end of the ride in New

I reach Fort Scott, Kan., after sunset.

York. Mom had chartered a bus for family, friends and guests. The bus would follow my route the final day, from Freehold, N.J., to the Brooklyn Bridge. Friends and family would be on the bus to cheer as I crossed the finish line on the bridge. Then it would be off to a big celebration dinner at the Hilton Garden Inn on Staten Island.

Great news. But at this point I really didn't think I'd make it through today.

I TALKED WITH MOM AND DAD as I pedaled the final gruesome 10 miles. I would tell them when I completed each mile. It was now completely dark out. I had not been riding this late since the second day of the ride. The wind seemed to decrease a little as the sun set. I talked a long time with mom and dad – ten miles, to be exact. Then, at exactly 7:53 p.m., I reached the city limit sign for Fort Scott, Kan. Man, what a relief! It was a late arrival after an extremely long and exhausting day on the road. I took my city limit photo and headed to the fire station.

I was beat — with a capital B. By the time we got to the station, we had completed 122 miles for the day, a few miles less than planned. Firefighters and their families were waiting for us with a home-cooked dinner. We would stay at the fire station tonight.

After dinner, we did the evening blog with Chief Paul Ballou and his wife, daughter and fire crew. Chief Ballou mentioned in passing that we were only three miles from Missouri. I thought how amazing it was to have nearly made it through windy Kansas. We talked about our plan for the next day. We'd shove off at 5 a.m. so we'd have time to take in an NFL Chiefs-Chargers football game. Tony, you see, was a Chargers season ticket holder for the past 24 years. Before we began the journey, Tony said he would miss his Chargers home football games. I suggested we see if they were playing any away games on our route. It was a good idea. By chance, they'd be playing in Kansas City the day we entered Missouri. We'd be less than 50 miles away. Tony said, though, it wouldn't bother him if he missed this game.

He did so much for me I could wake up early and ride as far as I could, without taking a break, so that Tony could see his game. After the game I would return to my pausing point to finish the ride for the day. It would be similar to a long lunch break.

Now, here we were in Fort Scott. I pedaled almost 2,000 miles. An extraordinary feat.

Tomorrow will be a day of milestones. But will a football game knock us off track?

Miles pedaled so far
1,999

Chief Paul Ballou, his wife and daughter show up to greet me.

22

Sunday, Sept. 30

Leaving Kansas: to Camdenton, Missouri
Miles to pedal today
114

I AWOKE BEFORE MY 4:30 A.M. ALARM. Man, was I ready to roll! Surprisingly, I wasn't feeling tired. I gathered my things and we were off. I was excited for Tony and the things we would accomplish today. He had made so many sacrifices to be here on this ride to support me and my family. Every day on the road he was making phone call after phone call, stop after stop and doing so many extra things each and every mile. It was a ton of support work. I was realizing that Tony was perfect for the job. So having an opportunity to do something for Tony made me feel really good. As I said, Tony had been a San Diego Chargers season ticket holder for 24 years. I now hoped – and prayed — that I could pedal through Missouri without the wind that hampered me through Kansas.

We had a goal today of about 115 miles. We were now off to an early start.

We pushed off in total darkness. There was no one on the road at this hour and there was no wind. I could still see stars in the sky. I put in my first mile to reach the 2,000-mile milestone.

Two thousand miles. Hard to believe. What a feat!

Tony drew a 2,000-mile sign. I was thrilled. We took a lot of photos in complete darkness. It was still too early to telephone anyone back home in California, so I just kept pedaling east. In minutes I reached the **Leaving Kansas** sign. Another milestone. More photos. I couldn't believe I made it this far. Or I should say I couldn't believe I survived Kansas. Pedaling through Kansas had been a physical and mental struggle. And the culprit was the ever-present wind. We now reached the **Entering Missouri** sign. Kansas was now behind us. I wasn't sure what Missouri had in store for us. We were making progress each day, and so reaching each new state was an accomplishment.

The ride today seemed easier. Wind had disappeared so I had a positive pace of 22 miles an hour. I had not ridden this fast in more than a week. The scenery changed as we were entering Missouri. Trees and rolling hills were everywhere. The sun was beginning to come up; it was a sight I had not seen in a long time because of our later starts each morning. It was beautiful. Dark purples and blue colors in the sky.

All of a sudden, bad news: another flat. This time the tire had split. This was my first flat tire in darkness. Tony snapped photos of me as I made the repair. We were making good time, so a brief stop to fix a flat wouldn't really slow us down too much. It was my sixth flat so far. Not bad for traveling more than 2,000 miles, I thought. That's about one flat every 300 miles. I changed the tire and returned to pedaling. I felt refreshed without wind blowing in my face. There are so many things that could have gone wrong on this trip. I managed to overcome wind the past four days. Later I learned that a week before we reached Kansas the east wind had picked up to 50-to-60 miles an hour. We made it over what some would call a peak in a life filled with peaks and valleys, or did I make it through the valley? I'm not sure which one is better.

I didn't want to stop for breaks today. I just wanted to keep going as far as I could so that Tony could reach his football game.

Weather today was cool. The Missouri topography led to a nice view. Tony went ahead to scout for a place to eat. While he was driving he ran into a woman named Sandy who was walking her quarter horse. This reminded Tony of his ranch and pets back home. He talked with Sandy about his ranch, told her about our ride and handed her a flyer.

Another milestone brings me closer to goal.

I don't know exactly why, but today I was feeling great. I think it was the absence of wind. Sure, there were more hills today, but I used momentum from the downhill speed to help make it up the climbs. I was so happy to be out of the Kansas wind! Did I tell you that? I don't think I can say it enough. The sun was now up. Today looked like a perfect ride day. My goal was to make as much time as I could so as to be ahead by the end of the day. The football game was in the afternoon, so I was like an animal as I pedaled. I powered through the hills just as though I was a totally-rested athlete in a race. After a few hours of riding across our new state, I reached a total of 75 miles for the day. That would be our stopping point. When we stopped, Tony told me we had made the front page of our local paper back home, the *Santa Maria Times*. Lauren's Ride was laid out over the entire front page. There were different photos taken at different times of the ride with an illustration of the country in the background showing the route we had traveled. I was quoted as saying "Every bad thing turns into something good." The story was written by reporter Jennifer Best. It was a well-done piece about Lauren's Ride!

We took a photo and headed for Arrowhead Stadium. After driving 40 minutes (my bike was in the chase vehicle with us) we were about half way to the stadium, so we decided to stop at the Clinton Fire Department. I wondered if I could leave my bike there while Tony and I went to the game. That's the kind of brotherhood we shared as firefighters. It would be no different if these firefighters came through California. The Clinton Fire Department crew welcomed us and gave us a tour of their station. I could tell Tony was excited to take in the game — he was dressed from head to toe in blue San Diego Chargers attire. A typical Chargers fan!

We got to Arrowhead Stadium a few minutes after kick off. We bought a couple of inexpensive tickets in the parking lot and headed in. Tony was like a child seeing Disneyland for the first time. He was charged like I had never seen him. He was just so happy as we walked to our seats. For me, this was the first Chargers game I had ever attended. We found our seats and greeted the fans sitting around us. Of course, we stood out because Tony was the only fan wearing all blue in a stadium of all red. Someone yelled at Tony, "A Chargers fan, huh?" He quickly explained that he was from San Diego, and they were surprised he had traveled from California all the way to Missouri. They thought he was even crazier when they found out he drove all the way here. Tony then explained why he had driven halfway across the country, and that I had ridden a bike halfway across the country. Then everyone sitting around us wanted to hear more about what we were doing. They were more interested in talking with us than they were about watching the football game.

Once they heard about The Ride, it happened. Like in every other place we stopped, money began to float toward us. Donations began coming to us from the people around us. It was like handing money from person to person when you buy a hot dog from a vendor. More than $100 came

Tony, a devout Chargers football fan, mingles with 'enemy' as Chargers play Chiefs in Arrowhead Stadium. Afternoon football game was relaxing break for us.

in. Again, as happened many times before, I just couldn't believe it.

The Chargers were playing great. They led the entire game and ended up winning, 37-20. After the game, we walked down to the first row. Tony yelled to his favorite players. He was so happy. He really needed this break. And stopping to see this football game was the perfect relaxation. The days had been long for him. I was so happy he was able to see the game. We took a victory tour around the stadium then headed to our car for the ride back to the fire station. This fifth day of the 100-mile sets was going pretty well. As we drove back, I closed my eyes and tried to rest.

When we got back at the station, the engine was out. The pet Dalmatian was lounging. On duty were Andrew Cary, Jim Halk and Jeremy Millan. The dog lived at the station. This was new to us, because few West Coast stations have Dalmatians anymore.

The history of Dalmatian dogs with the fire service dates back to the days when horses pulled fire steamers. Dalmatians, more than any other breed, loved to run with the horses. They wound up clearing paths as the horses pulled fire apparatus through the streets. We took a few photos. Then the guys gave us a donation. It was now about 5:30 p.m. We knew we had to get back to our stopping point earlier in the day. I began to feel really tired as we drove, but I only had 40 more miles to go to round out the day! I took the driving time to fall asleep and rest.

We arrived back at our spot sometime around 6:30 p.m. I figured I would just power through the final 40 miles. I had ridden strong all day. With an 18-to-20-mile an hour pace, I could finish by 8:30. The only problem was my body. It had worked hard early on, and I stopped for the football game. It wasn't ready to begin the ride again. Missouri was full of rolling hills. It wasn't like the hills of Colorado at all. Up and down, up and down. The elevation was never too high. Just 200 ft. up, then 200 ft. down. A flat mile or two, then another 200 ft. climb, then 200 ft. descent. This would have been easy if I didn't break for the football game. But I took a long break and now was sore and tired.

At 7 p.m. we came upon a **Watch Out for Buggy/Carriage** sign. I took a photo in front of it like I was the horse pulling this carriage. I discovered that each state had a different set of road warning signs. Sure enough, before long a carriage came into view ahead of me. This gave me a goal to ride to. Not exactly a race, just something to shoot for. Horses had a lot of hills to climb to get from one place to another. I gained and gained with a constant drive until I came up adjacent to the carriage. When it was safe, I passed it. I had never seen a buggy like this.

It was turning into a really long and tiring day. The sun was going down. It began to get dark. I could only see ahead because of Tony's head lights behind me as he followed. Remember, street lights were unheard of for most of the trip. I pushed myself though the hills. The hills were better than wind. I powered though until I made it to this brightly lighted bridge that crossed a picturesque lake with houses along the shore. We were almost at our goal of Camdenton, Mo. Another few miles and we finally made it to the city limit sign. A clear photo was impossible because it was too dark. I pedaled a few more miles to the fire station. The crew was waiting. It was now 10 p.m. What began as an

Daylight or not, I repair flat tire in no time.

easy morning turned into a tough evening. I had traveled 114 miles to-day. Ascent for the day was 6,421 ft. I climbed more than a mile. I covered more than I planned — and I was beat. I thought Missouri would be relatively flat, but it had a lot of rolling hills. As soon as we got in, Tony iced my legs to reduce swelling and soreness. They were really sore and tight. Tighter than I ever remember. I felt stiff and uncomfortable. The fire crew and some off duty members were waiting for us. They cooked dinner and we relaxed and ate. On duty were firefighters Jamie Hodlden and Chris Bockman. This was Mid County Fire Protection. First thing Tony did after dinner was to locate the department washing machine and wash all my clothes.

The guys gave us a package, addressed to me, that had been delivered earlier by a mail carrier. It was from Shannon King, one of Tony's co-worker's back in San Diego. It was a care package for us. Shannon had been supporting us from the day we began the ride. She had been raising money, sharing news of our ride with others and sending us constant messages of encouragement from home. A group of volunteers were helping her, too. In the care package were items such as suntan lotion, chap stick, snacks and chewing gum. It was a pleasant way to end the night — looking at the care package and thinking of everyone who "cared" for me as I attempted to bicycle across the country. Nice people.

Tony and I were really beat. No strength for the evening blog. How could we have strength? I pedaled more than 100 miles and got to see a pro football game in the deal.

The crew showed us to our beds. We hit the hay and went out like lights.

Miles pedaled so far

2,113

Day

23

Monday, Oct. 1

Missouri: Camdenton to Union
Miles to pedal today
121

TODAY I SLEPT IN. It was 10 a.m. and I was *still* in bed. Hmmmm. I wonder why? This is the latest I had gotten up. Everyone was up but me. I was pretty spent. Sleep was essential, but I really needed a full rest day today. Of course, a full rest day wasn't an option, so I got up and got ready for another 100-mile day. Just the thought of pedaling 100 miles today drove me nuts. Today was Day 6 of the long sets. If I could finish today I would be past half of them. Tony and I did yesterday's blog. Remember, we were too beat last night to even *think* blog. We then did our morning blog for today with the firefighters. I called Lesley back home at 11 a.m. to do our radio interview for the week, since it was another Monday. If I hadn't mentioned it before, Lesley called me every Monday for a radio update. I told her we just finished a tough week, and were heading into another tough week. I rode from the Kansas winds to the Missouri hills. It was nice to know so many people back home were following us and supporting our cause. Knowing that made me happy.

After our phone call I mapped out my route for the day. It showed 140 miles. A hundred forty miles? There must be a mistake. The original route we planned was much less than that. I double checked. It didn't look good. How did we miss this? It was 25 more miles than originally planned. How could anyone in his right mind pedal 140 miles in a day? I kept asking myself. Well, nothing to do except ride and put the miles behind me.

I called mom to see how everyone was back home. I vented a little about this most recent frustration. She told me she had talked to a woman named Sonia from Union Fire Dept. in Union, Mo., who told her the whole town was excited that we would pass through. The woman had been talking with mom all week about our arrival at Union. The one big thing I had going for me today is that I felt positive because people in Union were so excited about our upcoming arrival.

I pedaled out of town into the Missouri hills. Today an east wind was blowing. The wind was just strong enough to bother my face as I rode along. It slowed me down a bit. I tried to focus instead on the beautiful view. I kept thinking about my arrival at the end of the day. The temperature wasn't too hot or too cold; the day so far was perfect. There wasn't any rain so I was thankful. Somehow we just kept missing bad weather patterns. Today I felt a lot more determined than I had the last few days. While pedaling, I called Darrell for advice on the long day ahead. He was surprised that I had scheduled 140 miles. Not as surprised as I was, I said. He told me he'd check out the route and call back. Knowing Darrell had pedaled across the country gave me faith that it was indeed possible for me to do it, too. I knew today would be a day that I'd have to earn. I turned on the song "Yellow" by Coldplay and replayed it for a long time. Before beginning the ride, I had looked up what Chris Martin had written the song about. The song was written about brotherly love, where a person would do anything for someone he or she loved.

"I swam across for you. I wrote a song for you. It was all yellow."

Darrell called back with a new route. It would shave about 20 miles off the 140. Oh, baby! That was something I needed to hear. The only thing about the revised route was that it covered a few different roads rather than one main highway. We were always good at getting lost. Any extra mile after 100 was long, so I decided to take my chances by cutting out 20 miles, rather than risk getting lost. Hearing this made me really happy. I just knocked out 20 miles in a weird way. The hills weren't as massive as the Rockies, but were just enough to have to work hard climbing them. Of course, each hill had a downhill to it. The wind was still blowing easterly, but was better than the Kansas wind. I powered up and over these hills for the next few hours, then decided I needed food. We stopped, and I ate what we had in the chase vehicle. At this point it looked as if we were in the middle of nowhere. Earlier we had passed through several small towns. As I sat in the car and ate, I admired the green landscapes that surrounded us. Missouri was surely a pretty state. I still feel positive given the number of hills I encountered today. Tony, of course, offered encouragement. He read me more comments that had come in.

After lunch I returned to pedaling. I had a comfortable pace going, about 15 miles an hour. I was making pretty good time, moving at a pretty good clip. All of a sudden, a few deer darted out in front of me. This scared the you-know-what out of me. They quickly turned, ran into the woods and disappeared.

A few minutes later, another interruption: I came upon a turtle just resting in the middle of the road. The turtle surely would be killed if it stayed there, so I stopped and moved it off the roadway. Two deer, now a turtle. I was in my own animal kingdom!

Tony pulled up, spied the turtle and said he wouldn't mind company in the car. He said he missed his pets back home. Well, I wasn't sure if this was a good idea, but within minutes the turtle had joined us on our adventure to New York. We named the turtle Darrell after our team member back home who sent us on this road.

We came to a sign that read:

Route 28 Forward 8 Miles

Below that, it read:

Route 28 Left 10 Miles

I figured we should go straight and save the two miles, since they both apparently directed us to the same place. The map wasn't clear so we guessed. A few miles later, more bad news: a spoke on my front

Faced with conundrum, I chose the 8 mile route. The way I looked at it, two fewer miles on route is two fewer miles to pedal.

tire rim broke. Good news, however: this would be an easy fix. I simply took a wheel from another bike. I was lucky to have back up wheels. It was about 1 p.m. and I already knocked out 60 miles. I figured I had about six hours ahead. I powered through each mile and kept mentally strong, knowing that I didn't have to ride the 140 miles. I just kept heading east. I didn't want to ride in the dark, so I didn't stop for too many breaks. I looked forward to finishing the day and meeting everyone waiting for us. Really late arrivals made it difficult to meet everyone. People worked, children had school. Every time I made it up a hill I could see the next hill ahead of me. I would go down the hill about a mile, then start the climb again without much momentum from the last hill because I was getting tired. I must have done this 50 times to-

Darrell the turtle joins us to become Tony's carmate.

day. It was one hill after another, one pedal down, then the next pedal down. When we stopped for a break, Tony said, "You seem to be determined today, John." I felt really good when Tony complimented me. By now I figured I had to earn compliments from Tony. He continued, "I feel bad for you today. Every time I see a hill ahead, there's another one past it that you have to climb. You're doing really well, John. Keep it up. We're almost there."

It was getting late and I watched the sun set. We were now about seven miles from the finish. Really close. I rode another half hour in the dark until 8 p.m. when we finally reached the city limit sign. Today's total ascent: 9,396 ft. We still had a few more miles to go to reach the fire station, but just seeing that city limit sign was such a huge victory! I kept pedaling. We came upon a fire engine on a call. I wondered if the crew would even be at the fire station when we reached it. We were now really close. Two miles to go. From afar I could see the fire station lit up with flashing lights. The department had moved its engines out of the station. The flashing lights drew our attention. A bunch of firefighters with their families were waiting for us. To them, this was a big deal! What I thought was a fire engine on call a few miles back was actually their engine ready to guide us to the station. What a great welcome! I was charged. I had just pedaled 121 miles, and it was only 8 p.m. I had climbed almost two miles in ascent and I still felt great.

Sonia was there to greet me with a big hug. She had been getting updates most of the day from Tony and from my mom. So she knew the exact time I'd be arriving. I felt so happy to be here. The firefighters were happy I made it, too. I think Tony and I doubted whether we'd arrive today. But we did it!

With updates going to Sonia all day, the crew knew I had a tough day on the road, so they really catered to our needs. First, we took a group photo with Sonia. Then the chief presented us with a donation on behalf of the department. While this was going on I could smell dinner being cooked. They said they had been cooking all day. Let me tell you, it was one of the biggest firehouse dinners I have ever seen! They brought in RB, a firefighter who was also a professional chef. What an honor it was to be here with these guys! I felt so blessed. But I also felt sore all over. The guys gave me ice for my legs, and I ate and talked with everyone about our journey.

I finally turned in about midnight. Believe it or not, I was finding it difficult to fall asleep. I guess I was still excited about the nice people I just met — and the wonderful reception they had given us!

And that dinner......mmm!

Miles pedaled so far

2,234

Union, Mo., firefighters greet me at station.

Day

24

Tuesday, Oct. 2

Leaving Missouri: to Greenville, Illinois
Miles to pedal today
108

WHILE I WAS SLEEPING, RB and the crew were in the kitchen making breakfast for an army. The smell of the bacon wafted through the fire station. It wasn't even 7 a.m. yet. I was awake and getting out of bed. I walked to the kitchen and to a warm welcome. The guys had just finished cooking breakfast. All kinds of delicious looking food spread out before me: bacon, sausage, pancakes, biscuits, gravy, coffee, milk, orange juice. You name it. Large portions! RB was busy at work. I definitely would consume the calories I'd need for today. I wolfed down two plates brimming with food. What a meal!

After breakfast we began our morning blog estimating we had about 110 to 130 miles ahead of us today. It was the seventh day of the 11-day grind. I was almost out of the woods. Today we're heading for Greenville, Ill. Finally entering yet another state! We were noticing that time spent in each state was getting shorter and shorter. Probably because each state was smaller and smaller. After talking about general details we wished my mom a happy birthday. Sonia had come up with a bouquet of flowers for us to present to her "live" during the blog. We included several department members and Sonia in the blog as well. They talked about their department. The department was established in 1890

— and still had its original apparatus. Wow. Talk about history! We closed the blog singing "Happy Birthday" to my mom. She had been following every move we made, so I was glad we recognized her on her birthday.

Now for the difficult part: today's route. No one I had talked to was an avid rider. Nonetheless, a few good ideas did come our way. We began heading east, as usual. That's about as smart as I was. Tony checked the map. He hung back for a while to finish up the wash, upload the blog and prepare the vehicle. He always had a lot to do. With long days on the road, he had little time for rest. The wind today was gone, which was a welcome change. The hills became just small rolling hills. The more I pedaled east, the more the traffic increased. Tony caught up with me about 10 miles down the road. I wasn't hungry at this point. I'll be stuffed for the week with all the food I ate this morning. My bike for the most part had been holding up pretty well. Gears changed smoothly with little skipping. My body had a hint of soreness. Nothing Ibuprofen didn't fix.

Then, like in earlier days, all of a sudden we somehow ended up on a highway that we shouldn't have been on.

We continued on the highway because we didn't know where else to go. The shoulder was bumpy. Trash covered the side of the road. The problem with freeways was we had to cross exits and entrances. With traffic increasing, this was dangerous. After a few miles, there it was — a **Welcome to St. Louis** sign. Tony snapped a photo as I pedaled past. A few more miles on this major freeway and traffic conditions got worse. I almost got hit by two different cars in only one mile of travel. This kind of riding was illegal and dangerous. It was the closest call I had so far. Of course, there was a lot of horn blowing, yelling and even cursing. I decided this route wasn't working, so I took the next exit. Tony pored over the map for an alternate route.

The exit we had just taken would bring us right through the city of St. Louis to the famous Gateway Arch. We decided to go that way. A few miles into the city, we came upon a bike shop, South Side Cyclery. I figured this would be a good time for a tune up. And I'd have the spoke on my broken wheel repaired, too. The shop was loaded with customers. I went to the front desk and waited in line until I was helped. I asked how long it would take to get a tune up. He told me he'd have it tomorrow or the following day. Gulp! I explained that I was riding to New York and two days was out of the question. But I'd buy a few spare tubes for my journey, I added. The guy got excited and motioned me and my bike to the back of the shop. He introduced me to the staff, told them I was in the middle of a bicycle trip to New York and "urged" them to tune the bike right away. It was great, because they immediately stopped their work and began working on my bike. Wheels and tires came off. They added a new chain and lubricated gears. They even fixed my rare broken spoke. Before long, my bike was back in racing condition. They gave me the extra tubes I needed. They didn't charge us a dime! We took a photo before we left. Then I was back on the road heading north, parallel to the Mississippi River.

I kept pedaling northeast till I was in the center of the city. I knew we were in St. Louis. I could see the Gateway Arch. The arch wasn't in our plan, but by almost getting hit by two cars we were kind of guided to this place.

The Gateway Arch was high. Tourists from all over the world come to see this attraction. And here I rode my bike from California to get here. It's the world's biggest arch and it's called the Gateway because it's gateway to the west. Tony and I took an opportunity for a lengthy photo shoot. After all, we reasoned, it isn't every day you ride your bike here. We shared our story with tourists, then eventually continued our journey. We still had a lot of ground to cover today. Not a day passed when we didn't end up in an unusual location. I just wished we had more time to enjoy it.

I pedaled through busy St. Louis at a slow but steady pace. I had no idea where I was going. I just kept an eye on the heavy traffic. Tony said we needed to head about 10 miles north, then cross the Mississippi. That would take us into yet another state — Illinois! I did the 10 miles with little effort. At different times on the trip I was actually surprised at what we were doing. This was one of those times. Here we were crossing the Mississippi River — over a bridge, in fact, that prohibited bicycle riders. Sure enough, there was the Illinois state sign. Tony took the photo. I kept riding.

I pedaled for a few miles illegally, then pulled off the road to regroup. I still had many miles left for the day. Tony looked at the roads and thought they were complicated and confusing. He'd ride ahead of me, he said, to guide me. I was going through different areas: private roads, county roads, sometimes freeways and sometimes highways. Traffic began to thin out as we left St. Louis.

We had our first Illinois encounter as we moved through a small town. A driver began blowing her car horn at us. Tony wasn't blocking the road and I was surely off the roadway. So I wondered what we were doing wrong. The car passed me and pulled up next to Tony. I didn't know what was going on. A woman in the car was talking to Tony. I couldn't hear their conversation, so I just kept pedaling. As I followed, Tony and the car pulled into a driveway. A woman and two children got out.

She was beeping not to blow past us but to find out what our ride was all about. Another case of meeting the nicest people in the country. The woman introduced herself as Pat. Her children were Riley and Porter. Tony gave the children fire department stickers and coloring books. We talked about Lauren's Ride and what we had accomplished so far. We snapped photos with Pat and the children. Such nice people, we thought.

I couldn't wait to be beeped again.

Like the past few days, the last half of today's ride was challenging. The hills weren't too steep, but my legs were sore. Each day they felt tighter and sorer. The key to success was that I'd take a break every 10 miles. I absolutely had to do it this way. I would ride, power through, then pause for a break. As I rested Tony would read comments that came in from back home, then encourage me to keep pedaling. He would update me on the route with the number of miles left for the day. This always made the goal seem achievable. And it gave me a visual goal. For example, I'd tell myself I have only three more sets of 10 miles.

Rams mascot shows up as I pass through town.

Then only two more sets of 10 miles. They were manageable sections. At rest stops I would sometimes telephone my friends, my family, my co-workers. Thank God for mobile phones! One thing that pushed me was the thought of finishing for the day. I knew the sooner I finished the sooner I could rest and meet people to share our cause.

It was 8 p.m. when we finally reached our goal — Greenville. I didn't see a city limit sign. This town was really small. The chief, Bill Johnston of the Greenville Fire Protection District, met us at the hotel where we'd be staying. He had set up the lodging and had organized a small dinner for us. Since we didn't have a fire station or city limit sign here in Greenville, I decided that I would just take a photo next to the chief holding up my bike.

I had pedaled 118 miles for the day and had an ascension of 4,435 ft. Still a comfortable amount of hills, but nothing compared to the hills in Missouri. So day seven of the 11-day set was complete. I had now completed 24 out of 36 days of the trip. Which meant I had finished two-thirds of the trip. No turning back now, we joked. Not only that, but we were still on schedule despite the lengthy detours we encountered. I figured I was pretty much home free if I could just complete the next few days. Just four more long days of 100-mile sets left. Then Mike DeLeo would be back riding with me.

After our photo, Tony and I checked into the hotel. Dinner was next. We walked to the local restaurant where Chief Johnston and his friends were waiting.

At the table with the chief were his old friends Scott, Christy and Sherri. The chief first explained to us that Darrell had contacted him a few weeks back. When he heard that a firefighter was riding his bike to help his injured sister, he offered to help. He reminded us that the fire service is a brotherhood that looks out for each other. We told Chief Johnston we were thankful.

Sherri was a writer who owned a tractor business. She had just traveled by tractor more than 2,000 miles. She said she just steered; she didn't have to pedal like I did.

Christy worked with Scott and Sherri.

Like my sister, Scott had suffered a spinal cord injury when he was younger and was now in a wheelchair. His was also an injury that happened in water. We talked about his injury and how he adapted to live a normal life. He told us, for instance, that he designed his truck so he could automatically be lifted into the cab to drive. He said he would show us the truck after dinner. We talked about Lauren's injury and how it had affected her and my family. That's when the conversation got really deep.

He told me that when he was injured his brother had the hardest time accepting it. He and his brother had been so close. He said when someone you love so much is hurt it really hurts you, too, because there's nothing you can do to help. He said he thought being a firefighter made it even harder because we're paid to help people, and that a spinal cord injury is something that I could not fix. I remembered the conversation I had years earlier when Lauren explained to me that it was almost impossible for me to know what she was going through, as Scott explained to me that no one could ever feel what I must have felt when she was injured. He explained that so many people were there to help him and he knew the effect it had on his brother. What helped me the most was seeing Lauren accomplish so much and refuse to settle, not living like everyone else. Setting new limits and never settling. My sister had inspired me. Talking now with Scott made me realize how difficult things had been for me. I felt justified for feeling some of Lauren's pain.

Our dinner conversation moved in different directions. Sherri then decided she would ride a few miles with us the next morning. So we did a blog together at the restaurant, then headed out to see Scott's specially-equipped truck. Like Lauren, he was so inspiring. The truck was set up perfectly, and we shared these options with Lauren. I was so happy that Chief Johnston introduced us to his friends.

That night I finally got some needed rest. I would be seeing Sherri and Christy the next morning for the start of the eighth set of the 11.

We now had 24 days behind us. Only 12 days to go.

Miles pedaled so far
2,342

Day

25

Wednesday, Oct. 3

Illinois: Greenville to Sullivan
Miles to pedal today
124

SHERRY SCHAEFER IS THE OWNER and publisher of *Oliver Heritage* and *Heritage Iron* magazines. Her shop was a perfect place for us to shoot our morning blog. In the blog, I explained how I felt about the beginning of any journey in life. Every journey begins with a first step, but, before you can even take that first step, you must have confidence and faith in yourself. You must believe you are capable and good enough to do the job. You must then surround yourself with people who also believe in you and in your dreams. The steps then play out on their own. I am thankful for the whole team and what everyone has been doing to make this ride such a success. I am not an expert in the many facets of this ride. But so many people who stepped up to help were experts.

WHILE I WAS RECORDING this blog, so many things had been happening behind the scenes. Some I knew about, and some I had no idea about. For example, I learned that interested people from around the world were planning to rendezvous with us at the end of the ride. Much of this was a complete surprise to me. Each day these people called my mom and dad to ask where to stay in New York City, and where to be and what time to be there. My mom and Lauren were spending hours each day still sending thank you cards to the growing number of donors. It certainly looked as if these donations would help us get Lauren her car. My mom was trying to organize this big ending where our family and friends would be at the Brooklyn Bridge finish line to greet me. Each day more people called to tell her they were coming. Mom didn't know New York that well, so this was becoming a challenge. The Brooklyn Bridge is busy with foot traffic to begin with. It would become a real busy place for me to finish the ride. Believe me, the logistics were complicated for putting the finish-line celebration together.

How do we get 100 people, coming from different parts of the country, to Staten Island for a welcoming ceremony, then to the Brooklyn Bridge finish line, and then back to Staten Island for a celebration dinner? My mom had a lot to figure out. Andy Meuerle in New Jersey and Bobby Williams in Staten Island had now jumped into the picture to work out final route details for The Ride's last two days. For these last two days I'd be pedaling through heavily congested areas. New York City alone had rules and regulations for bicyclists that you couldn't believe.

For a bike to make it from New Jersey to the Brooklyn Bridge is no simple task. It may look simple, but it's not. Believe me! To pull this off, Bobby for the past weeks had been in touch with the Port Authority of New York and New Jersey, New York City Police Dept., New York City Fire Dept., Staten Island Lodge of Elks, Fire Riders and Rolling Thunder motorcycle groups, Wagner College chorus singers and assorted and sundry other organizations.

Andy was dealing with the New Jersey State Police and the Jersey side of the Port Authority of New York and New Jersey, which had jurisdiction over the Outerbridge Crossing connecting New Jersey to Staten Island. Both Andy and Bobby on the East Coast, and my mom on the West Coast, were now talking by telephone to come up with the best plan. Andy had ridden a road bike most of his life, so he was familiar with logistics the pair faced.

He said later that just the thought of bicycling from Freehold, N.J., to the Brooklyn Bridge sounded nearly impossible. He had several discussions with my dad to see if maybe we could think of a different place to end, if the planning got too crazy. Andy began with a letter to the New Jersey State Police. When he and Bobby talked for the first time he thought Bobby was crazy thinking that these agencies would work together to close lanes on major roads in New Jersey and Staten Island as we came through on bikes. Bobby Williams, on the other hand, was on the New York side. He felt sure everything would work out the way we wanted. It was truly a good balance of these two guys working together. It was sort of how Mike DeLeo and I initially planned things. I shot for the moon and Mike kept me grounded with the finer details and worst case scenarios to my plans.

So Andy was quite surprised that the New Jersey State Police even responded to his letter. Yes, the police said, they were certainly aware of Lauren's Ride. And they agreed to cooperate with us. First, they told Andy, they needed to know our exact travel route. But at that point Andy and Bobby hadn't yet devised the final route.

The question before them was how to get an unknown number of bike riders — it looked like maybe 50 bicyclists planned to join me for the last leg — through the busiest city in the United States? This is the planning stage they were working on only 12 days before my finish. When they spoke with me by phone, however, they were excited and told me all the details were being worked out. I found out later they never mentioned the problems, concerns and worries they faced. Bobby would tell me that everyone in Staten Island was excited and ready to give us a big New York City welcome. Hearing about this incredible ending kept me driven. The only thing they stressed was that I absolutely positively had to arrive in New York on the planned date of Sunday, Oct. 14. Not Saturday. Not Monday. No other day would work, what with heavy city traffic and the multiple agencies coordinating this event. Sunday would be *the* day to pull this off. So it looked as if I couldn't vary my schedule. After the New Jersey State Police contacted Andy, he and Bobby decided they would drive over a few possible routes from Staten Island to the Brooklyn Bridge to get a feel for what would work best.

MEANWHILE, BACK HOME in San Francisco, Lyn was still busy every day uploading photos and blogs, updating the donor list and speaking with business firms. Donations continued to pour in. She was working two full time jobs — hers and this one.

As we progressed, many of my friends, such as John Reynolds, told me he was so sorry he couldn't make it to the Brooklyn Bridge finish. Ha, ha! In reality, he and his family were planning to travel to the New York finish. John was editing a video that he hoped to play at the Staten Island celebration dinner. I remember talking with him explaining how much it would mean to me if he could make it to New York, and that I would even help pay for the airline flight. He said, "Sorry man, I just really can't make it because of work and family. My daughter is too young and I need to be here for my family."

I believed him.

Nick Ciardella, my first fire captain, his sister and her daughter had bought plane tickets and were getting ready for the trip to New York.

Cousins from England, John and Rachael Byrne, bought their tickets weeks before and were preparing to travel to New York.

Relatives from all over California were preparing to travel to New York.

Everyone did a beautiful job of keeping it all quiet. They even lied to me when we spoke.

Lauren was finishing up school and getting excited. This would be her first time on a plane since the accident. Lots of things were happening night and day, really too much to capture. Mike DeLeo finished up volunteering at the cancer camp and was anxious to rejoin me on the road. He realized, by watching our daily blogs, that my days were becoming more difficult. Darrell was like a hawk with his roadmaps, checking daily from his office back home to make sure we would encounter no curve balls or surprises.

My relatives in New Jersey were offering their homes to those who would need a place to stay.

Meanwhile, I had more than 1,000 miles still to travel, and another tough day ahead of me on the schedule.

TODAY WAS DAY 25 of my 36 day ride. It was the eighth day of a string of 11 days that I'd never forget. I was worn down physically, but was be-

Sherry Schaefer rides with me for a few hours.

ing held together with nothing more than love and support. I was really sore today, more than normal. Just knowing what was being planned for my finish, I now had to complete each day on time. I had planned a tough schedule for myself, but the outcome of this ride was worth the pain I was experiencing. We were meeting our fundraising goal. My biggest fear was not raising the money. Chief Bill had planned a radio interview for me after the morning blog. Today I had a 110-mile day ahead of me. Manageable, I thought. Only ten more miles than the usual 100. On the blog I delivered my thoughts about the upcoming day. Then Sherry told viewers about her barn. She would begin the day riding with me. She had a lot of energy and loved what she did. She was passionate about life. She explained her family business and was happy we did the blog in her barn. Tony explained the tough last few days and we tried to focus on the day ahead. That concluded our blog.

As we prepared to leave, I noticed the rubber tube in my tire was sticking out of the sidewall, so I changed the tire with a spare. We took photos with the group, then shoved off. Whenever someone else rode with me, our conversation usually would divert me from thinking about the miles ahead. Today was such a nice day to ride. Illinois was beautiful. The roads were smooth. I encountered little or no traffic. There was no wind, just a calm sunny day. It must have been the nicest day of the ride so far. Sherry and I kept a good pace together, and Sherry brainstormed on who she could contact about this ride story. After all, as a writer she had a lot of media connections. We had a nice ride together for 18 miles. Then we stopped for lunch at Denny's. We took a photo together holding our bikes in the air. We ate lunch. Then it was back on the road. By now it was 1 p.m., and I still had about 90 miles to go.

Reaching the end of the difficult 11 days would give me mental relief. If I could just get through these last few long days, an 80-mile day would be simple. I had 90 miles left for today so I started doing the math. Ninety divided by 15 equals six. If I rode for six hours, at a pace of 15 miles an hour I would arrive in Sullivan, Ind., about 7 p.m. That seemed doable. I was taking 800 to 3200 MG of Ibuprofen throughout the day to kill pain and reduce swelling of different parts of my body. Although my hips and IT band really hurt, my whole body was sore. I didn't realize it during the morning, but today I would be entering yet another state — Indiana. I talked for several hours by phone with mom and dad. Mom told me some things she was organizing for my finish, and I realized she was excited — and really overwhelmed. She always had good news to share with me. She just couldn't share all the secret things that were happening. She always asked me for the names and addresses of people who made donations so she could thank them. We would talk about who each new donor was, and we would try to figure out how they found out about The Ride. I was on schedule for my day's goal. After getting off the phone I kept my pace and figured I'd arrive on time.

I hit Indiana hours later. A large blue sign proclaimed:

Welcome to Indiana
Crossroads of America
Lincoln's Boyhood Home

Now here I was in the state in which Abraham Lincoln grew up. To think, he was the person who changed so many lives. Every state had a different look and feel to it. I mean, it was all the same United States, but I always felt small differences as I rode through each state. Sometimes it was the topography; sometimes it was the people; sometimes it was the wind. Indiana had a feel that was different than other states. It felt special to me.

I kept focused on my pace all day. It was paying off. We were on track. I could see the sun setting. Limited sunlight remained. And I still had about two hours to go. My IT bands and hips really hurt now. I could feel the pain every time I turned a pedal. According to Tony's GPS, we had about 30 miles to go. It would take about 2 hours at a 15 mile-an-hour pace. It was now 5:30 p.m. We would arrive just before dark. We decided to go with our ten mile strategy: I would ride 10 miles, take a break, then resume. Three sets of those and we were there. I powered through the first ten miles. I was in pain, but the beautiful scenery, and the fact that I was almost there, kept me pedaling.

Time for a break. I got into the car, spread out on a seat, stuck my legs through the window and drank water. We had 20 miles ahead. It was strange, but it was hard to picture finishing the ride today. I was spent. I mean, really spent. Then Tony said it's time for 10 more miles. He read me some messages from back home, I put on music, then powered through the next 45 minutes. I couldn't wait to be done for the day. It was like I was *almost* at the finish line — but it was *so* far away. After some small hills and pleasant views, I watched my speedometer reach the 100-mile mark. I had 14 miles left. I then watched the miles roll up to 104. This was my break time. We had about half an hour of daylight left. It was working out nearly perfectly. I took a short break. Then it was back on the road. Tony was ahead of me as the sun was setting behind me. Looking in all directions was so beautiful, with shadows and colors jumping out as the sun set behind us. We were almost at Sullivan, our stopping point. As I looked at my phone, I realized we entered another time zone — and lost still *another* hour. I really didn't care this time, because we were almost there. A few more miles into riding, the sun had finally set. I was at 109 miles for the day. I had a mere five miles left. I took a quick break and sat in the chase vehicle.

Then Tony dropped a bomb: he said no, in fact I had *15* miles left.

I was crushed. I grabbed my phone and looked it up myself. Yep, Tony was correct: It showed 15 miles to go. I walked to the road and sat on the edge.

Maybe I bit off more than I could chew with this cross-country trip, I thought. Maybe I won't be able to finish it after all. I was confused. I didn't know what to think. Or what to do. Fifteen more miles?

It was dark. I took off my shoes. I felt I was finished for good. The news was too much for me. I was overwhelmed. I felt like I had just lost part of me. I didn't know how I would ever ride the next five miles, let alone the next 15! I lay down and closed my eyes for a while.

I had reached my mental and physical limit.

My legs were killing me. I couldn't take the extra ten miles. My eyes teared. I felt that I wouldn't be able to finish today's ride. I had come so far…and not to finish on time. Hard to believe. We had completed the first 24 days on time. Now I was having a really difficult time thinking of failure.

I was beat to you-know-what.

I faced the agony of defeat.

I asked Tony *how* his GPS could be so far off. I even thought that maybe he was changing it to help me in some way. He was silent. After a while I wanted to rest and not think of anything, so I lay there and just tried to focus on breathing.

My entire body was aching now more than it had at any other time of the trip.

I might disappoint everyone who is counting on me to complete this ride. The human body can take only so much abuse.

I didn't move for a half hour.

But I eventually talked myself into pedaling at least one more mile.

I put on my shoes and stood up, and I just felt kind of miserable and worthless. I was broken. This is the first time on the trip I felt this way. It was dark and now getting cold.

This was the most difficult point in the ride. It took everything I had to get back on my bike. I took off slowly. And yes, I somehow managed to complete the mile. I stopped the bike for a few seconds, got off, paused, then got back on and pedaled yet another mile.

Torture. Plain torture.

I repeated this routine each mile. Each time I stopped, I got off the bike and began telling myself out loud that, yes, I could keep going. In fact, I *had* to keep going.

I'd be kidding you if I told you it wasn't torture.

I did this for two straight hours. Two…straight…hours!

Then, all of a sudden, a fire engine, police car and ambulance — all with flashing lights — slowly came into view! *Yes,* I thought. The Lord has been watching! The emergency equipment had come to escort me to their city. They were there to carry me the rest of the way. OMG!

I had about five miles to go. I don't know how to explain it, but that sight instantly raised my spirits. I needed a mental push of support because I had run out. We were close to getting there, and they showed up to help me to finish the day. Oh, baby! Through the dark I could see the vehicles lighting up the whole night with flashes of red and blue.

We passed the city limit sign for Sullivan. Forget the usual photo, I told myself. I wanted to just keep riding. It may have been the only city on the trip that I didn't stop to take a city limit sign photo. It was now 9 p.m. We continued through the city and pulled up to the fire station. A noisy crowd was waiting. They had planned a large dinner celebration, and had been waiting and waiting. I could see barbecue being cooked in the engine bay.

I had pedaled 114 miles for the day, with an ascent of 2,661 ft. I was lucky to have made it. In fact, after these past few hours, I felt lucky to be alive!

I struggled to get off my bike. Picture it. I was paralyzed. I could just about move. I was so stiff and sore I could barely dismount and walk. Tony made my Fluid recovery drink and asked a firefighter for ice for my legs. After taking some Ibuprofen, I met everyone who had patiently waited hours for me to arrive. We sat down for dinner and chatted about the last few days on the road, and the struggles I faced.

The people could tell I was sore. Then Tony brought out Darrell the turtle — an instant hit with the children. They played with Darrell all night. During dinner guests offered donations. After dinner, Chief Rob Robertson presented me with a large official donation from his fire department.

Sitting with these wonderful people for a few hours, however, I somehow managed to forget my pain.

It was yet another enjoyable dinner party. Later, we took group photos and cleaned up. I drank as much water as I could to flush out the lactic acids. Tony went to work laundering two days of dirty clothes while I routinely checked my bike. The bike looked good and ready for the next day's ride. It was holding up for me, I reasoned, so *I* need to hold up for Lauren.

After everybody left for the evening, the on-duty fire crew showed us to our beds.

Usually I would fall asleep easily after a long day's ride. But tonight for the first time I questioned myself as I lay on my back in bed. I had gone through physical hell today. How could I travel another 125 miles tomorrow, I wondered? I couldn't picture myself pedaling another day. I wasn't ready to accept failure. But I couldn't figure out for the life

Sunsets are absolutely breathtaking as I pedal across the country.

of me how I would physically continue pedaling. I kept thinking and thinking and thinking about it. Perhaps the end is near, I thought.

THEN IT HAPPENED. Chief Robertson returned to the fire station, knocked on the door and entered our room. His young daughter, Shaelyn, was with him.

"I'm sorry to wake you guys up, but I have another donation to make," he said.

He explained that when he and his family returned home after the dinner celebration, Shaelyn quietly walked to her room to fetch her piggy bank. With her small piggy bank in her outstretched hands, she told her father she wanted to donate money to "help them."

Shaelyn and her dad emptied the piggy bank and now returned to the station to give me this special donation.

"Shaelyn has something for you, John," the chief said.

Shaelyn held out her hand. It contained some pennies, nickels, dimes and a single quarter. Every cent she had saved.

I was speechless. We all watched in wide-eyed silence for a long minute.

"Tell you what, Shaelyn. I'll take this quarter and I'll tape it to my bike," I said. "Your quarter will ride with me across the country, and if

Little Shaelyn Robertson is all smiles as she donates piggy bank savings to help my sister Lauren.

the going gets tough as I pedal along, I'll look down at the quarter for help, and I'll remember you."

The youngster smiled sheepishly.

Who could sleep after that?

So we all went downstairs to my bike. With Shaelyn and her dad watching, I taped the quarter right next to Kaden's quarter. "Thank you, Shaelyn," I said.

Then little Shaelyn gave me a big, long hug.

I went back to bed.

Tomorrow might not be such a bad day after all, I thought. And I fell asleep in no time.

Miles pedaled so far

2,466

Day

26

Thursday, Oct. 4

Leaving Illinois: to Greensburg, Indiana
Miles to pedal today
124

I WOKE UP AT 8 A.M. feeling horrible. I thought I would go back to sleep. But I smelled bacon cooking in the kitchen. Adele Russell, an ambulance paramedic, had gone to a store after dinner last night and bought food so she could make breakfast for us. Pancakes, bacon and a few other breakfast treats were on the stove. I was thankful. So I joined the gang for breakfast. It was so nice of Adele to go out of her way for us. Breakfast really hit the spot. I ate — then I went back to sleep. I asked Tony to wake me up at 9:30. I woke up and tried to convince myself to ride today. Just three more long days, I thought, and a few shorter days will follow. Tony brought me Ibuprofen. I finally got out of bed. I was so tight and sore, mostly in my legs. After I stretched out on the floor, we shot our morning blog to include the on-duty crew and fire chief. In the blog I explained that I was really worn out and sore. We related events that occurred the day before. Then it was time to begin the process of getting on the road.

It was 10 a.m. when we finally went outside. I decided that today I would keep a slow pace and end up wherever I ended up. I know I had a lot of love and support behind me, and if I didn't arrive at the appointed time tonight, everyone would understand. I had to tell myself this to get going, but in all reality, I knew I would keep pedaling until I couldn't pedal anymore.

Today's route showed me pedaling 140 miles. I thought it would be a 130-mile day. I was wrong again. The extra 10 miles would be a lot of extra riding, given my beat-to-hell condition. The "Hey, let's just ride east" idea wouldn't hold water today. I really had to cover the least possible number of miles.

So we looked at alternate routes. We talked with the fire crew for ideas. Bingo! They charted a route of 111 miles. That was great. I mean, we began the day with 140 miles. Now we're down to 111. With that I started pedaling. I had covered 2,466 miles so far from day one! If all goes well, I'll hit the 2,500-milestone sometime today. And it's only 34 miles away. So I decided to focus on this short-range milestone. Tony checked the weather and saw signs of rain, but the mass seemed about 100 miles away. I was already at my physical limit. Rain would have driven me over the top. I'm sure I'd have a meltdown.

Tony ran some errands in town as I began pedaling. He bought snacks. He was always on the lookout for new hats for us to wear in our blogs. The ice chest again needed refilling, so he had to hunt for ice every day. His job was never done.

As I rode, the pain in my hip grew worse. It went down the side of my legs. Meanwhile, Mike DeLeo had finished his service at the camp. He had been watching the daily blogs, and he could tell I was now hurting. To cheer me up, he and his daughter did a music video to let me know he was there for me. He began the video by saying he noticed that I had a few rough days, and that he couldn't wait to be back riding with me. He was never one to be on video playing the guitar and singing, but for this video he played the song "Home" by Phillip Phillips. The song had come on the radio the morning we were heading to the Golden Gate Bridge. As it played, everyone in the car stopped talking and just listened to the words. We thought the song was being played just for us.

> *Hold on to me as we go,*
> *as we roll down this unfamiliar road.*
> *Just know you're not alone,*
> *I'm gonna make this place your home.*

His video was everything I needed for today's ride.

I stopped focusing on my soreness, pain and the miles I had left today. Instead, I focused on the present — where I was. It was a beautiful day. The air was crisp, the sky cloudless. I thought about how lucky I was to do this for Lauren in a place as beautiful as this! I thought about all the people who were volunteering their time and energy to make this dream possible. I had no idea how this ride would affect us. The ride had grown larger than I had ever imagined. The more I thought about these things, the happier I became.

Tony finally caught up and drove behind me. We were cruising through Indiana. As we rode, I couldn't believe that we were about to complete 2,500 miles. Twenty five hundred miles! This was an accomplishment. As the speedometer changed from 33.9 to 34, we ended up next to a grassy field. Twenty five hundred miles! Even with our slower pace today, we were making good time. Tony drew a 2,500-sign. I made a few phone calls telling people we had finally reached a special milestone. We took photos. One was with Tony lying on the grass looking dead, with the 2,500 mile sign resting on him. I don't know which of us was getting beat up more. After our exciting — but short — victory, we continued on.

The low rolling hills with fall colors were beautiful. I took no real rest stops today. I just kept focusing and pedaling. My fear was that if I stopped I wouldn't be able to get going again. So I just kept moving. I called and talked to my friends and family. Each conversation took me a few more miles. Mom gave me a progress report: plans for my finish at the Brooklyn Bridge were coming together. She was talking with so many relatives, even some she had never met. Every conversation she had was so positive and exciting, she told me. Every relative she spoke to was so excited to be traveling to Freehold, N. J., and then to the Brooklyn Bridge in New York. It made me feel really good to hear this. I figured, if they were going to be at the finish line, I just *had* to be there, too.

Physically exhausted or not, I couldn't quit.

I spent most of the day in phone conversation. At the 80-mile mark, I felt really sore. I knew I had to stop for a break. I sat down and called dad to talk. He told me that if I needed a break, take a break. So I took a short break. When I returned pedaling, I talked with him for more than two hours, until I reached the 100-mile mark. I had about 11 miles still to go today, so I told dad I could take it from here. I checked with Tony. He showed 11 miles, too.

I took more Ibuprofen, then started pedaling to finish the final 11 miles. Like the day before, the sun was starting to show signs of setting. 101, 102, 103, 104, 105, 106, 107 miles. I knocked off seven miles while Tony was taking photos of the sun setting behind me. I felt really good knowing we were near the end. I didn't want to ride too long in the dark, as I did the night before. When the sun set, I put on a reflective safety jacket and again checked the number of remaining miles.

But this time Tony told me his GPS was showing 17 miles to go. What? Rats. Here we go again, I thought. How the hell could this happen two days in a row? No way I could pedal 17 more miles. Eleven would be torture enough.

I sat down on the side of the road as I did the day before. A few minutes passed. I stared at the quarters taped to my bike from little Kaden and Shaelyn. And I thought about each of the two children, and about how excited they were to help my sister.

A few more minutes passed in silence.

I got back on my bike and started riding in silence. And I couldn't help looking down at the taped quarters from the two kids. I was determined more than ever to keep going.

After a few miles I came upon a fire chief's car on the side of the road. Wow! It was the light at the end of a dark road. He was there to escort me into town, he said. From that moment it took me about 90 minutes to reach the city limit sign. Seeing that city limit sign made me cry. I really didn't think I would reach Greensburg tonight. And I never thought I would ever cry. I was having such a struggle the past few days. The miles were taking a toll on my body and mind. I had a huge sense of relief knowing that I had made it. That I hadn't failed.

I was finishing the ninth day of the 11 long-day stretch. Tomorrow would drop back down to 100 miles again. It was now really dark. We

Tony shows just how excited he is to reach 2,500-mile mark.

had to use headlights from both vehicles to light up the photo. It was again difficult for me to get off the bike. I walked over to the sign and composed myself for a few photos. It was even difficult to raise the bike up with my arms. Now my shoulders and arms were sore and stiff.

I got back on the bike and pedaled to the fire station. We had traveled 124 miles for the day. I felt so sore, but I felt so much better knowing I had completed this day. Most of the Greensburg Fire Department was there — on-duty and off-duty firefighters. When Chief Scott Chasteen got out of his car I gave him a big hug. I don't know if he knew how badly I needed his escort into town. We took some photos, as usual. Then, good news: Chief Chasteen told me he had arranged for chiropractor Deanna Pacilio to help me out. Perfect, I thought! I'm ready to collapse.

We ate dinner with the crew. Then Dr. Pacilio arrived. She set up her table in the engine bay and did a head-to-toe assessment of my body. I was "off" and had a lot of swelling in different areas, she told me. As if I didn't know. Just touching some areas on my body hurt. The doctor made adjustments from my neck to my toes. After riding a bike 2,500 miles one's toes get sore. Believe me. They do. I know what I'm talking about. As I was being worked on, Chief Chasteen said the department had contacted local newspapers and radio stations about my unusual cross-country bicycle ride, and that a few would contact us tonight or tomorrow for interviews. Sure enough, as the doctor finished adjusting me, the press began to arrive.

Dr. Pacilio told me to drink a lot of water tonight to release the toxins. She said she would return in the morning for a few more adjustments. The nighttime would allow some of the swelling to go down.

IT WAS 10 P.M. and I was being interviewed for the next day's paper. The newspaper interview procedure was exciting. What seemed like such a rough day was turning into a positive one. These are the things I remember today. After the interview, I received a phone call from the *Greensburg Daily News*. As I said before, the more coverage I received, the more donations came in. After the press interviews, we did our nightly blog. Participating were Tony, Chief Chasteen, Firefighter Chuck, Darrell the turtle and me. I looked as if I was really beat up. I explained the day's ride. Tony talked about the rough day on the road. The chief thanked us for staying with them, then gave a brief history of his department and town. He explained that the courthouse had a tree growing out of its roof, and that we should see it before we left town in the morning. Firefighter Chuck spoke last. He was the one at the station who was most excited for us to be there. He related that he had spent most of the night contacting other fire stations along our route to see if any other fire company could pitch in to help. He started off saying to viewers, "If you're watching this and you have any family issues, ask yourself, would you ride 3,500 miles on your bicycle for your sister?"

His statement brought up an important point. People who met me thought I was the most wonderful brother in the world. Parents used the Lauren's Ride story as an example of what it was to be a brother, and how family members should treat each other. Believe me, I wasn't always this kind of brother. My family is like every other family. We had our struggles. We fought. We were mad at each other.

But, when it really mattered, we were there for each other. Every time. My parents did so much for Lauren and me as we grew up. They taught us values and work ethics.

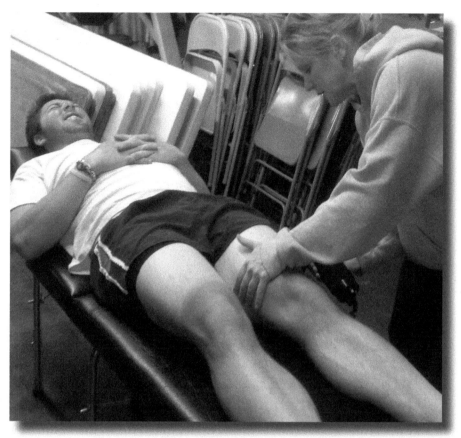

Chiropractor Deanna Pacilio gives me a painful —
but needed — 2,500-mile tune-up.

I heard stories as I pedaled across the country of family members who hadn't talked to one other in months or years over some minor disagreement. Lauren and I at times shared that same relationship. We didn't always have the relationship we have now. You learn from your parents, friends and your education about how to communicate in relationships. Each parent tries his or her best, from what they learned from *their* parents, to raise their children. Some people can break the chain of bad habits; some pass bad habits on. Having attention-deficit disorder as a child, I grew up to become scared of rejection and of being vulnerable. I was told that I was a baby if I cried, and that I didn't understand how to communicate correctly. This carried into my adulthood until I grew as a person and learned to take risks by opening up and communicating. Early on, if someone hurt me, I wouldn't talk to that person for days, weeks or months, or until I really needed to. I always hoped the problem would just resolve itself.

When that didn't work, I turned to drinking. Believe me, liquor just leads to more depression and unhappiness. And to more problems.

It took years for me to be comfortable with communicating about how I felt, especially when I was sad or hurt. Attending college and talking with Mike DeLeo helped a lot. I had problems with rejection and self-worth. My defense mechanism simply was to be angry, or short. I would assume things would fail or I was already not good enough to avoid the chance of rejection. The funny thing is that would lead to failure each time.

The changes for me were small changes that can change anyone. The ability to communicate is the biggest one. Letting people know how you feel. Don't assume. Talk things out. Don't hold expectations. Understand that everyone fails at one time or another. Doing your best is all you can do. These small changes turned my relationships with family, friends and co-workers into much healthier relationships. My life took a different path and my life became a happier one with healthier relationships. We just have the ability to learn from one another and we try to do our best. These small changes turned into bigger changes, and into a chain of healthy events that led to this cross-country bike ride to help my sister. As I said, change starts off small. The small decisions can have a magnitude of something bigger than we would ever imagine.

We ended the blog. I spent the rest of the night drinking water and shooting the breeze with Chuck. Eventually I fell asleep.

Miles pedaled so far
2,590

27

Friday, Oct. 5

Leaving Indiana: to Blanchester, Ohio
Miles to pedal today
100

I GOT UP SEVERAL TIMES during the night to use the bathroom. I must have been flushing all the toxins out of my system. I woke up around 8 a.m. and felt better than I did the day before. I had good things to focus on this morning: media interviews and interesting conversation with guys at the station. Dr. Pacilio changed her morning office schedule for me, and after breakfast she made even more adjustments. After she did a head-to-toe again, she said I was looking a lot better, but that I still needed a few more adjustments. She made the adjustments, then checked Tony out. He had been sitting in a car for 26 days. She made a few adjustments on Tony. After we were both tuned up and ready to go, we did our morning blog.

We blogged from the kitchen with the crew in the background cooking while getting ready for a chili cook-off fund-raiser. They were cooking 100 pounds of ground beef. We talked about today's planned route and all the media coverage we received. It must have been six interviews either in person or on the phone. Our route for today looked to be about 100 miles. The crew told us there were few hills between here and Blanchester. That was good news. Today was the next to last day of the 100-mile days. And today we would reach another state — Ohio.

Bad weather was still forecast near us, but it wouldn't cross our path. I looked and felt so much better today. The guys told me that I looked a lot like National Football League quarterback Andrew Luck of the Indianapolis Colts, so there were a lot of jokes during the blog, such as I had a game this week and had to cut the bike ride short. Tony said, "Have you ever seen John throw a football? Andrew Luck can't pedal a bike like this man." I closed the blog feeling thankful, and I said we have the right luck in the right places on this ride.

It was 10:30 a.m. when we were ready to go. I felt that today I would finish before sunset, so the late start was okay. I didn't feel as if I was racing the clock today because we only had about 100 miles, and this would be obtainable. I didn't feel as stiff. Overall I felt really positive and thankful for what everyone had done for us. Before we left, I had one more telephone interview, and then we took a few photos together.

MEANWHILE, AS I WAS GETTING READY to leave Indiana, Andy and Bobby were meeting for the first time in New York. They decided to meet in person at the Staten Island Lodge of Elks to plan final details of the route from Staten Island to the Brooklyn Bridge. Andy had co-ordinated our route with the state police from Freehold, N. J., to the Outerbridge Crossing which connects New Jersey to New York. They would spend the day together driving the roads through Staten Island and Brooklyn directly to the Brooklyn Bridge. With that they'd choose the best bicycle route for me. This was an exciting day for them because each detail had to be reviewed and coordinated by multiple municipal agencies. As the vaudeville comedian Jimmy Durante used to say, "Everybody wants to get into the act."

Bobby and Andy were busy planning what they called my New York Welcome.

BACK IN INDIANA, I WAS OFF to conquer the day. Our first stop was down the street at City Hall. We had to see this tree growing out of the roof. Sure enough, it was just as they had explained, something I had never seen before. We took a few photos and then left Greensburg. Unlike most of our previous stops, tonight we would be staying with the

McFadden family rather than at a fire station.

The McFaddens had learned about Lauren's Ride from the RAAM website. As I explained earlier, Race Across America provides a predetermined course for cross country bicyclists to follow. The course went straight through the town where the McFaddens live. Early on in our planning stage, someone mentioned RAAM to me. I needed a route in that area, so I looked at the RAAM website. RAAM had routes posted, complete with elevations and mileage between different cities. I called and spoke with a company executive who explained that the route required no road closures and it covered roads that were generally safe. I asked if I could use their route for my ride and they said it shouldn't be a problem. That took care of most of our cross-country route. We needed that before anything else could get moving. I just had to plan from San Francisco to Needles, and then somewhere in West Virginia to New York City. Luckily, Amy and John McFadden were a time stop for this ride and were avid bike riders as well. Amy and John were a stop for many riders doing RAAM who rode 3,000 miles in 12 days. They had made several unsuccessful attempts to contact their local fire station, so they offered us use of their own home instead. They had been following our ride from the beginning. Darrell had been in contact with them a few times as we rode. Today he told us that John McFadden would ride with us later in the day.

As I rode, today felt a lot better. I felt looser, but just slightly sore. As I said time and time before, every mile after 100 became harder and harder. For example, miles 110 to 120 are much more difficult to pedal than are miles 100 to 110. The outside temperature was 75 degrees. It turned out to be a gorgeous day. I could see clouds in every direction except ahead of us. It was like we had someone looking over our journey. There was a storm on its way. As I pedaled, I knew today would be a good day.

We put in about 30 miles before I stopped for a break. I sat in the car while Tony showed me a car tire that was leaking air. We decided to keep going and find the closest tire shop, only a few miles down the road. We found the C and C Tire Firestone. Tony spoke to James from the store and explained we were short on time because we were on a special bike ride. Tony wondered if James could squeeze us in for a tire repair. He dropped what he was doing and brought us in. I ate lunch and napped in the car while the tire was repaired. Tony went to the thrift shop next door to look for more hats for the blogs.

I looked at my phone, then checked our location on Google Maps. We were so far east now. Last time I really looked we were in Kansas. That was hundreds of miles ago. We were so close now to our destination. I couldn't believe where we were on the map. It made me happy.

Tony returned as they were finishing the tire repair. James said the tire had to be replaced because workers discovered four holes in it. He refused to accept payment from us. We were both surprised by his kindness. Not only did he donate his time, he donated a brand new tire. We were meeting the best people in the world. We took a photo with James in front of the shop, then resumed our trip.

I was making good time today. I rode for another hour and a half, then checked Google Maps for my location. We were now in Ohio. I stopped to talk with Tony. But when he pulled over I could tell something was wrong. I asked him what was going on.

He said his sister called to tell him his mom was ill and had been rushed to a hospital. He said she wasn't doing well.

This was horrible news. I asked him what he needed and he said we just need to keep moving forward today and get to our destination.

I pushed hard and was making good time. No major events or pain as I rode, but I tried to figure out what we would do if Tony's mom got worse. At 5 p.m. we reached a restaurant to meet John McFadden and his buddy, Bobby Collins. We were at 80 miles for the day. John and Bobby were on their bikes. The first thing I asked them was how many more miles we had to go. John said about 15 or 20 miles. That was perfect. I was hoping it wasn't going to be another 120-mile day. No surprises today. We used the restroom, decided to skip eating here and finish the day pedaling instead. They took me on a bike-friendly scenic route. John said that parts of the ride were part of the RAAM route. Being on these roads, we lost Tony, who headed directly to the

Race Across America enthusiasts Bobby Collins, left, and John Mc-
Fadden cross paths with me at McFadden's home.

McFadden home. The pathways were beautiful. The leaves were vibrant.

MEANWHILE, IN NEW YORK, Bobby and Andy had arrived at the
Brooklyn Bridge on their test run. They were still having problems with
the overall route, but were now concentrating on the bridge part. Bad
road conditions were widespread in Brooklyn. After they had scouted
out a few options, they talked with my dad. The best and fastest way
to get to the Brooklyn Bridge was to bicycle over the Verrazzano-Narrows Bridge — which did not allow bikes. So they scratched that option.
My dad suggested the Staten Island Ferry to Manhattan. Bingo! That
was the answer. They all agreed. This way, we could visit Ground Zero
in Lower Manhattan as we passed it. This was an important logistical
solution. It cut a few miles off the ride for the day and made the ride

a much nicer one. So that was the route Bobby and Andy finally proposed. Bobby sent me a photo of the Brooklyn Bridge, telling me that everyone at the end of the line was ready for my arrival.

BACK IN INDIANA, WE PULLED UP to the McFadden home as I reached the 100-mile mark for the day. Just then rain began to fall. Tony was on his phone trying to learn more about his sick mom back home. I tried to see if I could help him, or if he needed anything, but he said no. Inside, I met John's wife Amy, their two children and a Spanish foreign exchange student who was staying with them. Their home was full of photos of bike riders from around the world who had traveled the RAAM course. They shared stories of these riders who had pedaled the course in eight to 12 days. I thought to myself, if they can do this course in eight days I can surely do coast-to-coast in 36. What was I complaining about? These riders would pedal 300 miles in a 24-hour period. The McFaddens had been part of the RAAM since 2009. Realizing what these riders accomplished made me feel stronger, and gave me faith that I would indeed finish.

I had the 10th day of the 11 tough days behind me. I only had one more tough day to go. I had completed 2,690 miles. I was feeling sore, but I felt like I was recovering from the pain. I had been lucky with the weather, but it was pouring outside now. I thought that tomorrow could be rough, with the rain, but I could do it.

We had dinner and did a blog together.

Afterwards, Tony went outside and just sat quietly on the porch the rest of the night.

I sat with him for a while, until we both went off to bed. He was in bad shape. I didn't know how to help him.

Miles pedaled so far
2,690

Day

28

Saturday, Oct. 6

Ohio: Blanchester to Athens
Miles to pedal today
117

I WOKE UP EARLY. I was sore and dehydrated. Figures, because I had been subjecting my body to a full race each day with no time to rest.

I looked outside to check the weather. As I opened the door I felt cold air hit my face. I was up before Tony today, which was unusual. It wasn't long before Tony appeared. I checked in with him to see if he needed anything, and he said no. We ate breakfast in the kitchen with the Mc-Fadden family. John McFadden would ride the first few miles with me today. We skipped the morning blog and I dressed warmly. I doubled the layers of clothing I usually wore. Forecast called for rain today, so I prepared for it. If I can get through today I'll have two low-mileage days ahead, I thought.

We finished breakfast at 9 a.m., and I was ready to face the day. We had 117 miles planned for today. John said the miles seemed about right. I took it slow as we started off because of icy condition. It was nice having John riding with me. We began to pedal. I felt really strong. I could usually tell by my fast pace. We were riding at about 20 to 24 miles an hour. It had been a long time since I had ridden at that pace. John planned to ride with me to the Martinsville Clark Township Fire Dept. station in the next town. He would have his wife pick him up there. The station was 10 miles away. He would be hitting 30 miles and I would be hitting 2,700 miles. That was an accomplishment in itself.

It was open house at the station when we arrived. Focus today was on fire prevention. We tried not to bombard them as they were getting ready, so we introduced ourselves and took a few pictures. John made a sign reading 30 miles and I made a sign that read 2,700. I thanked John for all he and his family had done to help us, including his riding with me the last two days. He knew how badly I needed company when pedaling.

I had the eye of the tiger today.

This would be the final day of the 11 straight over-100-mile days.

I felt I was out of the forest, so to speak, so was now able to see myself successfully arriving to New York on time. From day one, I insisted that I would actually *ride* every mile — and I was a man of my word. I kept my fast pace. I asked Tony if he was up to doing bottle exchanges today. He said he was. The few times we stopped I checked my phone for updates about his mom. Tony had 11 siblings so he needed to be in constant contact with his family about medical decisions. His mom had been moved to intensive care. I asked Tony if he wanted someone to replace him. He insisted we would complete the ride together. He just hoped that his mom would be able to see him when he got back home. Truly, Tony was making sacrifices for The Ride.

All I could do was power through without issues, which would give me necessary time to rest. I continued my pace until I began to feel a drag. I looked down and, sure enough, the back tire was going flat. This is flat #7. I had been knocking the miles out, so I actually welcomed this brief break.

It just so happened a hiker was walking by as I repaired the tire. I talked with her, telling her about my cross-country ride. And, of course, I gave her a flyer.

Five miles down the road the same tire went flat again. Flat #8. Rats! I had checked the tubing and wheel for punctures and penetrations the last time, and had not seen or felt anything. I took a closer look this time, and again found nothing wrong. The side of the road did have a

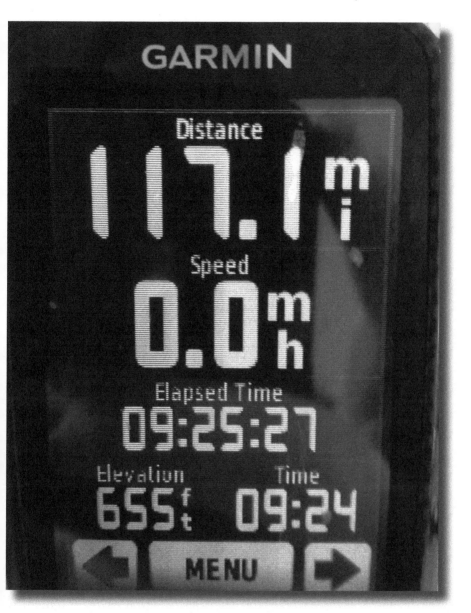

My trusty Garmin shows a 117-mile day. Electronics keep me posted with latest information.

lot of debris on it. I took a few spare parts out of the chase vehicle to
repair this flat. In no time I was back at my pace of 20 miles and hour.
I felt strong, and I focused like the eye of the tiger. I could finally see
the end. A few sprinkles hit us, but it was no real rain. Today was an

aggressive day. I think a few elements factored into this: it was the end of my 11-day set, the chiropractic adjustments, focusing on Tony and his problem instead of on myself and The Ride, and finally being able to picture the probability of success over failure.

I powered through until I approached the Athens city limit sign. I had pedaled 110 miles today, and had now chalked up a total of exactly 2,800 miles.

I can't believe that I pedaled an average of 100 miles a day for the past 28 days!

I think it hit me at this point, more than at any other point of the ride, about how far I was traveling, and what a special feat it was becoming. We took a few pictures. Tony told me he couldn't reach anyone at the Athens Fire Dept. He suggested we stop now to find a hotel instead. I asked him if it was okay if I pedaled seven more miles to meet the 117 miles for the day. It would give me a shorter day tomorrow, I reasoned. He agreed. A few hours of daylight remained.

I powered through the next seven miles with no problem. Today's ride completed four weeks of riding, and it marked completion of eleven 100-mile-plus days. I had an ascent of 5,114 ft. today. We realized Athens was a college town. The University of Ohio was right there. We checked into a hotel and decided to dine out. We had another nice milestone to celebrate, while Tony needed time to relax and unwind. With that said, we had decided before we began the trip that we would not drink alcohol. We represented many different elements, such as our fire department. We drove through Athens to see what the country's #3 college party town looked like. Nothing unusual. Eventually we discovered Cutlers Restaurant.

We entered and sat near guitarist Dale Kulchar. It was a relaxing evening so, we figured, why not go for a steak dinner? Might as well live high off the hog at least once, we told ourselves. We enjoyed dinner and talked with Dale during his breaks, telling him what we were up to. He gave Tony a music CD.

Back at our hotel we were receiving messages from people asking us if we had made it. We showered and shot our evening blog. I was feel-

28 days. 2,800 miles. Pretty good. We're getting there.

ing great, the best I had been feeling in days. It was a cold day, with light rain to annoy me. We learned later that heavier rain was falling all around us. But I lucked out. Next would be two short back-to-back days. Then we'd reach the Eastern Continental Divide, the hydrographic divide that separates the easterly Atlantic Seaboard watershed from the westerly Gulf of Mexico watershed.

Tony closed the blog by asking followers to pray for his mother.

Miles pedaled so far
2,807

29

Sunday, Oct 7

Leaving Ohio: to Ellenboro, West Virginia
Miles to pedal today
70

I SPENT THE MORNING sleeping in. Boy, I really needed the rest. Today's distance will be much shorter.

Tony had been up for some time now making phone calls for medical updates from back home. We did our morning blog. We only have eight days to go to the finish line. Yipee! What a relief! I knew Mike DeLeo was on his way to join me. What's more, I was now pretty certain that we would raise money for Lauren's special car. So the ride *is* working out, I thought. The simple thought of a bike fund-raiser for Lauren eventually turned into a major event; it turned into a beautiful ride. The universe took us in many directions the last few months, and it allowed me to experience exciting things from people.

It was then that I glanced out the window: rain.

I began pedaling at noon. Later than usual. In fact, *much* later than usual. All I had to do today was just keep an average pace and not injure myself. I was prepared for the wet weather with a few layers of clothing. A few miles into the ride it was still raining lightly. It was the first time I had gotten this wet on the trip. We had avoided rain for days. I was glad the rain at least hit on a day with minimal mileage. I was pedaling cautiously. Before long I reached a bridge that took me into West Virginia. Yes! Another state!

I could taste the finish line!

Tony took some photos at the city limit sign, and we continued on. A few miles of pedaling and, sure enough, another flat tire. This time it was my front tire. If you're counting, this is flat #9. The flat tires are coming more frequently now. I don't know why, but they are. I was cold and I wanted to repair the tire quickly. Luckily, it turned out to be a quick fix. I was about 50 miles behind our schedule for the day, so I kicked it up a notch to pick up speed. By 4 p.m. I had only 20 miles to go. Not bad, I thought. Even with the rain, the day was an easy one. Finally, time for a break. I really needed this break. At a rest stop Tony said he was unsuccessful in his attempts to contact the fire station where we were scheduled to stay. So we weren't sure if anyone would be there for our arrival. I decided to keep my fingers crossed and ride to the station anyway. Although Tony had a lot on his mind, he was still focusing on my safety.

MEANWHILE, LET'S LOOK IN at Mr. Tindula's 4th grade class in California. Mr. Tindula was playing guitar and teaching his pupils a new version of "This Land Is Your Land." He changed lyrics to reflect my cross-country bike ride — which the class has been religiously following. Mr. Tindula used my ride as part of his daily lesson plan. Each day the class would watch our blog. From the blog they learned more about each city and state through which we passed. And they talked about the different families we met. The class even made cards for me. Many of their parents sent messages to me, telling me what a positive impact my trip was having on their children. The whole thing really touched Tony and me.

I MADE EXCELLENT TIME TODAY covering the 70 miles to Ellenboro. We didn't see a city limit sign. So no photo. I headed to the Ellenboro fire station, but no one was there. I took photos outside the fire station, then went in search of a hotel. The closest hotel we found was about half an hour away. I wanted to be finished with the day, but it seemed as though a bit more travel was our only option.

We stayed at the quaint Hacket Hotel. It had five rooms, each decorat-

I feel wild and wonderful, too, because I'm closer to the end.

ed in a different theme. We stayed in the Williams room. Tony found a massage place, so he booked another massage for me. This would keep me loose for the rest of the trip. I was excited about another low-mileage day ahead of me. Now, with only seven days left on the entire trip, I felt so close to the finish line.

I thought about the next few days. A lot of friends and relatives were planning to be at the Brooklyn Bridge when I arrived. I was excited that I would finally get to see my mom and sister. Dad was staying home in California to anchor things there. And I thought about training for this journey. It's difficult to work a full time job while planning a cross-country bicycle ride. Looking back now, I don't know how I did it. But somehow I did it. I was thankful my body was still holding up.

The massage felt soothing. Just enough pressure so as not to be too sore the next day.

After my massage, we discovered that the chase vehicle had a front left flat tire. That was flat #3 for the chase vehicle. Tony had driven over a lot of debris. Luckily, Tony is a 20-year member of AAA. He called, gave our location and, like before, was transferred from one city to another. They were trying to figure out how to get help to us. Finally, they gave us an ETA of about four hours. But they asked him to hold on while they transferred the call again.

That's when he lost it.

He screamed into the phone at the AAA representative, yelling how upset and unhappy he was with the service. Tony had been generally composed during the ride, but he began to come apart the last few days. And this telephone call was the straw that broke the camel's back. A four-hour wait! Phew!

He threw the car jack lever across the street and started screaming, then slammed the receiver down. We'd have to figure out how to fix the flat ourselves, he muttered. We didn't have a car jack.

About 10 minutes later, a guy who lived a few houses away, and who had heard the commotion, came over with an offer to help. He went home and returned with a car jack. Problem solved.

We thanked the friendly man. Tony then dropped me back at the hotel while he searched for a tire place. He told me he wanted to cool off alone. He returned later and told me he found a tire place, but it was closed and would reopen in the morning. After this hassle, our enthusiasm was really low. We managed to knock off our evening blog anyway.

Tomorrow would be a better day, we hoped. For one thing, my friend Mike DeLeo was flying in from California to ride with me. That meant company on the road. I felt great and was looking forward to another "easy" low-mileage day.

Miles pedaled so far
2,877

Passing motorist helps Tony change flat tire. Each time we
needed help, motorists pulled over in minutes.

30

Monday, Oct 8

West Virginia: Ellenboro to Grafton
Total miles to pedal today
61

THIS MORNING TONY MADE TRACKS to the tire shop right away. I asked him to wake me up when he returned. He got back about an hour later with good news: he had a new tire. And with bad news: it was raining, much harder than the day before. I had anticipated rain, so I dressed with two layers of clothing. We knocked off our morning blog, then headed to the fire station. It was raining and 38 degrees. Rats. Looks like today will be a beaut. At least I don't have many miles to pedal, I thought.

We got squared away at the fire station. We then hit the road. The rain was still coming down. My route today was not over a single roadway. I would be pedaling on different roads, so Tony led the way. Road conditions were horrible. Debris was everywhere along the shoulders. Sure enough, with all that crap, it wasn't long before I got another flat tire. Four flat tires in the past three days! I couldn't believe it. This was flat #10. I was cold and I stopped on a lousy stretch of roadway. Tony came up with repair tools. I was now freezing. I repaired the flat. While I was working I noticed both tires were pretty worn. Something else to worry about.

I was cold and wet. I asked Tony if he had a jacket I could borrow.

He rummaged through the vehicle and, sure enough, came up with a heavy jacket. I needed something to keep my core warm. I didn't want to get sick again. Today was supposed to be an easy day. Already, my feet sloshed on every pedal movement. Visibility was difficult. The topography was changing. Now I had rolling hills ahead of me. I put my phone into a zip lock bag. I tried to listen to music as I rode. I told myself that I had to travel for only a few hours, and that I would finish. I guess I was lucky it rained on the low-mileage days and not on the 100-mile-plus days.

Before long, the route took me to a freeway. Riding illegally on a freeway is dangerous. But it was our only option. Crossing the entrance and exit ramps was the problem. It's scary by car. Imagine doing it by bike. Thank God traffic was light. I knew I just had to get through today because tomorrow Mike would join me. I really needed company.

I looked down at the quarters taped to the bike, thought about the two kids, smiled and kept riding. I was cold and I was worried that I'd get hit by a car or truck, or maybe slide with the bike and get hurt. This was a lot to focus on all at once. I was cold and hurting, so I was already distracted. Now with traffic to worry about. . . . . oh, well. Can't do anything about it, I thought. Just pay strict attention. I pedaled several miles and exited the scary freeway. We stopped for a break and a chance for me to warm up.

Tony blasted the heater while he looked for alternate routes. But the best route was on the freeway. I didn't have many miles to go today. I warmed up, then got back on the road. Now, after being warmed, I felt even colder. I pedaled up hills as rain hit my face and worked its way down to my sloshing shoes. I couldn't wait for the rain to end.

A FEW HOURS LATER we reached the Grafton city limit sign. This was the most interesting city limit sign of the trip so far. It proclaimed:

Welcome to Historic Grafton
The Birthplace of Mother's Day
May 10, 1908

Overcast weather is respite
from scorching sun.

Adjacent to the sign was a dedication. It read:

Dedicated to the memory of Thornsbury Bailey Brown
CO B 2nd VA Vol InT
First Union Soldier Killed in the Civil War
He lost his life on this spot May 22, 1861

Seems like this historical town could be quite interesting. So we decided to stop here for the night. I was still cold and tired. Mike DeLeo would be flying in tonight. We'd pick him up at the airport. We thought it would be nice for the three of us to begin tomorrow from this historical location.

We checked into our hotel. First thing I did was to take a nice hot soak! We ate dinner. I took a nap, then cleaned my bike. It was covered with dirt and grime. Just a few more days for the bike to hold up, I thought. So far, so good. We uploaded our videos and prepared the Go-Pros. As I lounged in bed, I checked the next day's weather: the report said clear and about 15 degrees warmer than today. Yes!

It was now time to pick up Mike, so we drove 45 minutes to the airport.

Mike had been traveling about 12 hours, with layovers — on small planes, to boot, because he was heading for small towns with small airports. Despite the grueling journey, Mike was excited to see us. And I was excited to see him because now I'd have someone to ride with. I brought him up to date on the last few days of riding. We realized we had a rough few days ahead just to make it over the Eastern Continental Divide. We dozed during the car drive back.

At the hotel Mike and I tuned up our bikes. Tony talked with his wife, then bought an airline ticket for her to fly to the New York City finish. That really brought up his spirits. He was excited. His wife had made a huge sacrifice by allowing him to participate in this unusual 36 day cross-country adventure. After all, she had to keep up the ranch back home for more than a month. Now she had to find someone to ranch-sit while she flew to New York. In our evening blog we shared struggles of the day while we pointed out how close we were to the finish.

Memorial plaque in West Virginia denotes exact spot
where first Union solder died during Civil War.

We learned earlier today that the Raiders cheerleaders had sent us football jerseys that we'd receive at our next stop. Gary Williams, the Raiders game announcer, and my friend cheerleader Kelly Lack, had for weeks been spreading the word about my ride.

During the blog, Mike introduced his comical walk — he looked as if he was walking down a flight of stairs. We told followers that we had been having trouble the past few days loading our blogs, and we thanked them for hounding us and for their understanding. We realized hundreds of interested people were following our daily progress. Tony closed out the blog by thanking everyone for their messages of support for his hospitalized mom.

He told me later that he understood what it meant to me when I said incoming messages from followers were really helping get me through the ride. With Tony's mom hospitalized, and him being helpless thousands of miles away, he needed all the support he could get. And the incoming messages really helped!

We hit the hay feeling we were now on track for a really strong finish.

Miles pedaled so far
2,938

31

Tuesday, Oct. 9

Leaving West Virginia: to Cumberland, Maryland
Miles to pedal today
107

WE ALL HAD A GOOD NIGHT'S REST. I felt better because we would now be three riders. Two of us could help Tony. But, on the other side of the coin, Tony now had to look after two riders — me and Mike — which meant twice the work for him. I took my time getting out of bed while Tony scanned his phone for the weather forecast. He told us it looked like a dry day.

I triple-checked my bike. I would have replaced both balding tires, but I didn't have a spare. The spare I had was worn. We decided that since we had a 100-plus mile day today we would skip the morning blog, get right on the road and pedal directly to the Grafton, W. Va., sign. A few milestones were in the cards today.

Air outside was cold and the sky was partly cloudy, but at least it wasn't raining. We started at the marker signifying where the first Union soldier was killed. Mike hadn't ridden a bike since he left me a few weeks earlier. He had been so busy with his camps that he had no time to work out. As soon as we began pedaling, we hit hills. It was like we were climbing the Rocky Mountains again. I kept a slow but constant pace and rode next to Mike. The pace was about 10 miles an hour. It wasn't too bad, considering we were climbing. The air began to warm up; clouds still dotted the sky. Temperature was about 70 degrees. It was turning into a beautiful day.

Not too far into the ride, I got yet another rear flat tire. Flat #11. I changed the tire quickly and then returned to riding.

We reached the 30-mile mark about three hours later, then stopped for lunch. While we ate we talked to people about our cause. Sure enough, donations came again. I was surprised at the generosity of people we met. We ate lunch, did some stretching and checked for tightness. Then it was back to pedaling. I was apprehensive today because I hoped we wouldn't get caught in the dark. We would be staying overnight at a fire station, a relief after staying in hotels the past few days. We continued to climb, and I told Mike the start would have been much easier on him if he had come two days earlier.

Several hours later we crossed the state line into Maryland. West Virginia was now history. Ahead was only Pennsylvania, New Jersey and the finish in New York. We're down to three states.

Mmmm. I could taste victory!

We took a few photos of our new state. Tony took a lot of photos as we rode through the beautiful countryside. I had never been to most of these states. We passed green fields with cows and trees. It was a perfect day to be riding, with a warm, comfortable temperature, good company and scenery. A lot more enjoyable than the rain of a few days ago. Scenery or not, however, one thing was certain: we had a lot of hills to climb. We made it into a nice town where we found a bike shop for new tires. The shop worked quickly. We returned to riding. We pedaled for a few hours, then arrived at Oakland, Md. It was funny because the Oakland Raiders in California had sent us a care package that would be waiting for us at our next stop — Oakland, Md.

We were so excited about the Oakland sign that we didn't realize we had taken a wrong turn.

We pedaled for some time, then hit another great moment. I had now traveled 3,000 miles. What an exciting feeling to think I had pedaled 3,000 miles on a bicycle! We took a few photos.

Then even better news came from Lyn back home. She reported ex-

I can't believe I pedaled 3,000 miles. I can almost taste victory.

citedly that Lauren's Ride had just hit the $50,000 mark in donations!

I was really happy at the news. It meant we would *definitely* have money to buy a car for Lauren. Fifty thousand dollars! It was turning out to be an outstanding day. This ride was working!

I took a look at our mileage and ascension for the day. A lot of climbing ahead. We took our short but sweet victory and continued on — the wrong way.

We rode for 10 miles to a major highway. Highway? I was confused. I checked my phone map, then realized that further back at the Oakland city limit sign we should have made a *right* turn. The three of us weren't paying attention and instead turned *left*. Looking at the highway I could see it wasn't designed for bicyclists. I was edgy. We had a choice: we could turn back for 20 miles or take the highway. Getting on the highway back in Kansas could have led to trouble, had it not been for the nice police officer who allowed me to ride to an exit ramp.

Our map showed there were no highway exits for miles, so if we were stopped again by police, we'd be out of luck. What to do? It was late in the afternoon and having to face hills again on the way back, I choose to ride the highway. I told Mike and Tony that I would ride ahead of them. This way, if police came up on them, it would buy me time to reach another roadway without getting stopped. At this point I'll admit I was frightened. If I did get stopped and ordered off the highway, the result would be a lot of extra time and extra pedaling. Our schedule really didn't allow for a lot of extra time and extra pedaling.

The highway route covered huge rolling hills. I was really moving because I couldn't wait to reach a safe place. I crossed entrance and exit ramps cautiously watching for traffic. Tony stayed back with Mike to protect him by riding close behind him. I pedaled and pedaled till I finally reached the East Continental Divide. I continued for 90 minutes until the highway ended. Phew! I made it. It was a horrible feeling to think that I was in jeopardy of not completing every mile of the cross-country trip just because of a wrong turn. I relaxed and waited for Mike and Tony to catch up.

The sun was setting as we completed the scheduled 100 miles for the day. It was nice now because we reached some long downhills, so we just flew. The difference between hills and wind was that hills gave you something to look forward to on the way down. The last few miles had been fun. We reached Cumberland city limits about 7 p.m. and found our way to the host fire station. I had covered 107 miles for the day for an ascent of 9,403 ft. It was a lot for Mike to ride on his first day back. But the three of us were happy we made it.

Now it hit me. I had been riding across the country for 31 days. I had only five days to go. I thought I'd be excited, but I wasn't. I was a bit sad.

I needed shoulder massage. 'Doctor' Tony was quick to help.

This unusual cross-country experience that I was into was coming to an end. Every day I was meeting different people: adults, children, fire-fighters, shopkeepers, other travelers. All friendly and nice.

Now, in a few more days, this wonderful experience would end.

Believe it or not, I had come to enjoy the daily struggles and adverse conditions to complete each day. I had survived through it each pedal of the way. Now it was hitting me. Sure, I was excited to have completed today, but I never thought I'd feel this way. I stood there silently for a minute thinking about it.

We took photos with the fire crew. They showed us our sleeping arrangements. Then Tony, Mike and I — and the fire crew — went into town for dinner.

As we ate we shared our cross-country story with the crew. Darrell, the turtle, made his usual appearance and, of course, was a hit. We looked over the next day's schedule. It was only 81 miles for the day. After dinner we returned to the fire station to collect the package sent to me from the Raiders. It contained two Raiders jerseys and an auto-graphed photo from 1984 Hall of Famer Willy Brown. Tony and I wore the jerseys for our evening blog. We reminded viewers that we had been on the road now for a full month. We were getting close to the finish line. Tony said the experience gets better and better every day.

I said I was getting excited, and was really looking forward to the next five days.

Miles pedaled so far
3,045

Day

32

Wednesday, Oct. 10

Maryland: Cumberland to Smithsburg
Miles to pedal today
81

I WOKE UP SORE, but it really didn't matter to me today because I knew I had only a few more days ahead of me. As long as I could pedal, I told myself, I'd be fine. Today's schedule listed about 80 miles to cover. A mere bag of shells, compared to some of those 100-plus days! So relaxing a few extra minutes this morning would be okay, I reasoned.

We skipped the morning blog and began the day. It was a warm, pleasant day. We would be following Highway 70, but actually staying off it as much as possible. We had a good climb to begin the day. Looks like it will be another day of climbing. But I was up for it. Mike and I rode side by side. We began to joke as we came upon hill after hill. The hills and the surrounding countryside were gorgeous. Tony pulled ahead and looked for a place where he could buy us breakfast. Eureka! Thank God for McDonald's! We feasted on orange juice, Egg McMuffins and hash brown potatoes as we pedaled. Now that I think of it, I spent a lot of time eating as I pedaled. Not the best way to eat, but, what the heck.

About 10 miles into the day we came upon a bicycle rider sound asleep on the side of the road. We quietly left a handful of biking snacks and drinks next to him, so that when he awoke he would be surprised — and resupplied. It looked as if he was on a cross-country ride, too. And he looked low on supplies. What would we think if we woke up with all that stuff around us, we wondered? We laughed.

We continued pedaling. I realized today's the day my mom and sister would be flying to New Jersey for the big rendezvous. She had completed the bus plans and everything else with everyone involved. Now, as I pedaled through Maryland, she was on her way to meet me in Freehold, N. J. She and Lauren were really excited about the whole ride.

We continued riding until we came upon a bike trail through the woods. Along the secluded trail we saw a lot of deer. My phone continued to ring as I pedaled along. Friends and family were calling to cheer me on. One fact was almost for certain: looks like I will finish this 36-day cross-country journey. Some days I felt as if it was over, that I couldn't go on. But now, the fear of failure was being replaced by a beautiful vision of the Brooklyn Bridge, with me crossing the finish line to cheers from Lauren, my mom, relatives and friends.

Now I have Mike and Tony supporting me. My bike was performing well, and I felt great. My soreness had gone away. I learned from phone call reports that we were right on track with donations. Speaking of donations, Mike said from the beginning he hoped the ride would raise enough money. He wanted to know early on if, instead of spending money to fly out and ride with me, he could instead donate that money to the ride fund. Actually, Mike had made a few donations already. I told him I really needed him with me on this final leg of the trip. He was happy to be here, he said. He just wanted to make sure we hit our goal.

From day one, Mike couldn't do enough to help. And here he was offering to donate even more money to make absolutely certain I succeeded.

That's my best friend!

We continued up and down the hills for a few hours until we paused for lunch. Tony said today it would be pizza. We pulled up to the pizzeria and went in. Dave Latham was there to surprise us. Dave had worked with me the day I considered the idea of a cross-country ride. Actually, it was Dave who said "Why don't you do a ride for your sister?"

I didn't know he was coming, so I was surprised, to say the least. He

I came across absolutely beautiful scenery on 36-day journey.
Mike DeLeo rejoins me here for final five days.

bought an airline ticket to meet us, and had already ordered lunch for all of us. It meant a lot to me that he joined us. Dave talked about some of the stories and blogs he had seen, and he told us that so many people back home were rooting for us.

The pizza was huge, but we managed to make it disappear. Then we again hit the road. Mike was riding next to me and Dave was driving his car close to us. Now the squad is up to four — including Tony.

Dave rode with us for about an hour. Then, he veered off to visit relatives. Kind of like killing two birds with one stone. He said he would re-join us in New York.

BY MID-AFTERNOON WE ARRIVED at the Smithsburg, Md., city limit sign. Engine Co. 71 was standing by to escort us into town. Mike and I took a photo giving each other knuckles, then fell into line behind the engine.

It was exciting riding into town behind a fire engine with lights flashing and siren wailing. Mike and I were riding side by side. Tony was following, taking photos and enjoying the new city. It took about 30 minutes to reach the fire station. Smithsburg was a small town. Firefighters Andy and Phil told us they were taking us to dinner and hoped that we were hungry. That was a foolish question. I don't know about Tony and Mike, but I was hungry every day of the journey. My GPS showed I covered 81 miles today, with a 7,278-ft. ascent. Today and yesterday combined were 16,681 ft. That's more than three miles of climb.

We showered, then joined firefighters for dinner.

BACK AT THE FIRE STATION, I talked with my mom and sister. They now had arrived in New Jersey. My phone was ringing non-stop. Everyone under the sun was calling to tell us we were soooo close. Like we didn't realize it!

I talked with Bobby Williams in Staten Island and Andy Meuerle in New Jersey. They had worked together to coordinate my final pedaling day to the Brooklyn Bridge.

Bobby said everything was ready to go. The excitement was building, he said. "We have a fire, police and motorcycle escort ready to pick you up the moment you touch Staten Island. They'll lead you about five miles to the Elks Lodge grounds for an official welcoming ceremony. Vocal Synergy, an a cappella student singing group from Wagner College would kick off the event," he added. I was beginning to believe that my hard work was paying off.

The crew at this fire station had received a package from Stephanie Dininni. She sent us more fire shirts to share with firefighters at stations along the way. What a nice thing to do for us.

We turned out our nightly blog, this time focusing on the feelings of success we were beginning to taste. Today brought us to the 90% mark. Despite challenges ahead, we kept moving east. Now we were close to the end. So close!

According to our map, our route the next few days would be relatively flat. Weather looked stable. Could this be, I wondered? What a great

Smithsburg, Md., firefighters welcome Tony, me and Mike to quarters.

way to finish!

Tomorrow we'd reach Pennsylvania.

I was charged. Tony was excited. Mike was ecstatic! OMG. So close to the finish!

Miles pedaled so far
3,126

Day

33

Thursday, Oct. 11

Leaving Maryland: to Lititz, Pennsylvania
Miles to pedal today
100

WE WERE ALL UP EARLY FOR PHOTOS with the fire crew. We skipped our morning blog and hit the road by 9 a.m. It was shaping up to be another gorgeous day. I knew this was Day 33. I also knew I had a mere four days remaining.

I was having mixed emotions. On one hand, I was excited to finally reach New York, with friends and relatives on hand for the finish. I even pictured Lauren receiving her car.

On the other hand, I met such terrific people, and I was sad because my journey was coming to an end. I never met so many nice, helpful, friendly people in all my life!

As we pedaled, our conversation turned to silly things. We were getting giddy now that the end was near. We made up different scenarios. What if Lauren was resentful during the time we did the ride? What if, during every press interview, she just talked about how unhappy she was about the bike ride? We had some laughs. Most of all, we recognized how lucky we were as firefighters to be able to help people. We loved our jobs and we loved the people who chose this line of work. We both were fulfilled being able to serve the public.

As we pedaled and talked, Tony pulled up to tell us we were only

Sign is music to my ears because I realize I'm so close to finish line.

about a mile away from the National Fire Academy, which was to be our next stop.

The National Fire Academy was protected by security guards and gates. Firefighters from around the country travel here for classes to enhance their skills. The academy is also home of the National Memorial. Every firefighter who died in the line of duty is recognized here. We had planned to stop here to pay tribute to the fallen firefighters, especially four from our station back home who died in the Spanish Ranch wildfire, in 1979.

At the gate we announced we were firefighters from California, here to visit the academy. We were required to submit our drivers licenses for a background check. The guards finally cleared us to enter.

We visit the National Fire Academy in Pennsylvania.

We rode to the memorial, a large structure. Firefighter names were listed in chronological order by year. Each year had the names of more than 100 firefighters who died in the line of duty that year. These were the men and women who made the ultimate sacrifice.

The three of us wandered around, reading all the names and departments. There was also a memorial to lives lost at the World Trade Center in New York on Sept. 11. We learned that for more than half the year the National Fire Museum's American flag flies at half staff due to the high number of firefighter line-of-duty deaths that occur nationwide. Reading the names was sad. We realized the many sacrifices that were made to save lives and property. We came to the section from our department. Mike and I found the names of four firefighters from our station: Edwin M. Marty, Steve R. Manley, Ronald T. Lorant and Scott Cox. The fire in which they died had gone into instant area ignition and quickly trapped and burned the firefighters, killing three instantly. Scott Cox survived the fire but died from his injuries a few months later.

We left the campus slowly and quietly.

We got on our bikes and continued riding. Mike and I talked about how we never realized the large number of firefighters from across the country who died in the line of duty. As firefighters, we spend a lot of time training for, then responding to, dangerous fires. After a while our response becomes normal. We really don't think much about how dangerous the job really is. Despite our training, death occurs.

We rode without speaking for a while.

We rode side by side, then reached the Pennsylvania state sign. It read,

Pennsylvania Welcomes You
State of Independence

It was our 13th state to ride through. Two more states to go to the finish. We snapped photos. We learned that historic Gettysburg was only a few miles ahead.

Fencing around Gettysburg seemed to change. It looked war-like. We pedaled past statues and cannons. Then we spied the statue of a firefighter. We stopped and walked our bikes. Actually, there were two statues: the subject in one wore fire gear while the other wore a military uniform. It was called The Second Fire Zouaves. It was a statue dedicated to more than 1,000 New York firefighters who had joined the Union Army during the Civil War. Seven hundred eleven of them had died.

We came upon a large statue of a man on a horse. It was Maj. Gen. George Gordon Meade, who defeated Gen. Robert E. Lee at the Battle

Historic Gettysburg becomes reality for me and Mike.

of Gettysburg in 1863.

We slowly rode through Gettysburg, passing statue after statue of soldiers from different states who died in the war. Hard to believe that so many died fighting for freedom. We were riding over battlegrounds on which men our age had killed each other. We stopped at each statue to read the names and stories.

What history! I was speechless.

The State of Pennsylvania Memorial, largest in the park, listed names of Pennsylvania residents who had served. Stars represented lives lost in battle. On top of the monument, markers pointed to where various battles had taken place. Battles at Little Round Top and Devil's Den, for instance. We took photos from on top of the monument. I just couldn't believe so many Americans fought and killed each other in these fields. What a history lesson come-to-life!

We wished we could spend more time here in Gettysburg, but we still had 50 miles to cover today. We had little time to tour. We tried to absorb as much Civil War history as we could as we pedaled out of the park.

We continued riding east on Highway 30 to increasing traffic. It was comforting to know Tony was traveling close behind us. Before long, Mike experienced his first flat tire. Flat #1 for Mike. Welcome to the club. It was a dangerous place to stop and change a tire, but we did it. Cautiously. We continued toward Lititz. The day wore on and we made good time. Mike and I were both feeling strong. Having Mike share these last few days with me will be one of my favorite memories of the journey. As we approached Lititz, Tony tried a few times to contact the fire station at which we would be staying, but to no avail. We stopped for dinner when we were about 10 miles away. My GPS showed I had covered nearly 100 miles. Today would be my final 100-mile day. Phew!

We ate dinner and headed to the fire station. If the crew is there, fine. But if the place is empty we'd just have to find a hotel for the night. We took the last few miles nice and slow. We rode into town and were greeted with the smell of chocolate. The scent of chocolate permeated the entire town. I learned later that the Lititz plant of Cargill Cocoa and Chocolate, founded in 1865, produces hundreds of millions of pounds of chocolate and confectionery products a year. We reached the station to find no one there. Tony searched and found a hotel. I had ridden 100 miles today and had an ascent of 5,643 ft. Sure there was a bit of climbing today, but I hadn't realized it. That's how strong I felt. It was now 6 p.m., so we took photos at the empty station and headed for the hotel for showers and telephone calls to our families. We uploaded photos and GoPro videos and prepared for tomorrow. I had only three more overnight stops ahead: here at Lititz and Conshohocken in Pennsylvania, and at Freehold in New Jersey. I was getting really excited as we drew closer to the Brooklyn Bridge. Google maps said I was less than 200 miles away as the crow flies. Yes!, I thought. We're going to do this! Mike and I routinely checked our bikes. I had no idea how we would get to Conshohocken. Meanwhile, Tony called Chief Stephen Phipps of the Conshohocken Fire Department to confirm tomorrow night's lodging. Then Tony put me on with the chief.

The chief said he had been following the ride from the day we began. He was 50 years old, he said, but tonight feels like Christmas Eve and he thinks tomorrow will be Christmas! Sounded crazy to me. But he said he had never been so excited for a day to arrive. I was thrilled to speak with someone as excited for us to arrive as I was. He then asked how we would be coming into town. I told him I had no idea yet, but that maybe he could help with directions. I asked if he rode a bicycle. He replied that he had, and that he would welcome the opportunity to ride with us. We decided to meet in the town of Phoenixville, which was near his town. He gave us directions, then told us we'd be riding through Valley Forge on the way.

When I finished the phone conversation, I told Tony and Mike that the chief said he felt like it was Christmas Eve. Tony said the chief told him the same thing. The chief sounded so excited you'd think he was crazy.

Little did we know what the town had in store for us tomorrow.

Miles pedaled so far
3,226

Day

34

Friday, Oct. 12

Pennsylvania: Lititz to Conshohocken
Miles to pedal today
62

I KNEW I HAD THREE BIG DAYS AHEAD, so I decided to sleep in. It was 9 in the morning before I even got out of bed. I ate breakfast, joined the others to get our things together, then headed to the firehouse to knock out our morning blog.

We had a mere 70-mile day ahead of us. Nothing compared to our earlier long-run days. Meanwhile, I learned that guests were already arriving in Freehold, N.J., our second and final overnight stop. Three more days left! We only had to make it to Conshohocken, Pa., tonight, then on to Freehold, N.J., the next day.

At Freehold I'd be within striking distance of my goal — the Brooklyn Bridge!

Chief Phipps in Conshohocken was now getting his bike ready. My sole focus this morning is simple: how close am I to New York, and what route must I follow to meet Chief Phipps in Phoenixville, Pa., about 40 miles away? We hit the road by about 10.

We headed out of the chocolate-aroma city along country roads. The day was shaping up to be a perfect Indian summer day. We were so lucky with ideal weather this entire trip. Sure enough, we made it to

Phoenixville in a mere four hours. And, sure enough, there was Chief Phipps with his mountain bike.

He was sporting a Cheshire cat smile — one of the widest smiles I had seen so far. His bike was still covered with numbers from his last ride. Before last night, he said, he hadn't planned to ride with us. He was wearing a bright yellow riding vest. His back pack held a radio, with the microphone drooped over his right shoulder. We were miles out of his jurisdiction, but he had his radio handy just in case he was needed, I guessed. He was so excited to see us! After introductions, we headed toward his town. Just then, Mike got a flat tire. Flat #2 for Mike. Our luck. Right opposite a place to eat. Pretty convenient. So we walked the bikes over to the Dunkin' Donuts shop and ate while Mike fixed his flat.

MEANWHILE, BACK IN SAN DIEGO, Dottie Shaw and Shannon King had organized a fund-raiser for the trip. In real life, they worked with Tony in the Cal Fire San Diego unit. They had been following our journey from day one. And today was a huge fund-raiser at San Diego fire headquarters. I was told that people came from all over. The result: Dottie and Shannon raised more than $1,000 for Lauren's Ride. I was stunned that back home, 3,000 miles away, our friends and co-workers had been following our progress and raising money for the cause. They sent us photos of everyone who showed up. What a nice event!

Back to lunch. We ordered. Chief Phipps paid for everyone. We were now ahead of schedule, so we relaxed and chatted with the chief as we ate. Chief Phipps explained that Conshohocken was a tiny town that covered only one square mile, and was just a pinhead on a map. He said he couldn't believe that, of all the neighboring towns, we chose *his* town for an overnight stop. He was honored with our presence. I felt even more honored. We had been fortunate to have people across the country go out of their way to ride with us and then invite us to stay overnight at their fire stations and homes. The excitement these people had displayed charged me up more than anything else. A lot of them were more excited about Lauren's Ride than I was!

Mike repaired his tire, we ended our coffee break, then began a slow and easy pace.

We rode single file until we came to a sign for Valley Forge. It was here that nine North Carolina regiments under General George Washington wintered from December, 1777, to June, 1778. We were now entering the land of General George Washington. In the past few days we had ridden through locations well-known from days of the Civil War. Now we're riding through the site of the Revolutionary War. We stopped and read every sign. I really hadn't known much about Valley Forge before now. We were all mesmerized, including Chief Phipps who said he lived so close yet never spent time here.

As we pedaled along, Chief Phipps kept checking in with his dispatch center. Mike and I joked when we saw him check in it. During our first days, we made up things to make it look like people we came across were there for us, when in reality the people had nothing to do with us or with the ride. For instance, when we passed a fire engine parked off to the side, we'd say it had come to see us off. Fact was, the fire crew was just shopping at a store. We devised fictional things that were being planned for us, like fireworks displays, or helicopter flyovers whenever a helicopter flew overhead. If nothing else, it kept us entertained and broke the monotony.

That being said, we still thought it a bit unusual that the chief was in contact with his dispatch center so often. Then again, we had no idea of the work he had, or what he was discussing with his dispatch center. But each time he spoke to the dispatcher, he would casually fall behind us as he spoke. So we really never heard his conversation. Quiet shop talk, we figured, and never gave it another thought.

We pulled up to a few small wooden cabins. The winter of 1777-1778 was brutally cold. We learned these were the cabins in which the troops lived as they tried to survive. We found out that more soldiers died that brutal winter in Valley Forge than in actual combat. The structures were small, holding five or six soldiers. We spent time reading about the cabins. I thought a lot about what it was like to have been General Washington and his men. That winter was brutal.

Next was the Washington Memorial Chapel built in the early 1900s. It overlooked the training battlefield where troops trained during the winter. We entered the chapel, took photos and talked with the staff. I'm sure I read about Valley Forge in school. Like a lot of the other kids, I didn't remember much about it. But being here in person. What a history lesson! It was an interesting place that I didn't want to leave, so we took our time browsing and walking around. We were ok, because we had only about 12 more miles to pedal today. We were actually ahead of schedule.

We left the park and headed to our overnight stop. As we pedaled, Chief Phipps told us that a month before we arrived, Police Officer Brad Fox of nearby Plymouth had been shot and killed in the line of duty. His police dog had been shot and wounded. I asked if we could pass the memorial site.

Chief Phipps explained how it happened. Officer Fox, in his patrol car, had been following a hit and run suspect. The suspect ditched the car and took off on foot. Officer Fox chased him down an alley, where the suspect turned and fired. It was the police officer's 35th birthday. He had been a U.S. Marine and a hockey player. He is survived by his pregnant wife and five-month-old daughter. It was sad. We briefly prayed for the officer's family, and we thanked him for service to his community and country.

We rode down the alley, then onto a road to the local fire academy, where we came upon a police car and vintage fire engine. Ah, ha, I thought! We had an escort to the fire station. We pulled up to the engine and met the officer and firefighter who had been waiting for us. As I gazed past them, I could see an ambulance — and another fire engine. Chief Phipps said he wanted us to have a "nice escort" into town. We toured the fire academy, then checked out the vintage fire engine. Boy, I thought, fire engine technology has come a long way. The apparatus reminded me of the fire engine my grandfather rode years earlier. I have photos that were taken of me at his firehouse in Freehold, N.J. The chief said we'd see the vintage fire engine in action tomorrow. He then pulled me aside and confided that he was sorry we were delayed because he was trying to interest the local press in covering our arrival. But the press couldn't make it, he said. I told Chief Phipps not to worry. (Later

Chief Steve Phipps, left, organized and executed super duper welcome to his one-square-mile Pennsylvania town. While we received welcomes from many fire departments, the welcome to Conshohocken is one I'll never forget!

Part of unusual welcome reception in Conshohocken. From left, fire-fighters John Drozd, Bob Phipps, Chief Steve Phipps, me, Mike and Tony, Walt Curll, Chris Heleniak, Ryan Comber, John Costello and Bill Weber.

I learned that he had received information from the local news station that he wasn't sharing with us.) This turnout was more than I expected.

A few pieces of emergency equipment were on hand, and he was accompanying me on his bike. What more could I ask?

With Chief Phipps in command, the apparatus moved into formation.

Mike, Chief Phipps and I rode side by side. Tony, as usual, drove behind us. But as we moved ahead more fire engines and police cars appeared and quietly fell in ahead of us and behind us. We were slowly heading for town. After about a mile, all the vehicles turned on their lights and sirens. What a sight! What a surprise!

But wait. I could see ahead. Still *more* fire engines and *more* police cars appeared at each intersection we approached! As we passed, police cars, ambulances and fire engines fell into line.

I'll tell you right now. I never experienced anything like this before. My eyes and my mouth were open wide. Mike, too. I turned, and Tony was smiling and shaking his head in disbelief. Mike, Chief Phipps, and I all looked at each other as we continued to pedal. We were all smiling.

This continued, not for a few blocks, but for a few miles. At each intersection more ambulances, fire engines and police cars joined our parade. Where did all this emergency equipment come from? I wondered. I glanced ahead, and there were two ladder trucks with their ladders extended to form an arch. A huge American flag hung from the crossed ladders. Oh my God!

Now I was beginning to understand why Chief Phipps was so excited about today.

Remember, he said last night felt like "the night before Christmas."

Well today was his Christmas Day!

We approached the ladder trucks that stretched over the street, then pulled up to the fire station. A throng of firefighters, police officers, community members, an NBC News camera crew — even the mayor — was on hand to greet us.

Chief Phipps had surprised us. *Totally* surprised us with his secrecy.

Now it all made sense. Earlier, as we pedaled, he kept going on his radio to secretly coordinate this turnout. That's why he dropped back as he spoke to his dispatcher.

I had not met the chief until today. To think he would mobilize his entire town, and surrounding towns, just for us stunned me. The only thing he had known when he decided to put this welcome together was that we were brothers in the fire service, and that I was riding my bicycle across the country to help my sister. But apparently that was more than enough for him to move into action for weeks of planning and coordination. Words can't explain how I felt as I pedaled through the streets. In town, I thanked everyone for being there for the welcome. NBC News interviewed Tony, Mike, Chief Phipps and me. The world was turning so fast, I thought. But this great welcome was just the start of things to come for the day. I spent a few hours outside talking with everyone. At one point Tony discovered a flat tire on the chase vehicle. Chief Phipps got on his phone. In minutes a guy shows up to fix the flat. He fixed it in what seemed like record time.

When the crowd thinned, we toured the fire station, then headed to the nearby Boat House Restaurant. Loads and loads of food awaited us. So did a $500 check toward Lauren's Ride from the town.

Today was another one of the best days of my life! I mean, all these people who never met me turned out to give us this fantastic welcome!

I felt so much support. Now I knew for sure that I'd complete the ride and raise the funds required for Lauren's special car.

After we dined and fraternized, we returned to the fire station. In the conference room, people were wearing T-shirts proclaiming Lauren's Ride. The chief told us his department had created and was selling special shirts. The money they raised was being donated to Lauren's Ride. I shook my head.

His little fire department in this small town had done *so* much to help us.

Now, we were taken downstairs to the engine bay. Firefighters were ready to give us a special ride through town on their classic 1924 American La France pumper.

The historic fire engine was driven by chain. To think, years ago firefighters responding to alarms stood on the back step of their fire engine. They didn't have the luxury of sitting in an enclosed cab, as firefighters today do. Chief Phipps said that was exactly how we'd ride tonight. We'd stand on the back step as the engine paraded through the streets.

Tony, Mike and I put on fire helmets, the driver fired up the engine, and the three of us hopped on the back step. We drove through town, with the town's people beeping car horns and waving as we slowly rolled by. Townspeople knew we would be given the fire engine ride because television news programs had announced it for days. I felt like a famous athlete. The three of us were holding the support bar tightly, careful not to fall off. Riding a fire engine this way was a new experience for me. I felt as if I was experiencing 1940s history.

The rig took a few laps through town and returned to the station. Tony announced he had a surprise. Earlier, he had contacted rapper Dr. Geek who agreed to make a special You Tube video just for Lauren's Ride. Tony played it. The rap was really good. Dr. Geek told Lauren's story well, highlighting what a disability really means. He told how Lauren lives such an active and positive life. She is limited in some areas but lives life more than most people do, and he explained all of that in his rap. It was a moving video. By now, my emotions were on system overload just thinking of the love given us by so many people here in this tiny Pennsylvania town. I couldn't be happier!

The only thing missing from this unbelievable reception was my family. Boy, oh boy, did I wish they could be here with me. I knew I'd see them tomorrow, and I'd tell them all about the parade and reception. But oh how I wished they could be here in person.

Rather than wait until tomorrow, I decided to call my family and tell them right away about the big parade into town that we had just received. And about the big dinner. And about the ride through town on the back of a fire engine. And about everything else that was happening to me and the guys. I was so excited! Lauren was so excited when I told her she would definitely get her special car. As I talked with her and my mom, I glanced at the miles I covered today. I pedaled 61 miles. We did the math. I already pedaled 3,288 miles.

Later that evening, when things settled down, Chief Phipps told me that tomorrow morning he set up a breakfast interview with reporter Jenn Bernstein of CBS 3 Philly News. I kept telling him I couldn't believe that he did so much to help us. He kept telling me that *he* couldn't

Television reporter interviews me in Conshohocken, Pa.

We sport special t-shirts. Note happy junior firefighter at lower left.

believe I had selected his small town for a stopover.

We formed a friendship that day I feel will last forever.

Tomorrow will be a big day. I mean a *big* day! It'll be the final day before I take Manhattan and the Brooklyn Bridge. Mike, Tony and I talked as we tried to fall asleep. But who could sleep after all the excitement today, and thinking about tomorrow?

I kept thanking Mike and Tony for helping make this a really successful cross-country ride for Lauren. I knew I couldn't have made it this far without them.

What a day! And the finale is still to come.

Miles pedaled so far
3,288

Day

35

Saturday, Oct. 13

Leaving Pennsylvania: to Freehold, New Jersey
Miles to pedal today
72

THE GUYS WERE DRINKING COFFEE and watching television when I made my way to the living room. CBS, Channel 3 News, was on. Reporter Jenn Bernstein was covering the ride live from right outside the fire station. I wasn't awake 10 minutes, and here it was the beginning of another fabulous day. Chief Phipps said the television reporter would join us for breakfast for her in-depth story about the ride. So I walked downstairs to the engine bay and, sure enough, there was Jenn. I felt honored that CBS was devoting so much air time to our story. Yes, it was a story about brotherly love. Coincidentally, today I'd pedal through Philadelphia — the city of brotherly love. We walked with Jenn to the Conshohocken Cafe for the breakfast interview. The cafe opened early just for us. We had the entire restaurant to ourselves.

We told Jenn all about The Ride. Chief Phipps described his excitement because we chose his one-square-mile town for our stay over. "Smaller than a pinhead on a map," he added. I told Jenn about the challenges I faced, and about the many interesting people I met along the way. I explained how positive my sister has been about her injury, and how her positive attitude and drive inspired me to jump in and help. As the interview continued, I couldn't help but think today was shaping up to be one of the most memorable days — if not the most memorable day — of my life. We placed our breakfast orders. The waitresses told us they were donating to our cause by paying for the meal.

Something amazing happened every single day, from the time we got the idea for a cross-country ride six months ago. Here, for instance, Chief Phipps had organized the biggest surprise of the trip, with his community doing so much. I just couldn't believe the amount of nice things people were doing for us. In just one day here, we raised a few thousand dollars and were part of the largest welcoming ceremony so far. And it was all done for Lauren's Ride.

Meanwhile, my family, including Lauren, had already arrived in Freehold, N.J., which would be our *next* stop. They were waiting for us at the Freehold Fire Dept., which had been my grandfather's fire company. Now I was really excited about finally seeing them!

Jenn asked question after question.

"Were you a big bike rider before this?"

"No."

"Have you ever planned a major ride before?"

"No."

I had little knowledge or skill with this, I told her. It was the hearts of so many that got us to this place. People could see that Lauren was an unusual young woman, and a new car would give her a more independent life. Thousands of people across the country were helping make our dream come true. I could have spent hours talking with Jenn. But we both knew that a lot of excited friends and family awaited our arrival in Freehold later today.

We returned to the fire station for our morning blog. It was almost impossible to include everything we had experienced the day before in a 10-minute blog. But we did it with smiles. And with excitement! Chief Phipps offered to escort us out of town on our way to Freehold. We had about 70 miles to cover today, and it now was only about 10 a.m. So far so good.

If it weren't for family and friends waiting in Freehold, I may have just stayed in Conshohocken another day. Tony agreed. He said on the

A CBS television news crew is on hand to tape my adventure story.

blog that if Conshohocken was a state, it would be his favorite state of the whole trip!

The chief gathered all of us in front of the fire station, where he snapped photos of the group and of me raising my bike into the air. As we pedaled out of town, the television camera crew shot footage of Chief Phipps leading the way. Chief Phipps planned a scenic route to take us out of Pennsylvania into New Jersey. He guided us to a pathway that ran adjacent to the Schuylkill River. So here we were pedaling along the water's edge on yet another gorgeous day.

The universe was surely looking out for us!

COLLEGE ROWING TEAMS WERE RACING in the river as we rode along the path. This went on for several miles until we made it to Philadelphia. Chief Phipps had another stop for us. It was the Rocky statue in front of the art museum. "Rocky" was the movie I had watched time and time again about a guy who beat the odds. He ended his training by running up the stairs. We took several photos with the statue. Like everyone else, we just had to run up the stairs with our bikes. Mike and I took turns running to the top.

We made our way through Philadelphia. Chief Phipps was still escorting us through the traffic lights and stop signs to a neighboring fire station, where we dropped in. We talked with the on-duty crew and took some photos, then continued on. Every time we told people we were riding from California, they were really surprised. Chief Phipps took us all the way to the Benjamin Franklin Bridge. This was his stopping point.

I got off my bike and we hugged. Neither of us said a word. We just hugged. It was difficult for me to say goodbye to him. He'll always have a place in my heart.

He's now family.

Mike and I pedaled across the Benjamin Franklin Bridge into Camden, N. J. We called Tony, and he was heading in our direction but was a bit behind us. We needed direction. We decided to just start heading north. After a few miles, we stopped and looked at the map to see if we were going the right way. There were some rough roads and, like most days, we were again lost. I again called Tony to give him our location and direction. He had no idea where we actually were. I wanted to get through this city. Tony sounded a little frustrated not knowing where we were. He had to stay back to upload the last blog and had trouble so he was delayed. Mike and I continued to ride, honoring stop signs and traffic lights. During these times, we would see what a possible route might be and if we were heading to Freehold. We were not sure if we were even going in the correct direction. At an intersection we came upon a man who just stared at both of us. He yelled, "Hey, you." I wasn't sure if he was going to cause trouble. Why was he yelling? I was a little concerned because a few miles back we met a guy who glanced at our bikes and said "nice bikes," as if he wanted to grab them. This guy yelled again, "Hey, you." His car looked beat up. I answered "Hey," and waved. He said, "You the guy I saw on the news today who's riding his bike for his sister, right?" With a sigh of relief I replied that he was right. I asked him which way to Freehold, and he confirmed we were heading in the right direction. I thanked him, the light turned green and, once again, we were on our way.

I called ahead to Andy Meuerle, the guy who originally gave me the bike, to see if he had a better route for us. I told him where we were — and he gave us a few possible routes. He said we were coming in from a different direction than we had planned. This would cause the guys at the fire station to change the location of the escort they were planning for us. Mike and I just kept pedaling hoping we were heading in the right direction. The roads were not easy to ride on. We had to dodge quite a bit of traffic. At one point, my front wheel went into a rivet in the uneven roadway. By some stroke of luck, it popped out in an instant. I was surprised I hadn't fallen. Again, someone from above was looking out for me. After some time, Tony called for our location. I told him the roads and cross streets. He was getting closer to us.

In the middle of all this directional confusion, my second cousin Melissa showed up. She had been dropped off to ride with us. Of course, she knew the rest of the way — she was from the area. It was a big relief.

It was now the three of us heading to Freehold. Tony was catching up to us and Andy was heading towards us from Freehold. Ten miles later: there's Andy. Tony pulled up. We were all together now. The fear of not making it had disappeared.

Thoughts of success filled my heart.

FREEHOLD WASN'T JUST ANOTHER TOWN to me. It was the New Jersey town where my mom was raised and where my grandfather John Quigg served as a volunteer firefighter for more than 30 years. He was even fire company president. He died of a heart attack before I was born. I was honored to have been named after him. When I was a child, every time we went to New Jersey I would wind up visiting his firehouse. I remember climbing on the engines and petting the Dalmatian. Three or four engines were quartered there. My grandfather belonged to Engine Co. 2. They also had a hook and ladder unit and a yellow fire engine donated by Freehold resident Bruce Springsteen that had "Born to Run" painted on the door. My parents still have a picture in their living room of me on my grandfather's engine when I was six years old. The reason I became a firefighter, I think, was because of those visits to the firehouse. I wanted to be like my grandfather who was a hero to many and a friend to so many more. For many of the guys, he was their Little League coach when they were young, and a great mentor. I would hear story after story about his courage and heart.

Making it to Freehold will be a powerful moment, and we're so close.

IT WAS SUCH A WONDERFUL DAY OUT. After almost falling, I wanted to pay attention to making it safely. Mike, Melissa and I were talking as we rode. In less than 20 minutes of riding together, we saw a Freehold fire engine ahead of us. Mike Crawford had organized our arrival. Mike was my mom's next door neighbor growing up. My grandfather used to take Mike to the firehouse when he was a boy. Sure enough, Mike grew up to be a firefighter, too. It was extra special for me knowing Mike knew my grandfather. I talked with him a week into the idea of the fund-raiser and explained to him that it was important for me to stop at the Freehold firehouse. With that, he organized our arrival. He could not have been any nicer. The lead engine was the engine that carried my deceased grandfather from the funeral home to the church to the cemetery. Years ago mom explained to me what his funeral was like. He died much younger than anyone had expected. He was only 62 years old. Hundreds of people came to his wake and funeral. Not only was he a volunteer firefighter, he was a member of the American Legion and the Elks Lodge. His first priority was always his family.

Now, the engine that carried him to his resting place was the same one leading us into town. I couldn't help but tear up. Many more engines came out to follow, as well as firefighters on bikes. We had escorts several miles through town to the station.

Sirens started up and emergency lights lit up the streets even though it was the middle of the day. It was a huge welcome into town. Tony was behind us and the escort was in front of us. The guys rode next to us and congratulated us on the accomplishment of making it to Freehold. As we got close to the firehouse, I could see a large crowd in front of the station. Police had closed the roadway. Now I could hear shouts of joy over the sirens. As we drew closer, the noise grew louder and louder. Then I spied my mom, sister and family. We pulled up, and the cheering crowd mobbed us in the middle of the street. I could hear Aunt Jean literally screaming. Lyn, who created the Lauren's Ride web page, was there taking photos. We made it. We made it! He's here, he's here they were yelling. We did it! We arrived. Lauren in her wheelchair and mom ran over and hugged me. Mom started crying. Tony's wife, who had flown in from California, gave Tony a long, long, long hug. They had been away from each other for six whole weeks. Our arrival caused a traffic jam. Everyone was in the street in front of the firehouse. I saw people who I never thought would be there. Nick Ciardella, his sister and niece came from California to surprise me. My cousin Marisa had flown in from Hawaii. *Hawaii!* Cousins John, and his daughter Rachael, made the trip from England! I was flabbergasted when I saw them. Many of my aunts and uncles were there. My Aunt Susan, who is my godmother, was there. Even the mayor came to greet us. It was such a special moment. Among the most meaningful moments of my life.

We made it! We made it! We made it!

Thirty five days of riding, and we made it safely. After 30 minutes of celebration in the streets, we had to clear the way so police could reopen the street to vehicular traffic. The press was asking questions. Local residents were in awe of what we had done. Some of the guests knew my grandfather. It was the first time I would meet them.

We made our way to the engine that led us in, now parked in front of the station. Tony and I took photos in front of the engine and then some with my sister and my mom. It was such a powerful moment in my life.

As I said, anything is possible if you believe.

I would never have imagined six months ago that I could have made it by bicycle to New Jersey. I knew my grandfather and grandmother were looking down on us. I'm sure they were proud of what we had done.

We made our way into the historic firehouse that was built in 1872. Walls were covered with photographs of firefighters and large Freehold fires. My mom led the tour, sharing stories of the fires my grandfather was involved in. During the time my grandfather was president, he turned an unused basement room into a multipurpose room. My mother told me a funny story. During the downstairs room renovation, my grandmother, Elsie, kept looking and looking for items in her house that she thought she had misplaced. She couldn't find them. Couldn't figure out where they were. This went on for months. The puzzle was solved the day the new firehouse room opened. During the open house, everywhere she looked she saw items from her house — the items that had disappeared. Most importantly, the room was named the "John Quigg Room," and a special plaque was created in my grandfather's honor. We spent hours socializing at the firehouse. We were told the fire station would host a dinner for us that night in the upstairs banquet room. The American Legion Hotel donated several rooms for us, so we went to the hotel to take showers and get ready for dinner.

Dave Lienemann arrived from California as we went to the hotel. He had ridden the first day with me and would be riding with me the final day. We had carried his bike as a spare the whole way on the back of the chase vehicle. Dave helped organize a lot of behind-the-scenes activities for Lauren's Ride. Tomorrow, we would have an official escort, so we wouldn't get lost, and it was only about a 40 mile day. I almost forgot to look at our daily mileage for today. I rode a complete 72 miles, putting us at 3,360 miles so far. Wow! I never could have imagined that was possible. We did it. We took showers, and I rested for half an hour before we returned for dinner. We were about a block away from the fire station.

At the station, family, friends, firefighters and supporters packed the room. I was reunited with cousins and second cousins I hadn't seen in years. I heard story after story about the wonderful man my grandfather was and how proud he would be of me today. I managed to talk with Lauren, who told me she was surprised at the outpouring of love and support she received during the event. She was so grateful. We were so excited that we had done it. This was going to change her life and our family's lives so much, providing so much more independence. This

Mom, Lauren and I sport Cheshire cat smiles as we finally meet after 35 days. That's the engine my grandfather, John Quigg, rode during years as a Freehold, N.J., volunteer firefighter.

turned into such a heart-filled story about love from so many people.

It certainly would change me.

We all had dinner together. You could feel the love in the room. The fire department presented us with photos of my grandfather and showed us the book he signed in 1947 when he joined the fire department. The book held the signatures of every member who volunteered for the station. The beautiful plaque that was created in honor of my grandfather was presented to me. I was really touched. At the end of dinner, we decided to do a blog with everyone there. It was the Day 35 evening blog. And it was a beaut!

In the blog, Tony thanked everyone who was with us tonight. The people here today were so happy to see us make it in one piece, especially my mom who had worried each day. Mom said hi to my dad back home, through the blog, wishing he was here to share this time with us. Lyn was happy we arrived here in one piece. Mike was humbled by the things he saw on the ride. We felt lucky to share these moments. I thanked Darrell Sales, Amy Jones and Corrin Lee — the ride was not possible without our team members. Tony thanked his wife for allowing him to make such a big sacrifice to make sure I made it safely. He and I were so thankful to be able to meet many kind people. I wasn't sure this was even possible. It was like a dream. It had been a long road. It was a journey filled with the most unusual and warm experiences found in so many different places. The messages and calls I would receive would really get me and Tony through the hard times and difficult days. We gave everyone a chance to talk in the blog. Most people explained how they were touched by the love and acts they viewed as we traveled across the country. We were experiencing things you see in movies or read in books. We closed the blog thanking everyone for their love and support. I was taking it all in. It was like a family reunion having so many of our family and loved ones together. We were the last ones to leave the firehouse at 10 p.m.

A lot is planned for tomorrow. I mean, we haven't even reached the finish line and the reception here in Freehold has been absolutely fantastic!

Miles pedaled so far

3,360

36!

Sunday, Oct. 14

Leaving New Jersey: to the Brooklyn Bridge!
Miles to pedal today
A mere 41!

THE FINAL DAY. IN ONE WAY I didn't want the day to begin. If I could live in this one moment for the rest of my life, I would. I felt like time had stopped for us all to be together, and I didn't want it to end. It was so magical. I lay in bed and was just so thankful the hard work was paying off. I was with my best friends and my family. If nothing else in my life took place, I could say that I had lived a full life from the things I had experienced and seen from mankind. There were many sacrifices from so many in different ways. The bond formed from so many people was real. I did not have a single bad experience in six months. It was like a fairy tale. I knew today would continue that story. It was day 36 of the ride. Bobby and Andy told me a few times they had a special New York City welcome planned. Tony walked in and said we needed to get up and get ready for the day. New Jersey State Police would meet with us as soon as we reached the Freehold fire station.

The joint was beginning to jump.

Today was 36 of 36.

The day we competed for gold.

The end of the line.

Whatever you want to call it. I was so happy that we had reached

311

our ending location each day for the past 35 days. Hands down, today would be the same.

At the fire station, we started preparing our bikes for this final run when the state police arrived. Tony and five bicycle riders met with them: Andy, Mike, Dave, Melissa and myself. The officers were all business. The escort through New Jersey to the Outerbridge Crossing into New York State would be a dangerous route, they explained. We would be bicycling on major congested roadways. One error could lead to injury or even death. The officers pointed out that we would be approaching one of the most heavily trafficked areas in the world — New York City! The police made it absolutely clear that we had to stay together as we rode, and we had to signal if we needed to stop or if we needed help. This meeting lasted about 15 minutes. Andy told me the night before that he never imagined the New Jersey State Police would do this for us because New Jersey highways are usually pretty clogged with traffic. There was really no other easy way to make it to New York either, so when they contacted him to confirm they would help us, he was thankful.

My final day began as another sunny and warm day. When we were ready, we took a few photos in front of the antique Freehold fire engine. After the photo session, I spoke with Mike Crawford who had organized our stay here. He asked me if I could take a photo with his daughter. I said I would be grateful to. I thanked him for making the last two days possible for us. It was so much more than I would have ever asked for or dreamed of. There was a little urgency to be on the road early because the later we left, the more traffic we would encounter. We would have a fire department escort out of Freehold. New Jersey State Police were ready to escort us to the state line at the Outerbridge Crossing. Interestingly in addition to the fire and police units, four Mini Cooper automobiles, courtesy of the Ray Catena Motor Corp. dealership in Edison, N. J., joined the motorcade. The small cars just added to the hoopla.

As we were preparing for our final ride, everyone else was getting ready for their parts in this special day. My mom was organizing details. A charter bus would shuttle guests from Freehold to an official

Fab five ready to roll from Freehold on this final day.

"Welcome to New York" ceremony at the Elks Lodge on Staten Island, then on to the Brooklyn Bridge finish. The bus would then carry participants back to Staten Island for a special celebration dinner at the Hilton Garden Inn. After dinner, the bus would return to Freehold.

Bobby Williams had set up a police and fire escort for us from the Outerbridge Crossing to the welcoming ceremony at the Elks Club. It was a distance of about four miles. Unbeknownst to me, many friends and relatives were heading to Staten Island to surprise me. My good buddy John Reynolds spent the whole night completing his video that he planned to air at the celebration dinner. He originally told me he and his family wouldn't be coming to the finish. And I believed him. But he was here. He tricked me.

After a final safety check at the Freehold fire station, we began moving out. Following was the Freehold Engine Co., then me and the other bike riders, Tony in the chase vehicle and the four Mini Coopers. We slowly snaked our way through Freehold. As we left Freehold and entered Route 35 North, the Freehold Engine Co. peeled out of the formation to return home. We were riding together at a pretty fast pace — keeping it at about 20 miles an hour. On the upgrades, Dave would drop back, and Mike and I would give him a hard time. "Come on Dave, you can't keep up!" we would holler. He was doing his best to stay in line with us.

We were flying. Both Melissa and Andy said they couldn't believe they were riding here. Never in a thousand years would anyone ever imagine bikes riding here on Route 35. Traffic flew by and we got many honks and cheers from people as they drove past us. People were probably wondering what was happening. I was focused on the road, which was not too smooth. We had to watch where we were riding, even more so for Dave who was having trouble with his pedals. We made a few road changes and turns, and before long we were climbing the Outerbridge Crossing into Staten Island. New York would be the 15th and final state we pedaled through.

We arrived at the Staten Island side of the bridge much earlier than scheduled. We were so early that no one was ready for us. Andy had given Bobby a conservative traveling time for us to reach the Outerbridge Crossing. Bobby passed that time to the Staten Island escort groups. But we did it half the time. As a result, no one in the Staten Island escort had arrived yet. So we cooled our heels when we got to Staten Island to await our escort. After all, welcoming activities at the Elks Lodge were timed. And we were ahead of schedule. So we had no choice but to wait. We were so focused on riding that we hadn't stopped for a break, plus we kept a super fast pace. We met police officers from the Port Authority of New York and New Jersey, the agency with jurisdiction over the bridge, and took a break on the lawn. We thanked the New Jersey State troopers for their support, and they returned to New Jersey.

We weren't resting too long before our escort began showing up in the parking lot. A New York City Fire Department engine company was the first unit to arrive. Then motorcycle groups, the Fire Riders and Rolling Thunder, showed up. Many more units than I ever imagined showed up. Getting there early gave us a chance to talk with everyone as they pulled up. In no time 20 roaring motorcycles pulled into formation. I talked with members, all of whom were firefighters, but most of whom were retired. Many of them told me they had responded to the World Trade Center and saw the towers collapse on that fateful Sept. 11. They were a group of motorcycle riders who participated in a variety of community ceremonies. I considered these men the bravest of the brave, and they had my highest regard. I was honored to spend time with these guys. In an amazing set of circumstances, they would officially escort me into their fine city — the city of New York! Mike and I spoke with one of the motorcyclists. He told us he thought it took a real hero to organize and pull off this cross country ride. I was breathless hearing his words. When we talked to firefighters of Engine Co. 167, their officer said he would like to make a donation on behalf of the New York City Fire Department. Not only were they escorting us through the city, they were also donating to help my sister. We were surrounded by an amazing group of guys. After taking photos in front of the fire apparatus and motorcycles, and getting to meet everyone, we began to move into formation. Our next stop would be the Staten Island Elks Lodge for a welcoming ceremony.

The official escort included FDNY Engine Co. 167, Richmond Engine Co. 1, Oceanic Hook and Ladder Co. 1, special memorial Engine Co. 343, which was a restored pumper, police motorcycles, and the Staten Island Chapter of Rolling Thunder, the Vietnam Veterans motorcycle organization,

In addition, the motorcade included the Fire Riders motorcycle club, auto dealer Ray Catina's Mini Coopers, Tony in the chase vehicle and all the bicycle riders. We had about five miles ahead of us before we reached the Elks Lodge.

When word was given, we all pulled out in formation. The engine and police led the way, with motorcycles blocking intersections as we rode through. It was most definitely a New York City welcome! What we were experiencing, people could only dream about. I had said once before, doing this ride allowed me to see first-hand the unbelievable amounts of kindness from people and organizations. Now we made our way through Staten Island streets. It was a Sunday morning, so traffic was light. We were looking at each other in amazement at what we were experiencing. I am sure it is the same feeling a Tour de France rider experiences when he or she is finishing the tour, or an Olympic athlete on a final lap. All the hard work and months of planning and sacrifice had led up to us finishing the ride and taking us to these moments in life. We reached many of our goals on this ride. We made it safely… we raised money to buy Lauren's special car…we inspired many people along the way, something we never thought about as we planned it…I rode every mile without gaps, and it was all done on the bike given to me by Andy Meuerle…we never had one bad experience. All the challenges would turn into great things.

As we approached the Elks Lodge, I could see Ladder Co. 87 with its ladder extended. A huge American flag fluttered from the raised ladder. It really was an honor to be riding for my sister, for my department and for everyone who was following us. I felt proud to be an American and to see what being an American meant to me. I could hear the crowd cheering as we approached. We were guided into the grounds and the escort and riders were directed to their locations. We rode under the ladder truck with the American flag and made our way into the center of a ceremony. As I looked around, there were so many people. Many more people had arrived to surprise me and join us for this special day.

Bobby Williams, the man who called me a few days into the idea of the ride and the person who inspired me to write this book, guided me into the place I needed to be. There I was, standing in front of the Elks Lodge with everyone surrounding me. Bobby was wearing a bright red jacket, and he gave me a hug.

"You did it John. You did it! Congratulations!" he said to me with a grin.

Two weeks into the idea of the ride, I remember Bobby telling me that if I make it to New York, "we'll give you a super special New York

I enter grounds of Staten Island Elks Lodge, passing under American flag fluttering from extended bucket of Ladder Co. 87.

City welcome." Boy, he was right. This reception was unimaginable. His original message inspired even more people hearing about this huge ending. Two weeks into the idea of the ride, people were saying in California, "New York is already planning his arrival." A few days after his call with this news, he said, "John, you'll experience something only one in a million people will ever experience in their lifetime, and if you take notes, you can write a book someday about your journey." I told Bobby that wasn't possible. I failed English twice in college because I couldn't write a ten-page paper. It took me a third time to finally pass English. He said, "You'll experience something great, something no one else ever will, and if you write a book, everyone who reads the book will get to experience it through you." I knew after he said it that I wanted to share the things I was experiencing, and I would do my best to write a book.

Now here I am today. And Bobby is hugging me and smiling. It was a special moment to see his face and to be here with him. "You did it John," he kept yelling as he patted my back. He was as excited as I was.

EVERYONE MOVED INTO POSITION for the outside ceremony. We got off our bicycles and stood at ease in front of the lodge podium.

Elks Exalted Ruler Tim Kuhn welcomed guests to the ceremony.

Vocal Synergy, the 12-voice female a cappella singing group from Wagner College, delivered moving versions of "The Star Spangled Banner" and "God Bless America."

Retired FDNY Batt. Chief James McGrath then took the microphone:

> Good morning everyone. I was the battalion commander of Battalion 32 in the Red Hook section of Brooklyn, which is not far from the Brooklyn Bridge where later today John will complete his special cross country ride. I am also vice president of the Staten Island Fire Department Retirees and a proud member of the Staten Island Lodge of Elks. On behalf of the New York City Fire Department, our retirees and my fellow Elks, I welcome John and Lauren, their family and friends and fellow firefighters to Staten Island.
>
> Ladies and gentlemen, John Byrne is a San Francisco firefighter. His family hails from Freehold, N.J., as well as from West Brighton here on the Island. As a firefighter, he's no stranger to helping people. So it seems quite natural that he would want to help his sister obtain her goal of independence. John's sister Lauren became paralyzed as a teenager when she jumped into a backyard swimming pool. She has been unable to walk without assistance and has relied on family and friends to take her everywhere.
>
> John had to figure out a way to raise money to purchase and maintain a car with hand controls so that Lauren could become independent of others as she completed her college education. He realized he could raise funds by obtaining sponsors for a bicycle journey across the country. He created Lauren's Ride. He would

bicycle 3,500 miles from the Golden Gate Bridge to the Brooklyn Bridge, stopping nightly at firehouses across the country.

Well, he did it. Here he is. He's down to the final 10 miles!

After 9/11, I had the occasion to travel throughout the country to meet many firefighters. It seems that we all shared each other's sorrows, joys and accomplishments. So today I feel I can speak for all firefighters in America as I congratulate John on his accomplishments of raising money for Lauren's special car and completing his 3,500 mile ride.

Rev. Alan Travers, pastor of Holy Child Roman Catholic Church on Staten Island, spoke next:

John, we owe you a profound debt of gratitude because what you have done reminds us of the potential we all have — the great glorious potential we all have. To take stock of the blessings that we have in life and the inspiration that can take hold of us when tragedy strikes. It's important to take stock and give thanks while putting into effect the faculties that we are left with. In your case, mobility, developing into an Olympian degree. So we thank you and we thank God for this revelation of human greatness and compassion. Through this, we just don't give thanks to God for the blessings that we are left with, but you went above and beyond to do something to address those persons, especially your sister, who are not sharing this particular blessing that we all take for granted. Compassion, concern, care and love. These are in the beautiful tail of the comet that flew across the nation as you pedaled these many miles. So we thank you for the inspiration that you gave us simply by acting, simply by doing. Actions speak louder than words and all the words here are a failed comparison to the wonder of what you have done and what we have seen and what we are about to see you do in these final miles. With many dangers, toils and strains you have already come. It is grace that brought you safely here thus far — and grace will see you through. And we are here with you on this last leg of your journey and from the inspiration you give us we are able to turn ourselves to God and pray.

Oh, Lord, may everything we do begin with Your inspiration, and with Your help be brought to perfection. We thank You for John

We made it!

and we thank You for Lauren and we thank You for this beautiful occasion that gives You glory for the care that Your people show towards one another.

Amen.

Vocal Synergy then delivered "America the Beautiful."

THE PROGRAM EVENTUALLY GOT TO ME. I was asked to speak. Believe me, by that point I was choked up thinking about all the love and support, and the feeling that we did it! I walked up to the podium, paused, looked out to my friends and family, and spoke:

From the beginning until now, I must tell you that I experienced the best in America. There are so many great people in the United States. The little acts of kindness and support have gotten us to where we are today. Just like when Lauren had her injury, we had family and friends there supporting us to get Lauren through it. This entire trip wasn't just me pedaling the bike. It was everyone pedaling the bike with me. Everyone helped get me through this. There were hard times, there were challenges. There were a lot of sacrifices from a lot

Battalion Chief Jim McGrath welcomes me to the Big Apple on behalf of FDNY.

of people who generated a lot of energy to help get us here today.

Lauren will inspire many people throughout her life. She has plans to become a teacher, and I have no doubt she will reach those goals to inspire so many people.

Thank you everyone here today. Thank you so much.

Audience is engrossed as I speak.

AFTER THE CLOSING CEREMONY, we eventually went inside for a brunch reception. I got to talk to everyone, including my friend John Reynolds, his wife Amanda and his brother Joe. There were other firefighters I worked with from different parts of my career who came from California to Staten Island just for today. We spent about an hour at the reception, then began to get ready for our final leg to the Brooklyn Bridge.

Our fire department escort would now lead us through the streets of Staten Island to the Staten Island Ferry.

The plan called for us to travel from Staten Island to Manhattan on the world-famous ferry. It would be extremely difficult, if not impossible, for us to bicycle across the Verrazzano-Narrows Bridge and through Brooklyn's heavily congested streets, we were advised. So early on, as I said, Bobby and Andy decided we'd go by boat.

We were escorted from the Elks Lodge by a fire engine and police car. Distance from the Elks Lodge to the ferry was about 10 miles. We made the run in less than 30 minutes. We thanked our escort and boarded the ferry. We stood together in the bow so we'd have an unobstructed view approaching Manhattan. We took photos, and I again glanced down at the quarters taped to my bike donated to me by the young children. They helped to keep me going on the long and tough days. I told them I would ride them all the way to New York. And here I was approaching the greatest city in the world!

From aboard the ferry we had a spectacular close-up view of the Statue of Liberty. I thought about my other grandfather, Thomas Byrne, my dad's father. It was the first thing he saw as he arrived in America by boat from Ireland. He came here for opportunity. Anything was possible in the United States through hard work, he was told. Seeing that statue meant so much to him.

After the 25-minute crossing, the ferry docked at Whitehall St. in Lower Manhattan. Andy wasn't quite sure how to reach the Brooklyn Bridge, a distance of about a mile or so. We could see the bridge, but how would we bicycle to it? Enter Melissa, who works on Wall Street and who knew the area inside out. She'd be our guide. We told her we wanted to stop at Ground Zero before we reached the bridge, if it was possible. She said that was no problem. She knew the city like the back of her hand. Today was the only day on the entire ride when we were not lost at some point, excluding our days pedaling through Kansas where there was just one road to travel for the entire day. New York City grew bigger and bigger as we approached.

Meanwhile, the loaded charter bus left the Elks Lodge about the same time we did, crossed the Verrazzano-Narrows Bridge and was taking local Brooklyn streets to the Brooklyn Bridge. The bus would arrive at the bridge long before we did, of course, allowing my family and friends to get into position at the finish line.

With Melissa guiding us, we pedaled to Church St., made a right and headed uptown. Our police and fire escort was gone. We were five bicyclists alone on a mission. Melissa explained she chose the perfect location for us to look in at reconstruction of the World Trade Center. We flew past yellow taxis and cars in the busy Manhattan traffic with Melissa leading the way. Bicycling in Manhattan was another unique experience! I've done a lot of riding, but this was something else. There were row after row of skyscrapers and hundreds and hundreds of people. We reached a stopping point opposite Ground Zero. It was a hotel. Melissa talked with the hotel valet and asked if he would watch our bikes while we went to the fifth floor. She told him we had come all the way from California and this was our last stop before we reached the Brooklyn Bridge. The valet agreed.

We took an elevator to the fifth floor. We viewed the 9/11 memorial and construction of the Freedom Tower. We took photos together and of the site. It was Mike's first time at Ground Zero. It was hard to imagine so many firefighters losing their lives that day. We spent time just taking it in before heading down to the street and our bikes.

Our next and final stop of this 36 day adventure: the Brooklyn Bridge.

We were lucky to have Melissa riding with us today. Getting through Manhattan is no easy feat, especially on a bike. The Brooklyn Bridge was now about a quarter-mile away.

Reception committee awaits my arrival on Brooklyn Bridge. Excited friends, relatives and co-workers traveled from throughout the country and overseas to whoop and holler as I crossed finish line.

We hit the 3,400-mile mark as we pulled up to the Manhattan side of the Brooklyn Bridge.

Here comes the final mile of my 36-day cross country endeavor.

As I rode onto the bridge, I thought of the first moment I crossed the Golden Gate Bridge talking with Darrell Sales.

I remember thinking I had the entire country ahead of me. I now have the entire country behind me.

I rode on the side wooden walkway, usually reserved for pedestrians and bicyclists. Just like the Golden Gate, the Brooklyn Bridge has a feel to it. The bridge stood tall, with hundreds of people walking and riding across. It was my final mile! I did it! As I pedaled uphill, I could see well-wishers at center-span awaiting our finish. A red ribbon stretched across the walkway.

Ta da! Cameras click, guests clap and fans cheer as I zoom across red ribbon finish line. How did I feel? Just look at my face!

YEP. IT FINALLY HAPPENED. After 36 continuous days and 3,401 miles pedaling a bike, I reached my goal. I rode through the red ribbon stretched across the finish.

The crowd was cheering.

For one final time, I held my bike over my head in victory!

WE CELEBRATED RIGHT THERE on the bridge in the midst of everyone and everything. There was so much excitement in the air. Some people were holding up homemade signs. We took loads of group photos. Dave Latham handed me a check for several hundred dollars. He told me that if I made it to the bridge, he would make a donation. He is a man of his word and a generous man. I excitedly talked with family and friends for a long time. It was a moment I didn't want to end. Standing in the middle of the Brooklyn Bridge. What a view! There was Manhattan!

There was Brooklyn! What a reception! We must have spent an hour or so on the bridge celebrating.

When the hoopla died down, I got on my trusty bike for one last time and coasted downhill to the Brooklyn side of the bridge to the waiting charter bus. Before boarding, I sprawled out on the grass for a good five minutes. I just couldn't believe it.

I did it!

We boarded the bus after our bikes were loaded, and we headed to the Hilton Garden Inn on Staten Island for the dinner reception. I don't remember much about being on the bus. I must have been so excited. I just remember getting to the hotel. We arrived early so we had to wait while they readied the reception room. The dinner reception was packed with friends and family. We sat down at our table and the food and drink flowed. We were about to eat when John Reynolds stood up to make an announcement. John, remember, had just completed a 30-minute video about Lauren's Ride. He managed to include footage of me completing The Ride only a few hours earlier. He worked with the hotel staff so that he could play it. The video, with background music, showed highlights from each state through which we traveled. He even contacted many followers and family members and persuaded them to contribute short clips. It was truly touching. Lauren spoke on the video about how much The Ride would help her independence. Even more important, she said, was that the cross-country extravaganza gave everyone a chance to see how special I was. I have the best friends and family. After the video was over, most of us were crying.

I thanked John Reynolds for creating a video that covered The Ride so well. At that moment I realized that in an hour or so it would all be over.

It hit me. For the first time in six weeks I would *not* be riding tomorrow.

Everyone worked together for six months to make every single day a magical day. Each day, for the past 36 days, we pedaled across our country and met interesting and exciting people. Tonight was the end of The Ride in that sense. It hit me hard. I thanked my family for being here

Lisa Ocasio holds creative poster.

onight and told them how thankful I was for their support.

I could relate to baseball player Lou Gehrig when he said he was the uckiest man on the face of the earth.

To be able to do something you love so much and to be supported by o many people is something quite unusual. It was such a sad moment hinking this dinner would end. I wanted it to continue forever, but also knew this was the start of the next step of The Ride. We would eturn to California and buy a car for Lauren.

Lauren spoke:

"I am really thankful. I am digesting everything that has happened,"

Historic Brooklyn Bridge never looked so welcoming!

she said. "It doesn't seem real. I just want to thank everyone who sup-ported us, and I am so happy John made it safely."

After we both spoke, I spent the rest of the evening socializing and

I raise bike in victory for final time. That's Andy Meuerle with me.

telling stories about the past 36 days. Everyone had questions. They were intrigued by the stories I told. Everyone wanted to know so many details. I spent the whole night answering questions about The Ride and filling in people on what happened on different days. I really didn't want this night to end. Eventually, it did.

One chapter of The Ride just ended. A new one was to begin.

Total miles pedaled in 36 days
3,401

PART III

Finally, the Car

RETURNING HOME, I TRIED to get back to a normal life. Believe me, after what I had just gone through, it wasn't easy. Everywhere we went, people asked Mike and me about the ride. My union contacted me, and I wrote about the brotherly love we shared across the nation and the support we had received. The union published my story on the front page of its magazine.

Tony's mom, who was hospitalized while we were riding, died a few days after we returned.

As I closed out the ride, I had one major step left. I still had to buy the car for Lauren. Little did Lauren know, but we *already* had a car being modified. Adaptive Driving Solutions in San Luis Obispo secretly had been working on a special Honda Element. We had to create a diversion for Lauren, so on Nov. 18 we decided to go "car shopping." Lauren, mom and I went to dealership after dealership looking at cars. We asked about the ability to adapt cars to make them work for Lauren. She didn't know we were close to having a car completed and ready to go.

ON DEC. 11, I WENT TO Adaptive Driving Solutions to officially purchase Lauren's special car. Damian and Patricia Juarez and their children met me there. I arrived before they got there and was the first one to see the car.

It was a black Honda Element.

The mechanic showed me how it was set up. You pushed a button, the doors opened and a ramp automatically came out. A wheelchair could go up the ramp and the person would then transfer to the driver's seat. They showed me how Lauren will drive the car with her hands and how another person could still drive the car with his or her feet. After the tour, we sat down and completed the paperwork.

I explained my vision for presenting the car to Lauren. I decided we would surprise her with the car on Christmas morning. We were excited. I wrote out the check for $51,885. I handed the check to the sales rep just as the Juarez family arrived. I gave them a tour of the vehicle. We took loads of photos and could not believe how sharp the car looked. The dealership made it look like every other car. Which is what Lauren had hoped for. She wanted a car like everyone else's. She didn't want her car to stand out. I was so happy to have my friends share this big moment with me. The presentation would be some surprise. I had to keep it quiet till Christmas.

Beep. Beep.

As Christmas approached I worked out details with my fire station and with Adaptive Driving Solutions. Luckily, I had Christmas Day off. Lauren and mom would be staying at my house in Nipomo for Christmas. We decided to have Christmas morning breakfast at the fire station. My station was only a mile from my house. Christmas Eve, mom and I sneaked off to the station to look at the car. It was the first time mom had seen it. Adaptive Driving Solutions had attached a large bow to the car. We notified the media of the presentation to take place, and I went over the plan one more time with the fire station staff. I know what Chief Steve Phipps of Conshohocken, Pa., felt like as he secretly planned our arrival. Now, for me, it was *really* the night before Christmas. This gift was going to change Lauren's life in so many ways.

It was difficult to sleep that Christmas Eve. I just kept thinking about the whole ride experience, and how excited Lauren would be to finally have her own car.

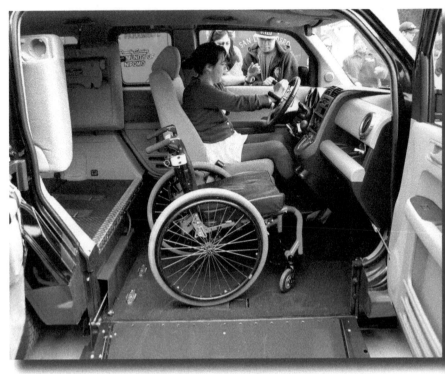

Lauren checks out her new car.

We woke up Christmas morning and routinely opened our gifts. I told Lauren we would go to the station for breakfast, then return to the house to open the rest of our presents. I apologized to Lauren that I didn't get many gifts for people because I was so busy with the ride. To keep Lauren diverted, I had a friend call her a few days before to tell her his shop in Los Angeles modified cars. The plan was to drive down a few days after Christmas to check out the shop. She had no idea what was around the corner. We all got into mom's car and headed for the station. I texted ahead that we were on the way.

A lot of our friends and co-workers came to my fire station that morning to be on hand for the big surprise We pulled into the fire station and parked. All other cars parked in the rear of the station, so it looked like no one was there. We got out of the car and put Lauren's wheelchair together. After she transferred into her wheelchair, the three of us casually moved towards the building.

That's Lauren behind wheel of her new wheels, with everyone who turned out for Christmas morning surprise.

Just another Christmas Day at the firehouse.

As we approached the building, the large station doors began to open. Nothing unusual about that. Three vehicles were parked inside: A fire engine on the left. A fire engine on the right. And a car in the middle.

Lauren's car.

All three vehicles slowly pulled forward simultaneously. The fire engines' lights were flashing. Lauren's car sported the big purple bow sitting on its hood. Then, just like a surprise party when the guest of honor walks in, a throng of people jumped out from behind the engines where they had been crouching.

Lauren shrieked and brought her hands to her face. It took a second or two for the picture to register in her mind. When it did, she realized she was looking at a car.

Her car.

I RETURNED TO WORK the next morning. Lauren took driving lessons. She did well. She still had to get her driver's license. Lauren and I tried to get in as much practice driving time as we could. She set an appointment for her driving test. Mom and I waited as we saw her pull out with the instructor. When they returned, the instructor spent some time talking to Lauren. Uh, oh. My mom and I thought it was a bad sign. But Lauren headed towards us sporting a really huge smile.

Lauren was now a California driver.

SO THAT'S MY STORY. Lauren's Ride worked out exactly the way we hoped it would.

Lauren drove her new car home at the end of the week. I escorted her out of town by driving next to her. She was so focused. I thought about the people she'd touch and inspire as she drove down the road of life.

My sister Lauren was now on her way in her very own Lauren's Ride.

Well, here's where we came in. Thanks for listening.

A lot's happened since our family photo in the beginning of this book. Despite what you read — and maybe because of what you read — we're still in great spirits.

Mom still keeps busy with community theatre...dad's retired now and spends more time in the garden and kitchen...I'm still chasing fires in the San Francisco area.

And Lauren? Well, Lauren graduated from Cal State East Bay College with a bachelor's degree in liberal studies. In fact, she managed to walk to the stage at commencement — with a little help, of course. But she's getting there.

No matter where Lauren goes these days — to the store, to a doctor's appointment or to hang out with friends — you can be sure of one thing: she drives in her very own Lauren's Ride.

Keep in touch.

Acknowledgments

A sincere thank you to everyone who contributed to The Ride and who helped me write this book, especially to: **Andy Meuerle,** my friend, who gave me the bike that started the chain of events leading to The Ride. Your act of kindness changed so many lives. My **mom,** for years of unconditional love and faith, for your hard work through the entire ride, and for sharing your love with everyone. My **dad,** for your work ethic, for our lengthy phone conversations during challenging times along The Ride, and for the countless hours you spent helping me with this book. My sister **Lauren,** for your constant positive attitude, and especially for your determination to never give up. Your love and belief in a successful cross-country journey kept me pedaling and pedaling. **Lyn Bratton,** for creating Lauren's Ride the moment you heard of the idea, and for your endless emails, phone calls, web page updates and outreach. My mentor and best friend **Mike DeLeo,** for making the impossible possible. **Tony Hernandez,** the stranger who gave up six weeks of his life to follow me in a car, providing everything I needed to get through each of my 36 grueling days. Thank you, Tony, for keeping me safe. **Darrell Sales,** for your unique help in organizing this gigantic event. **Bobby Williams,** for meticulously planning the New York City finale, and for your constant inspiration, guidance and patience to help me write this book. **Rob Lewin,** for being a great leader and role model. You empowered me, and you shared our cause with the department, the media and our union. **Steve Phipps:** I'll never forget what you did and what you continue to do for us! **Arnold Schwarzenegger,** for being the perfect role model, and a perfect example of what passion, dedication and hard work can accomplish. Your six rules of success helped me achieve a feat I felt was nearly impossible. **Matt Streck,** for your profound guidance. **Stephanie Dininni,** for being the very first donor to the Lauren's Ride fund. **Jean Byrne,** for your love and teachings that changed my life. **Margaret May** and **Joan Peterson,** my grammar school teachers, who taught me how to use my attention-deficit disorder as *a strength* instead of accepting it as a *weakness*. The **Ciardella** family, for your unending friendship. **Courtney Sarkisian,** for your love and support. **Bill Byrne,** for your unique editorial expertise. And to The Ride sponsors: **Fluid, Target Solutions, Shuster Oil Co. Inc., Tom's Equipment, Meals and Support Service Headquarters, Yamaha Generators, Davies Appliance** and **Home Motors**. Your belief in our cause led to my overwhelming success!

About the Author

John Byrne and his sister Lauren were raised by their parents Dan and Judy Byrne in Newark, Calif. John earned an Associates of Science Degree in Fire Technology from Allan Hancock Community College, Santa Maria, Calif. He is a captain with Cal Fire, the California Dept. of Forestry and Fire Protection, assigned to the San Francisco Bay area. An avid tri-athlete, John enjoys public speaking and sharing stories of The Ride. He feels blessed to share his story with you.

9 780991 186051